**BOCCONI
UNIVERSITY
PRESS**

Mario Ciunfrini · Claudio Scardovi

HANDBOOK OF MERGERS AND ACQUISITIONS

Foreword by **Antonio Arfè**

Cover: Cristina Bernasconi, Milan
Typesetting: Imagine, Trezzo sull'Adda (Mi)

Copyright © 2025 Bocconi University Press
EGEA S.p.A.

EGEA S.p.A.
Via Salasco, 5 – 20136 Milano
Tel. 02/5836.5751 – Fax 02/5836.5753
egea.edizioni@unibocconi.it – www.egeaeditore.it

All rights reserved, including but not limited to translation, total or partial adaptation, reproduction, and communication to the public by any means on any media (including microfilms, films, photocopies, electronic or digital media), as well as electronic information storage and retrieval systems. For more information or permission to use material from this text, see the website www.egeaeditore.it

Given the characteristics of Internet, the publisher is not responsible for any changes of address and contents of the websites mentioned.

The publisher, having completed the paperwork to acquire all the rights to the iconographic set of this work, remains at the disposal of those who would nevertheless claim ragiorni in this regard.

First edition: January 2025

ISBN Print Edition	979-12-80623-42-3
ISBN International Edition	979-12-81627-21-5
ISBN Digital Domestic Edition	978-88-238-8933-0
ISBN Digital International Edition	979-12-81627-22-2

Table of Contents

Foreword, by *Antonio Arfè*   XIII

Part I – M&A, Private Equity and Value Creation
by *Claudio Scardovi*

1 M&A: Driving Sustainable Values Creation   3
- 1.1 The death of M&A and private equity?   3
- 1.2 Flipping no more   4
- 1.3 A few fundamental questions   6
- 1.4 A quick rebound for M&A and private equity?   7
- 1.5 Sustainable life at the end of the financial tunnel?   9
- 1.6 What is M&A—and what critically defines it?   10
- 1.7 M&A as an art and (a bit) of a science   18

2 Private Markets: The Opportunity for Sustainable Values Creation   23
- 2.1 Too much equity chasing fewer and fewer opportunities?   23
- 2.2 Too many private assets with less and less equity to invest in them?   24
- 2.3 "Alpha" in private equity (and real assets)   25
- 2.4 Opportunities for asset and wealth managers   26
- 2.5 Opportunities for insurance companies   28
- 2.6 A new, emerging, systemic risk?   29
- 2.7 What it takes to become "master of the universe"   31
- 2.8 Real estate opportunities for private markets   32
- 2.9 Real estate as an investable asset   33
- 2.10 Infrastructure opportunities for private markets   38
- 2.11 Closing the funding gap for green transformation   40
- 2.12 M&A, private equity, and real assets for green transformation   42
- 2.13 M&A, private equity, and real assets: transforming stranded assets   44
- 2.14 Permanent capital: a link between illiquid assets and liquid markets   45

3	**Worth It? Delivering Sustainable Alpha in Private Equity**		**47**
	3.1 The past: was it true glory?		47
	3.2 The future: are there reasons to worry?		52
	3.3 Designing a "smart beta" strategy in private equity		55
	3.4 Developing an "alpha platform" in private equity		58
	3.5 A "decalogue" to drive sustainable values creation		60
	3.6 Primary research: creating "alpha" in mid-market private equity in Italy		65

Part II – Fundamentals of M&A, Private Equity, and Real Asset
by *Mario Ciunfrini*

4	**The M&A Process**		**69**
	4.1 External growth strategies		69
	4.1.1 Introduction		69
	4.1.2 Players involved in an M&A transaction		69
	4.1.3 Typologies of transactions		70
	4.2 The M&A process		72
	4.2.1 The buy-side process		72
	4.2.2 The sell-side process		76
	4.2.3 Post-closing considerations		80
	4.2.4 Other considerations		81
5	**Introduction to Valuation**		**83**
	5.1 Introduction		83
	5.2 The two valuation approaches		84
	5.3 The toolbox of valuation		84
	5.3.1 The time value of money		84
	5.4 Risk and return: CAPM and discount rates		88
	5.5 Deriving value with intrinsic valuation		90
	5.5.1 The weighted average cost of capital		90
	5.5.2 Discounting cash flows		90
	5.5.3 Estimation of future cash flows		92
	5.5.4 The growth rate		92
	5.5.5 The TV		93
	5.5.6 Net debt and other elements of the equity bridge		93
	5.5.7 Drawing conclusions: the two-step discounted cash flow		94
	5.5.8 Deriving value with multiples		95
	5.6 Conclusions		99

Part III – M&A and Private Equity in Practice

6 Legal and Tax Processes in M&A and Private Equity,
   by *Carlotta Robbiano* and *Daniele Cevolo* — 103
   6.1 Introduction to the legal side of M&A — 103
     6.1.1 The role of corporate lawyers in M&A transactions — 103
     6.1.2 Distinctiveness of M&A transactions in the private equity sector — 104
   6.2 The legal process in M&A transactions — 105
     6.2.1 The LOI — 105
     6.2.2 Auction process versus one-to-one negotiation — 106
   6.3 Overview of the share purchase agreement — 109
     6.3.1 Conditions precedent and covenants — 111
     6.3.2 Payment mechanisms: locked box versus price adjustment — 111
     6.3.3 Representations and warranties, indemnities, and guarantees — 112
   6.4 Introduction to portfolio companies and management mechanisms — 112
     6.4.1 Carried interest as a management incentive in portfolio companies — 113

7 The Tax Process in M&A and Private Equity, by *Valentina Santini* and *Gianmaria Leoni* — 115
   7.1 The structure of the transaction — 117
   7.2 Variables underlying how the investment is carried out — 119
   7.3 Asset deal versus share deal — 121
   7.4 (Merger) leveraged buyout: "typical" structure of the transaction — 122
   7.5 Optimizing the seller's tax regime: consequences for the buyer — 126
   7.6 Optimizing the tax management of acquired companies — 126
   7.7 Taxation of investment return flows — 128
   7.8 The taxation regime at the time of "exit" — 129

8 The Due Diligence Process in M&A and Private Equity,
   by *Tamara Laudisio* — 131
   8.1 Financial due diligence — 133
     8.1.1 Definitions and purposes — 133
     8.1.2 Valuation drivers: due diligence supporting deal pricing — 134
   8.2 Conclusions — 146

9 SME, M&A, and Private Markets in Italy: A Perspective,
   by *Ernesto Lanzillo* — 147
   9.1 General introduction — 147
   9.2 The critical role of SMEs in the Italian economy — 147

	9.3	The key role of sustainability	148
		9.3.1 Digital transformation and SME growth	149
	9.4	Role of private equity in supporting SMEs	149
	9.5	Trends and data on private equity in Italy	151
	9.6	Conclusions and future perspectives	154

10 Value Creation and Transformation in Infrastructure,
by *Francesco Checcacci* — 155

	10.1	Introduction	155
	10.2	Fundamentals of value creation in infrastructure	156
	10.3	M&A as a catalyst for value creation in the infra sector	157
	10.4	Value creation in infrastructure: how to manage the process	159
	10.5	Case studies of successful value creation and transformation via M&A	161

11 Value Creation and Urban Regeneration in Real Estate,
by *Andrea Mucchietto* — 165

	11.1	What is urban regeneration?	165
	11.2	ESG: from regulatory requirements toward drivers for value creation	166
	11.3	Challenges in urban regeneration: management of stakeholders	168
	11.4	Urban regeneration value creation and measurement	173
	11.5	An Italian example: the case of MilanoSesto urban regeneration	179
	11.6	Maximizing value through urban regeneration	184
	11.7	Conclusions and future perspectives	184

12 Value Creation and Post-Merger Integration in M&A and Private Equity, by *Tommaso Nastasi* — 187

	12.1	Introduction and importance of PMI	187
	12.2	Key challenges and strategic considerations	187
	12.3	Steps for a successful integration	189
	12.4	Cultural and human factors in value creation	206
	12.5	Conclusions	207

13 Sustainable Finance, by *Abulenta Librazhdi* — 209

	13.1	Introduction	209
		13.1.1 Integration of ESG principles in private equity	209
		13.1.2 Benefits of integrating sustainable finance principles	212
		13.1.3 Challenges in implementing sustainable finance principles	215
		13.1.4 Successful implementation of sustainable finance principles	215

	13.2 Overview of the current landscape	216
	13.2.1 Sustainable alternative assets	217
	13.2.2 ESG private equity and debt funds	220
	13.3 Key trends in the current landscape	222
	13.3.1 Increased ESG integration	222
	13.3.2 TCFD: valuation of private equity	226
	13.4 Conclusions	230
14	**Elevating Portfolio Companies through IPO Readiness**, by *Gabriele Arioli*	233
	14.1 IPO Readiness: the project	235
	14.2 IPO Readiness: areas of analysis	236
	14.3 Conclusions	237

References   239

List of Contributors and Their Roles   241

We extend our deepest gratitude to Elisa Galassi, Sara Natalini, Mara Pradella, Giacomo Crotti, Mattia Gatti, and Emilio Montardi for their invaluable contributions to and steadfast support during the creation of this book.

Foreword

In the rapidly evolving landscape of global finance, private equity and mergers and acquisitions (M&A) stand as two of the most dynamic and influential fields. These sectors are not only pivotal in driving economic growth but also instrumental in shaping the competitive structure of industries worldwide. As the world becomes increasingly interconnected, the roles of private equity and M&A continue to expand, bringing both opportunities and challenges that require a deep understanding and strategic approach.

Claudio Scardovi and Mario Ciunfrini, supported by a highly qualified panel of Deloitte partners and professionals, designed this book in order to provide a comprehensive guide for professionals and enthusiasts who seek to navigate the complexities of private equity and M&A. Whether the readers are practitioners looking to refine their strategies or newcomers eager to learn the fundamentals, the text provides both valuable insights and practical knowledge.

The world of private equity and M&A is marked by constant change and innovation. New technologies, regulatory developments, and market dynamics continually reshape the landscape. As such, this book also addresses emerging trends and future directions, equipping readers with the foresight needed to stay ahead.

The journey through these pages will equip readers with the knowledge and skills to navigate the complex world of finance, make informed decisions, and contribute to the success and growth of businesses and economies.

Antonio Arfè
Strategy, Risk and Transactions Leader, Deloitte

Part I
M&A, Private Equity and Value Creation

by Claudio Scardovi

1 M&A: Driving Sustainable Values Creation

1.1 The death of M&A and private equity?

Following the pandemic, and supported by extremely buoyant fiscal and monetary policies, M&A activity (or "mergers and acquisitions"—defined by Wikipedia as business transactions in which the ownership of companies, businesses, and organizations, or their operating units, are transferred to or consolidated with another company or business organization) rose to almost unprecedented levels, supported by the increasing role of a professional and dedicated subsector of the alternative asset management industry, that is, the private equity one. As lax monetary policies led to a multiplied quantity of monetary base in the economy being built up, with interest rates approaching zero or even negative territory and with abundant liquidity provided by central banks to the global financial system, potential M&A bidders were able, and indeed almost forced, to use leverage in order to be competitive in any open-bid transaction. This increased and easy recourse to leverage then had the effect of modifying the decision-making of the general partners of private equity funds (i.e. the investment managers of such funds, as opposed to "limited investors"—the end investors). For the former, the net effect was to pursue an even larger number of deals, with growing volumes negotiated and transaction prices signed at ever increasing multiples, as the total firm value agreed was also increasingly financed by debt. A first indirect effect of this was to shift a larger and larger portion of risk to lenders, whilst allowing equity bidders to retain an even bigger share of the upside linked to the possible buyout (the larger upside is for the limited partners, but, more importantly, for the general partners, as they gain money through a mechanism called "carried interest," which allows them to capture around 20% of any gain, despite having invested little or nothing). A second net effect came from the increased value of bids, because the greater number of potential bidders and their lower cost of capital (equity plus debt) led to an increased number of secondary deals, where basically a private equity fund exits an investment by selling a portfolio company to another fund, and this second to a third one, through multiple rounds or "flips" and with an average holding period of three to four years—with an unclear end state and final exit. In short, in the aftermath of COVID-19, we experienced a brief but very financially valuable golden age of M&A—mostly spurred by private equity.

This short but intense "golden age" was then followed by a few dramatic changes in the overall economic environment, starting from the rise in inflation (long overdue, because of the lax fiscal and monetary policies previously noted) and the consequential change in the interest rate set by the main central banks, beginning with the Federal Reserve System (Fed), and followed by the European Central Bank (ECB) (Figure 1.1). A radical increase in the interest rate, coupled with a less noticeable but still relevant reduction in the quantity of money in circulation (whether as M1, M2, or M3) changed all this, with 2023 defined by many as the *annus horribilis* of M&A and private equity at the global level. First, tighter conditions have been increasingly attached to the allowance of lending facilities, hence reducing the debt "dry powder" theoretically available to finance deals. Second, the cost of borrowing has meant prospective bidders are faced with a higher cost of capital and much less convenient options to do a bigger deal or pay a higher price. Third, even past deals have been put under strain, as the increased cost of debt has started impacting their economic sustainability, leading to more equity being required to rebalance the leverage equation and potentially suggesting an increase of troubled situations ahead (such as UTP (unlikely to pay) and NPL (non-performing loans)). These hence require restructuring and liquidation (if loans become non-performing, with the underlying company or asset becoming bankrupt and subject to liquidation, repossession and recovery are based on their residual value).

1.2   Flipping no more

From a private equity perspective, many things that were acting as key growth factors in the previous interest rate era also turned negative. As a start, private equity's mostly illiquid investment propositions had become very attractive because of the mid-teens targeted IRR (internal rate of return) promised to prospective investors—not just institutional but also, increasingly, private wealthy clients and even affluent and mass market retail investors. Hence, it was easy for them to raise capital, reaching an estimated $13 billion (according to investment date company Preqin) of "dry powder" (the capital available for deals that can be drawn down by private equity when the opportunity arises) at the end of the pandemic. Second, before the change in the monetary policies, it was easy for private equity funds to finance almost any kind of deal at very convenient terms (albeit with variable rates—hence exposing them to future raises in interest rates). It was also easier for them to exit the investments, as the number of secondary deals (i.e. where a private equity player sells a company to another one) with invested corporates often reached four to five "flips" in less than fifteen to twenty years and had increased leverage through time (more dangerously, from a governance and conflict-of-interest standpoint, some of these "flips" were even done between funds managed by the same asset manager and advisory company—or "general partners"). All this came to an almost complete stop, with fewer and fewer secondary deals and an increase reticence by limited investors to allow "flips" between funds managed by the same asset manager and advisory company. Third, in a world of global assets, which kept growing in nominal value anyway as lax fiscal and monetary policies were generously supporting econ-

1 M&A: Driving Sustainable Values Creation

Figure 1.1 The interest rates applied by the ECB for CITs (1999–2023)

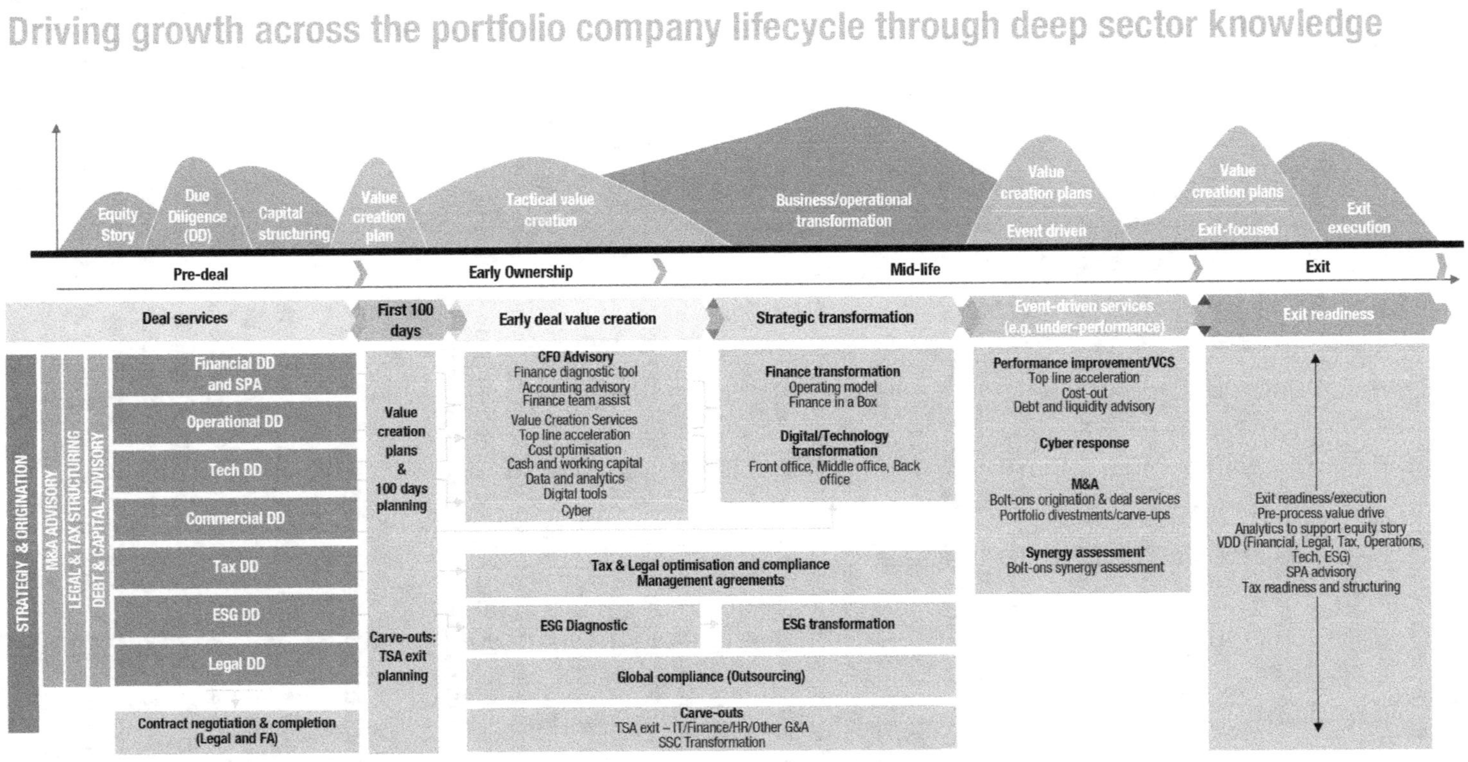

Driving growth across the portfolio company lifecycle through deep sector knowledge

Phase	Pre-deal	Early Ownership	Mid-life	Exit
Sub-phase	Due Diligence (DD) → Capital structuring → Value creation plan	First 100 days → Tactical value creation	Business/operational transformation	Value creation plans (Event driven) → Value creation plans (Exit-focused) → Exit execution

Pre-deal — Deal services
- Financial DD and SPA
- Operational DD
- Tech DD
- Commercial DD
- Tax DD
- ESG DD
- Legal DD
- Contract negotiation & completion (Legal and FA)

First 100 days
- Value creation plans & 100 days planning
- Carve-outs: TSA exit planning

Early deal value creation
- CFO Advisory: Finance diagnostic tool, Accounting advisory, Finance team assist
- Value Creation Services: Top line acceleration, Cost optimisation, Cash and working capital, Data and analytics, Digital tools, Cyber
- Tax & Legal optimisation and compliance / Management agreements
- ESG Diagnostic
- Global compliance (Outsourcing)
- Carve-outs: TSA exit – IT/Finance/HR/Other G&A, SSC Transformation

Strategic transformation
- Finance transformation: Operating model, Finance in a Box
- Digital/Technology transformation: Front office, Middle office, Back office
- ESG transformation

Event-driven services (e.g. under-performance)
- Performance improvement/VCS: Top line acceleration, Cost-out, Debt and liquidity advisory
- Cyber response
- M&A: Bolt-ons origination & deal services, Portfolio divestments/carve-ups
- Synergy assessment: Bolt-ons synergy assessment

Exit readiness
- Exit readiness/execution
- Pre-process value drive
- Analytics to support equity story
- VDD (Financial, Legal, Tax, Operations, Tech, ESG)
- SPA advisory
- Tax readiness and structuring

Cross-phase streams: STRATEGY & ORIGINATION · M&A ADVISORY · LEGAL & TAX STRUCTURING · DEBT & CAPITAL ADVISORY · Equity Story

omies across all kind of sectors and on stock markets (and also due to the transition effects caused by inflation: from products and services to revenues to companies' value), it was easy for private equity funds to justify increased an NAV (net asset value) appraisal of their portfolio companies and hence argue for very high double-digit IRR—with an high potential "carried interest" for the general managers, albeit not yet "closed" or monetized.

All of this has changed completely, given the new interest rate environment, as raising capital has become increasingly difficult because of the competition of government and private bonds offering higher and higher yields (whether linked to inflation or not) and greater liquidity (with coupons offering immediate and periodic payouts), and a "flight to quality" (here referring to the tendency of investors to invest in safer assets, e.g., government bonds, during periods of high volatility, market dislocations, and reduced growth (or outright recession) expected in the economy). In fact, not only it has become more difficult for private equity funds to raise their own equity capital to invest, but also to couple this with banks' lending—now more difficult to get, less abundant, and much more costly. The combined effect (less equity, less debt, higher cost of capital) has therefore not only put a strain on the deal flow and greatly reduced the potential economic payoff for both limited partners (i.e. the investors putting money into the funds) and general partners (i.e. the partners—whether an asset management/advisory company or single individuals—that are managing the fund and taking decisions on the investment/divestment cycle and on the portfolio company management). It has also reduced the chances of an easy, quick, and rewarding exit of the investment by the portfolio company, as the secondary market has also become less liquid and requires greater discounts to close a deal, not to mention the regulated stock markets that, whilst still approachable for an IPO (initial public offering) exit, have also become less liquid and convenient, as their pool of potential new capital sources has been reduced and sources have been demanding higher expected yields to match their higher opportunity costs All these effects have translated into lower EBITDA (earnings before interest, taxes, depreciation, and amortization) multiples, some companies delisting or being taken private through buyout transactions, not to mention increased volatility in the markets.

1.3 A few fundamental questions

The changed macroeconomic environment is not the only factor professionals working in M&A and private equity have to worry about, as increased geopolitical turbulence (with major wars going on in Central Eastern Europe and the Middle East) is also reducing opportunities for internationalization, let alone full-blown globalization of business. Bidders are therefore retrenching and willing sellers are also increasingly restrained by "golden shares," regulatory constraints, and retaliatory fiscal regimes—with further future "tit-for-tat" trade wars expected in the best scenarios. Climate change, a further engine of troubles ahead, is also posing new problems in terms of physical and transition risks that would need to be carefully considered by prospective buyers, with significant uncertainty on what could happen, where, and when (in terms of geographies, industries, and subsectors) because of the decarbonization process (or, more worryingly, the lack of it). Are M&A, as a strategy and as a process, a tool, and a driver of value creation, and private equity, as its main force and one of the market-leading movers and shakers of the recent past (and main driver of a secular trend we thought was just extending ahead of us), therefore both destined to die? Slowly suffering, year after year, and fighting to remain relevant, whilst companies, investors, and professionals are rethinking their intrinsic and long-lasting usefulness and even their raison d'être? Of course, death may be an exaggeration we use to make the point, but the main questions still stand—and it is worthwhile addressing them with some urgency:

- Has M&A lost its "cool" status and is it destined to become less and less relevant and more and more subject to criticism regarding its real contribution to value creation?
- Is private equity really a force for good to drive the transformation of businesses and their economic value creation, or just a new form of financial speculation at its worst?
- Are its asset managers the new "masters of the universe" or just temporary manifestations of the hubris of utilitarian economic agents pursuing their goals to the extreme?
- Finally, are they all good enough as they stand, or do they need to be rethought and redesigned—conceptually and for market action—to be able to truly deliver on sustainable values creation? And what is sustainable value creation really about?

1.4 A quick rebound for M&A and private equity?

Whilst in 2023 the total value of deal-making sank below $3 trillion for the first time in a decade (with total value of transactions down by 17% at the global level to about $2.9 trillion, according to the London Stock Exchange), the expectations are for some mid-term rebound, as the peak of inflation and of the accompanying restrictive monetary policies will start to deflate, with interest rates also expected to follow a decreasing trajectory. There is also widespread expectation that disruptive technological innovation—namely, the extended adoption of generative artificial intelligence (Gen AI)—will contribute to stronger growth fundamentals in the long term and an increase in productivity that, contrary to the well-known "paradox" of Robert Solow, will be visible everywhere, including in the statistics. In the meantime, heightened expectations are already justifying greater investments by front-runners and more aggressive moves by laggards. Finally, as the world is embarking on a climate-change-driven green conversion, with radical changes expected to infrastructures, business and operating models, and the full set of products and services used by consumers in their everyday life, more M&A-driven transformative work is also expected (e.g. think of the Chinese electric vehicle producers and of the German car manufacturers trying hard to adapt, and of the extensive required recharging infrastructure that will be required to operate those vehicles). Widespread geographical migrations, also a consequence of changes in the ecosystem that will make some regions unlivable due to their scorching hot weather or permanent inundation, are also likely to drive some radical movements of entire cities and of a relevant share of global population (e.g. think of Jakarta and of the new Indonesian capital being built in the north of that country; of the Indian Ocean islands that will be submerged; or of the large areas of Greenland that will be made hospitable), hence driving huge reallocation of capital, companies, assets, and people across megacities. The project of Neom–The Line, a net-zero futuristic linear city crossing the Kingdom of Saudi Arabia from the sea to the mountains, with a width of a few hundred meters and a length of hundreds of kilometers, is also pointing the way toward how investment in real estate development could change in the future, requiring M&A and private wealth to execute the visionary projects of these emerging "sustainable cities," with industries and companies also reorganizing as they develop.

These huge future transformations will not only require critical decision-making and radical changes, but also involve a sense of urgency, as this will need to happen within a few decades, and active management of the trade-off related to the transition and physical risks involved. Most importantly, it will require financing estimated in the hundreds of trillions, which the overall banking system does not have and most governments cannot afford, because of the limits to leverage imposed by the Basel Accord to the former and the high burden of public debt already shouldered by the latter. Private wealth will then need to be attracted, managed, and deployed for these kinds of investments, which could be operated through private markets because of their relative illiquidity, and following a direct approach that would also involve new forms of governance typical of the private equity industry (including, in this term, direct investments in real estate development projects and urban regeneration, not to mention digital and physical infrastructure). As it can hardly be expected that lower interest rates, increased availability, and the reduced cost of debt for deal-making—as experienced in the aftermath of the pandemic—will again happen in the next decade, we can also assume that buyers and investors will need to return to chasing returns "the hard way," that is, focusing less on hyper-leverage and financial structuring and more on real performance improvement drivers and synergies—something good for the overall economic sustainability of the economy, for the environment, and for our social development and extended civilization as well, and with a greater and greater emphasis on "real sustainability." Eventually, should the current geopolitical tensions and regional wars be contained and revert to the "normal" situation of the last decades, we could also expect a rebound in international across-bloc investment activities, with more opportunities for M&A and private equity to chase (and a greater opportunity to allocate resources optimally at the global level).

1.5 Sustainable life at the end of the financial tunnel?

Hence, there is life at the end of the tunnel of restrictive monetary policies and global decoupling for both M&A and private equity, with—no matter what the short-term turbulence is showing—most of the secular forces still pointing in that direction, albeit with cyclical up and downs. In fact, as greater and more rapid transformation is required, it follows that those inorganic moves (e.g. M&A, joint venture (JV), and alliances) and external capital and governance (e.g. equity capital on all kind of private market assets, with its related changes in governance and ownership) are needed more and more, as organic, incremental changes are just not enough to ensure the targeted change. As we experience this and the many other "bumps" that certainly will follow on the road ahead, we should always remember how each crisis, to quote Obama (and Churchill before him), is too good an opportunity to let go to waste (e.g. should not be overcome without some strategic rethinking and evolution that simply would not have been possible to implement in "normal" times). In fact, we believe that M&A and private equity need some serious rethinking in terms of their overall strategies, processes, and tools. In terms of strategies, they should more clearly define the sustainable targets of values (economic, social, and environmental) they pursue and try to achieve. From an approach-to-execution point of view, they will increasingly need an integrated end-to-end process that takes into account and interrelates with key stakeholders the sustainable values creation at hand. Tools will then also need to adapt, with vertical competencies and skills adapting fast to a world where the three important key factors of M&A and private equity are changing (from "price, price, price" to "sustainable economic, social, and environmental values"). As a consequence, we believe this mission-related, strategic rethink of M&A and private equity should start from their foundations, and by trying to answer some hard questions:

- Why is M&A still a relevant approach and tool to pursue the creation of greater and more sustainable wealth and related well-being, and how we should avoid the mistakes of the past? And on which kind of sustainable value should we focus to achieve that?
- Which of its main processes and tools need to change and adapt for M&A to be even more effective in pursuing these ends and avoiding the many speculative pitfalls observed—including financial short-termism, hyper-leverage, and misplaced market/agents' incentives?
- Why is private wealth so relevant, apart from the obvious reason of being needed to close the funding gap to drive sustainable transformation, and how we should involve this in M&A through private equity as a complement to (not substitute for) regulated stock markets?
- Why is private equity potentially the most effective way to recapitalize the real economy and preserve, regenerate, and transform real assets vis-à-vis the "visible" hand of the state? And why would the "invisible" hand of stock markets not be up to this challenge?

- Why are private markets potentially a very relevant "force for good" and what could determine their balanced development and contribution to the global change needed? Or how could they become, if managed badly, a new destabilizing, systemic factor within the global economy?
- Finally, why are M&A and private equity so related, with such intertwined destinies, and why might a synergistic and virtuous evolution of both, as the yin and yang of our global economic development, contribute so much toward sustainable values creation?

1.6 What is M&A—and what critically defines it?

As mentioned, according to Wikipedia (a great reference of the perceived shared "knowledge" in real life), by M&A we tend to refer to business transactions in which the ownerships of companies, businesses, and organizations, or their operating units, are transferred to or consolidated with another company or business organization. As such, as part of the strategic plan and management of a firm, M&A, as an integrated end-to-end process to generate synergies and value accretion, can allow enterprises to grow or downsize and dynamically change the nature of their business and competitive positioning as a result—in a fast and furious way. This generic definition needs, however, to be clarified to truly understand the potential benefits that an inorganic M&A move and its process can deliver to the counterparts directly involved in it and to the wider stakeholders that may be indirectly impacted as well (technically, a merger is the legal consolidation of two business entities into one, whereas an acquisition occurs when one entity takes over the ownership of another entity's share capital, equity interest, or assets). We also need to fully understand and gauge the potential risks related to this—not to mention the tendency to use M&A (still mostly an art with a little science underpinning it) for merely speculative reasons and to focus on the short-term asymmetric financial gains that may occur and be monetized (for owners, top managers, advisors, investors, and others). That is, to judge it, among many counterparts, by its effect on "value migration" (and not "value creation"), with little sustainability in the economic value transferred or marginally created, not to mention the limited or negative impacts on the other, social and environmental, dimensions. For this purpose, a few terms of our first definition need to be focused and better qualified, as an initial step to reset the real aim and expected outcomes of M&A:

- *Mission and vision*: Great companies are born with a mission—a larger-than-life objective that they are trying to achieve directly or contribute indirectly for the greater benefit of humanity. A company's mission informs its sense of purpose and ultimate ontological end, and both are then encapsulated into an ambitious but still actionable vision. A vision is an attempt to achieve this high-level mission and the ultimate purpose by translating them into expected results, which may include (but should not be limited to) profitability and growth targets, and other more detailed key performance financial indicators, such as EBITDA margin, market share, cost income, and so on; but also (and this is our thesis regarding sustainable values creation), goals related to social inclusion and wellness brought to the stakeholders of interest and—more broadly—to humankind and civilization and goals related to environmental targets—the rebalancing of the ecosystem, the preservation of species and ecological environments, the fight of climate change and pollution, and so on. All of these targets (or "sustainable values") should be pursued on the basis of the core values that the organization adopts, consistent with its culture. They should also be pursued while, typically with a sectorial view, taking into consideration the core competencies (financial, industrial, commercial, operational, etc.) of the company—to identify unique selling propositions that can make "that" company truly and distinctively competitive. The management and the board of the company then have the responsibility of translating this, with its subcomponents, into a strategy—all incorporated into a formal document often called a "strategic (or industrial) plan," describing the competitive journey the company intends to take over the next three to five years to reach its (economic, social, environmental) value creation targets, in accordance with its mission and sense of purpose as described in the vision.

- *Business model and business plan*: The "strategic plan" just discussed is typically a description of the business design of the company. This includes the business model and the related capabilities the organization intends to develop and adopt to generate revenue and address client needs and market opportunities in competitive ways. The business design, on top of the internally developed business model, also includes a definition of the phases of the value chain that the company is directly presiding over or is considering entering, or is just controlling indirectly through alliances, JVs, or "best horse race" commercial relationships with third-party suppliers. Furthermore, it includes descriptions of the on-, near-, or offshore markets it is selecting for its production-to-distribution value proposition model. This is particularly relevant and can drive M&A activities, as geopolitical tensions and the US–China decoupling is causing several Western companies to consider reshoring or friend-shoring (the repatriation of their capabilities from China to their domestic home market or toward other allied countries, such as South Korea or Taiwan). Separate, but underpinning the business model, that is, front-facing target markets and customers, the operating model of the company describes in turn its internal back-end organization—people, technology, and all the process-related capabilities it will need to master in order to be able to deliver on the supply of its core products and services and to fulfill its end clients' expectations. Business is an operating model, as revenue- and cost-generating conceptual blocs are logically interconnected in the business plan through the financial indicators analyzed and monitored for the planning horizon considered. Apart from revenues and costs, the focus is also on the equity capital and debt that are required to sustain the two, and on considering the consequential impacts on the balance sheet and profit-and-loss statement of the company. The business plan then defines in detail profitability, growth, and economic value-added targets—supported by other kinds of financial, operational, and commercial key performance indicators (KPI)—all broken down year by year and according to detailed annual budgeting plans. Finally, a master plan, usually represented through Gantt-like diagrams, showing actions, interconnections, milestones, and short-stoppers, and short- to long-term targets across a timeline, is created. The master plan shows in practical terms what the action plan entails and which working group should do what, when, how, and with which kind of required funding and help from which stakeholder (internal or external). Given the mission-related importance of focusing on a plurality of sustainable values, the current challenge is to augment the traditional business plan with multidimensional views of the impacts the company is having on society and the environment and how these could (and ultimately should) lead to a better competitive positioning of the company, hence reinforcing its economic dimensions as well. This challenge, which entails an extra valuation effort, a cultural shift, and an expanded management focus, could in turn ultimately introduce a new wave of M&A, which would be led by the sustainability repositioning of the company, and that could consider accelerating the company's transformation and managing its transition and physical risks (to focus on the environmental sustainability dimension) through the sale of certain "soon to become stranded" businesses and assets and the acquisition of others that could help in reducing its overall CO_2 footprint and making its value chain greener— across scope 1 (direct emissions from owned or controlled sources), scope 2 (indirect emissions from the generation of purchased electricity), and scope 3 (all other indirect emissions that occur in the company's value chain).

- *Strategy and M&A*: No matter how the management and board of a company define its strategic plan—as laid out deterministically for the long run or emerging dynamically through time, or as imposed top down or agreed bottom up, and so on—the key point we want to make here regards the company's role as the master-in-command, with M&A potentially acting as its servant (no matter to what extent this servant can be crucial for the successful execution of the strategy, it remains a tool informed by the end goals defined by the strategy). In fact, it is for strategy to decide and for M&A to execute all these decisions, even if, in some regard, with great latitude of choices, given what is practically achievable in terms of deal-making in the market. Hence, strategy is the head driving the many legs of M&A, as a tool and as a process, which can help in moving forward and, most importantly, aiding the company to change and evolve for the better. As strategy is the end, and M&A (or more generally, finance) is a possible (or sometimes required) mean to get there, there can be no excellent M&A if the strategy is not right. Good M&A could lead to the most successful transaction in history, with great financial gains created along the way, but it would remain an opportunistic, tactical move, not addressing the real transformation the company wants to pursue nor the ultimate reason d'être that brought the company into existence in the first instance. Strategy should therefore clearly specify which objectives, financial and non-financial, including the social and environmental key dimensions contributing to total sustainability, the company wants to achieve, and the multidimensional sustainable values creation it wants to execute. And then consider the main options to get to the desired results, which are typically actioned by industrial, financial, operational, organization, technological, commercial, and other levers, through a mix of "organic" or "inorganic" moves—as strategy is put into action.

- *Organic and inorganic*: A generally acclaimed company target is profitability, that is, the ability to return in full the company's capital costs and provide an extra yield that technically justifies the creation of economic value added. Another universally recognized target is, however, for companies to grow and keep growing over time and across economic cycles. The two targets are not necessarily linked as they also present some intrinsic trade-offs. It is easier to maximize a percentage profitability (such as the one measured by ROE—return on equity) by giving up growth and vice versa. Most importantly, (almost) everything can be done organically, that is, counting on the sole forces of the company—for example, driving profitability through cost optimization or by innovation in key processes and technologies; or promoting growth by entering new geographies, markets, and client segments and developing complementary products and services. But this usually requires a lot of time, with business and operational risks linked to the company's limited scale, insufficient scope, or partial business and/or technical knowledge. All of these goals can instead be achieved through M&A in an accelerated way, that is, via inorganic moves that may create scale at the stroke of a pen (signing an M&A deal), allow the penetration of a new region (with a few flights required to negotiate the deal), and build up institutional knowledge without hiring anyone (just retaining the employees and capitalizing on the key processes of the acquisition target). All this can happen with increased speed through M&A—leading toward everything the company wants to reach and achieve, albeit via navigation through unchartered waters and counting on the partnership of the merging entity or acquired counterpart. Hence, these greater potential returns naturally come with a much higher set of risks. These can range from the obvious one of overpaying the target, to doing well but then destroying the financial value gained through skillful negotiations in the post-merger integration (PMI) because of cultural clashes or poorly planned IT and process migrations, or other factors. In fact, a positive value migration in M&A can happen in hours and simply requires some help from investment bankers and lawyers. But truly incremental value creation can only happen over time (the first "1000 days"), as M&A fully unfold across multiple years with the help of the company's managers and of strategic and industrial consultants.
- *Synergies and dyssynergies*: Leaving aside bilateral value migrations, which naturally occur in deal-making because of differing contractual power, expertise in negotiation, and smart financial structuring, the real question is whether, and how, M&A can truly create additional and diffused value with a newly combined entity that is stronger and more profitable and able to grow faster and better than the two original counterparts would have been able had they remained separate. When this is the case, M&A is able to justify a fairer market value for the new-

ly combined entities (note—the two values are not necessarily moving together, as good or poor communication of the first can optimize or imperil the second; and because capital markets are still dominated by "animal spirits" and still far from the hypothesis of perfect information, full knowledge, and extended savviness assumed by the efficient market hypothesis we tend to use in academy). In fact, M&A can truly create additional value only if it is able to create, execute, and monetize synergies of a different nature. As a first point, economies of scale matter a great deal in driving cost optimization and enhancing operational productivity, especially given the indivisibility of certain investments (among which research and development (R&D) and IT stand high) and the greater efficiency a larger buyer can achieve on procurement or by managing the workforce with a greater pool of resources that can be deployed dynamically across key processes. As a second point, economies of scope, linked to leveraging the same distribution channels to sell diverse products, or gaining market power and brand recognition by using a sole umbrella brand to sell multiple value propositions coming from different companies, and so on, can also justify revenue synergies—hence also contributing to higher commercial productivity. Third, learning and knowledge economies can also be leveraged if different organizations contribute complementary knowledge to manage the same value chain, or extend from that to other complementary or adjacent ones—with shared and augmented intelligence. Finally, many other synergies, including those coming from risk and capital management, and diversification effects can also be considered. Whilst not always admitted by academic theory, in imperfect reality these financial synergies (that a savvy and skilled investor could create at the level of their portfolio) are also often valued and appreciated by pragmatic economic agents. Alongside all kind of synergies are, however, associated dyssynergies, as economies of scale bring more inflexibility and lower dynamism and a much greater complexity in managing a burgeoning organization; and as scope effects also bring the risk of overstretching, with overlaps and a less focused approach vis-à-vis pure, vertical players. Extended knowledge can also mean knowing a little about everything and almost nothing about what really counts, and so on. Hence, in this case every decision and move also need to attentively gauge any trade-off, which in turn can change over time and with the advent of new technologies, not to mention the relevance of the company's governance and the quality of its management.

- *Accretion and dilution*: Creating extra value is a good start but it does not guarantee to the single counterparts that they can be sure of having created and secured value for their original shareholders. In fact, by putting all the ingredients together, it is important to make sure we end up creating a larger pie, where synergies are larger than dyssynergies. But the dimension of the share of the pie also counts, and this justifies the "accretion" or "dilution" of the contributing companies (or of the buyer and seller—the ingredients in the case of an acquisition). An M&A can therefore become accretive for a counterpart (or eventually for both, if the monetary value of dividends they can expect from the combined entity is larger than their pre-merger one, considering not only the bigger pool of distributable profits—the larger size of the pie—but also the reduced entitlement in percentage to take home part of that money). Conversely, it can become dilutive if the net effect is making that flow of money shrink now and over time. Again, whilst in academic theory we may assume the way an investment or M&A deal is financed does not count toward determining this value creation, in practice it does—critically so. And, apart from choice about the mix of debt and equity used to finance a transaction, in M&A it is common practice to use shares to fund very large deals and other expensive transactions. The choice between an all-cash or an all-share deal structure (or a mix of the two) then contributes significantly to determining the accretion–dilution conundrum. A large company with undervalued stock market traded shares could in fact elect to pay cash when buying a smaller company. Or a mid-cap but well-appreciated company could also try to buy a much larger, but undervalued, one by offering a share swap that could still be accretive for its shareholders, whilst allowing the target to retain the absolute majority of the enlarged pie, and with an expected rerating of the stock coming from the supposedly better-managed bidder (in theory, the overall rerating of the newly combined entity could allow an accretion for both the bidder and the target company—hence creating financial value to both from Day 1).

- *Grow, downsize, change, and evolve*: In truth, the ideal M&A deal thus involves a friendly, pre-agreed merger between two major companies, or the acquisition of one of the two by the other, often following a hostile approach. In practice, typical and more frequent M&A involve the acquisition or sale of smaller businesses, whether already incorporated into a dedicated legal entity or as a subject of a required "carve out." A "carve-out" approach entails a piecemeal approach: taking out some part of the business and operating model of a company that is then contributed to a legal entity or SPV (special purpose vehicle). This is then ultimately bought and merged by the acquirer. In fact, M&A can obviously help a company to grow, by buying *tout court* a competitor, or by consolidating just some parts of their businesses, as the remains may not be of interest. A company can also use M&A to exit businesses and geographies that are not profitable or simply no longer strategic—to enhance its profitability, business model consistency, and stock market appreciation; or to ring-fence certain trouble-making assets and dispose of potential arising issues—that can be better managed and addressed by other third parties. Or it can just elect to sell some good enough but non-core business to address its excessive leverage or pursue a dynamic reallocation of capital, in accordance with its defined strategy and taking into account the macroeconomic trends it is betting on—often in response to discontinuities happening in innovative technologies, regulations, geopolitical equilibria, social secular (such as demography) shifts, and so on. In all these cases M&A is used as a tool to drive change and design a step-by-step evolutionary path toward the new target business and operating model and is less considered as a "great bargain" to be chased tactically, or as a truly "transformational opportunity" to be pursued at all costs. It becomes then the chisel in the hand of the sculptor, albeit creating a quick, effective, and sometimes rough "sculpture" that will need further polishing and smoothing, via the integration plans that will follow.

- *Value creation and monetization*: Eventually, M&A is not just used as a tool to merge large companies and build scale, scope, and other knowledge-based synergies. Or as a tool to change the business and operating models of a company. Or as a tool to chase arbitrage opportunities and financial short-term speculation. In fact, it can be used by owners and managers of equity capital to invest such capital in a more productive way, by pursuing a return through the better management of a company or of any other real asset they are buying from other owners and managers that—this is the underlying assumption—are not the best holders of these—or just need capital to keep going, do better, and/or grow more rapidly. The typical play of private equity managers is therefore to buy decent companies and good-quality real assets to manage them better and realize a multiple of the capital invested after a three- to five-year timeframe. Or to get control of good companies by injecting capital into them to allow these to grow more quickly—as they invest more and buy other smaller competitors. Or to buy excellent companies in order to then buy and consolidate other decent or poor ones, bringing them up to their mother company's higher standard and realizing, in this way, a rerating of the overall, combined company. Of course, private equity players can also make money by "buying low and selling high" (always a good starting point to consider for a successful M&A) but they are not truly adding value by this, just migrating some from the seller to the buyer (the buyer including themselves as general partners, and their investors as limited partners). And they can make even more money if they add a lot of leverage on top of the invested company, as they positively skew their expected return (lowering the amount of equity invested), shifting most of the financial downside to the lenders, not to mention the company itself, with its employees and ecosystem of suppliers, clients, communities, and territories served. Given these very diverse and paradigmatic approaches (often used in combination), it is therefore important to understand which kind of mission, vision, and strategy is driving the decision-making of the buyer and what kind of values (financial, i.e., speculative; or economic, i.e., long term, not to mention other intangibles) would really be migrated or created, when and how through the proposed M&A, and for which stakeholder.
- *Integrated end-to-end process*: M&A can be perceived as a flashy, high-profile, and high-octane business that can happen overnight, or over a weekend, with brutal acceleration and fast thinking, with sharply acting movers and shakers operating behind the scenes. In fact, it can take a few weeks to design and execute a great financial deal, and even less to implement a horrible one. But, speaking of true incremental value added that can be generated for all counterparts to a deal, it is usually safer to assume that a well-thought-out, well-executed, and fully realized synergies-driven accretive deal can take several years, with a "100 days" plan focused on the immediate, after closing, integration plan ("PMI") and

a further "1000 days" plan usually required to fully ensure that all potential synergies are targeted and addressed, whilst limiting any potential dyssynergy, let alone operational (and financial) risk from the integration itself. What is more important, and described in greater detail shortly, is that M&A as a process should be considered as an integrated one with a certain consistency across the different, and often very paradigmatic, phases, from end to end. It should start from the initial conceptualization of the inorganic move, progressing through its strategy definition; the targeting and screening of potential counterparts; the origination, development, and valuation of the actual opportunity; its negotiation, signing, and final closing, whilst considering in parallel the definition of the ideal funding and incentive structure. The PMI plan would then be addressing all kind of synergies and dyssynergies, until the full execution of all the main financial, industrial, operational, technological, and commercial levers considered to be drivers of added value creation (and risk management). On top of this integration, ad hoc restructuring, turnaround, and transformation plans could also be considered for the buyer and/or the seller, using M&A as a catalyst (e.g. sometimes this can work simply as an excuse to execute an overdue organizational overhaul, corporate service center trimming, migration of IT systems, etc.—where, given the two existing platforms, the target may be even be identified as a third, new one). This integrated and end-to-end process can then require multiple competencies and skills, including from specialized advisors, but would need only one "art director" clearly setting the direction and pace of the journey, and driving its values and momentum. The "M&A as an art director" should be able to integrate multiple managers and external advisors as a closely interconnected, albeit sometimes fully virtual, SWOT (strengths, weaknesses, opportunities, and threats) team—a team made up of people who will need to work together intensively and often come from very different professional backgrounds and cultures. In short, great fortunes can truly be gained (or wasted) over a short period of time because of M&A (mostly coming from value migration across multiple counterparts, including stock market investors). But eventually great creations of economic value added, not to mention other sustainability values, will take years to be achieved and safely secured, as the "M&A as an art director" is able to make the extended team run a marathon made up of thousands of sprints.
- *Economic value and total sustainability*: We should, therefore, not only distinguish between (existing) value migration as a zero-sum game and (incremental) value creation as a wealth accretion that can be distributed among the many counterparts involved (advisors included), but we should also enlarge the definition of the value being created, atop of the economic one (taking into consideration the capital-at-risk dimension and not just the profit-and-loss or cash flow ones). In fact, the economic value gained could be secured for the long run only if other intangible sustainability dimensions of value are also considered: from the social one (including, for example, the interest of employees, suppliers, and clients, and of the overall community and territory where the newly combined companies

happen to operate—a disgruntled workforce, or unhappy business partners, or a badly treated client base will hardly approve the M&A when implemented and tend to vote with their feet, i.e. moving away to competitors); to the environmental one (including, for example, accelerated plans for the decarbonization of the combined businesses, which would need to incorporate into their cost structure the negative contributions to the ecosystem and the depletion of natural scarce resources—to face the risk of becoming a "stranded business" and to make sure it respects in full the legislation, not to mention the requests coming from long-term environment, social, governance (ESG)-savvy investors and customers). Hence, our hypothesis for a successful M&A across time includes the definition and target of a set of strategy-driven, high-priority sustainable values, addressing and making up what we call "total sustainability"; and the idea that only a total sustainability approach can reinforce, from a competitive positioning perspective, the ability of a company to create incremental economic value in the long run.[1]

1.7   M&A as an art and (a bit) of a science

Our previous longlist of critical factors that can support a successful M&A execution, from thought to finish, is of course not exhaustive, as multiple other dimensions could be identified to better define what M&A is and, more importantly, how it can be developed to drive sustainable values creation, supporting a larger and larger impact on the many stakeholders involved (well beyond the shareholders of the seller and/or the buyer or of the two merging-of-equals counterparts). Before proceeding with an detailed description of an "M&A"-winning approach, we need to recognize that, no matter how much we use methodologies, frameworks, algorithms, and other technicalities that are at least partially science-based (analyzed in Part II of this handbook) and that practitioners need to know and master, M&A as a tool and as a process is still mostly an art, and will likely remain so—notwithstanding the many changes that new technologies (including AI) are soon expected to bring to the table and deliver through their go-to-market readiness and wider implementations. In short, economics as a "dismal science" is a social science where psychology, sociology, and philosophy, just to mention a few, are relevant disciplines that are usually learned by professionals the hard way, in the execution battlefield. Eventually, each buyer needs to have a clear vision they believe in and, even more importantly, each seller (particularly when the seller is the founder, top manager, and main owner of a company) will surely have a dream of what they want to achieve, beyond a great bargain and the money that comes with it. In fact, rarely, in our experience, has the final transaction price uniquely determined the outcome of a deal where an entrepreneur is selling their own business. As an art (as famously stated by Napoleon), M&A is therefore all about execution—and about winning the war of incremental value crea-

---

[1] Claudio Scardovi, *Strategy, Finance and Sustainable Value Creation* (Routledge 2024).

tion and accretion, even if some financial value migration battles could be lost during the bumpy road ahead. As such, M&A could be hardly expected to happen suddenly and quickly, as a grand revolution, as it will be more likely to fight its way to value creation via a "guerrilla war," à la Che Guevara. And, as a war, it should always be driven by strategy and by some superior political mission (as war is simply about politics brought to the next level, as famous general Carl von Clausewitz famously stated). It should also consider how any almost-perfect academic theory needs eventually to strike a balance with the imperfect reality of everyday life and the fabric of markets and societies. In short, M&A works through people, so their emotions and passions are also critical determinants to consider when making this happen successfully. With this in mind, a brief yet detailed description of the main components of the M&A life cycle as "one" (e.g. integrated and end to end) is worth considering:

- As a first stage, based on the mission and vision of the company and on its related strategic targets (profitability, growth, change in competitive positioning, etc.), an M&A strategy is defined based on the macro trends of the economy and the microeconomic ones of the industry and sector of relevance. Specifically, "game changers" such as climate change and green transformation, innovative technologies (from AI to biotech to 3D printing, etc.), or geopolitical dislocations (from trade wars to regional conflicts) can act as powerful catalysts, suggesting a refresh or entire rethinking of previous M&A strategies and accelerating the need for some inorganic offensive or offensive move—in short, they can bring back deal-making to the CEO and board.
- As a second stage, a longlist and then shortlist of opportunities can be built and screened, as aligned with the M&A strategy and matching most of the practical, actionable market and sectorial opportunities available. We have often used the tool of designing "M&A strategic forays" to stretch the discussion and consider also unobvious and apparently inconsistent options, to reinforce previous hypothesis or reject them altogether, to also overcome the "not market practice" automatic rejection temptation, and stretch the typical broker–dealer approach of many M&A advisors (usually trying to pitch to sellers what is already on sale and the market would already expect to happen, with little space left for imagination and creativity). In fact, great deals can also come from unexpected ideas. These shape—and do not follow—the market.
- As a third stage, proper homework needs to be done to get ready for the first interactions with the counterpart, the starting negotiations and following deal-making, and then prepare for the potential transaction ahead, splitting any irrational or less rational decisions into smaller elements of thinking and analysis that make these doable, manageable, and completely rational. The duty-of-care principle then requires (usually both) counterparts to perform deep due diligence on multiple fronts, from financial to operational, from ESG to commercial, not to mention regulatory, tax, and other legal dimensions. Whilst due diligence can raise some yellow or red flags, its target is not really to get the green flag on everything, but to understand all the potential risks involved, to address them preemptively

and plan for mitigants, and to also consider contingency and recovery plans. On the one hand, there is hardly any value to be gained from a deal that is plain and simple, with no risk attached—hence it will usually attract all kinds of competing bidders, who then push up the price. On the other hand, greater risk-weighted returns can be realized from complex situations that are offering the opportunity to create "alpha" (an extra return, uncorrelated with the market and able to beat it over the long run) if the owners and managers of the bought or integrated entity are playing well.

- As a fourth stage, all kind of transaction and closing risks need to be identified and addressed to successfully close the transaction, once the counterparts have committed to a price and to the related governance, which can make the potential value creation targets achievable and feasible. However, once the transaction is closed, the difficult part begins and preparatory work must start well in advance, with a clear definition of the Day 1 starting baseline and of a detailed plan regarding the targeted end state of the post-deal integration and its required journey (including a listing of required timing and investments, costs, and risks). In fact, all these elements of the post-deal journey should be factored in and considered, not only to justify the price a buyer is willing to pay, but also to start incorporating the elements using a proactive risk management approach that starts with the structuring of the deal, its financing, the governance, and all kind of other legal and regulatory provisions—from signing to closing and afterwards.

- As a fifth stage, a proper integration plan, ideally developed bottom up with the involvement of both the buyer and seller's management, need to be agreed and defined, with a "100-day" plan—to address emergency and immediate needs—and a "1000-day" plan—to pursue mid-term requirements and opportunities, which can then be fully targeted for the long term. This PMI plan then addresses the synergies that need to be realized (in the case of a merger) or the turnaround and transformation that need to be executed for an M&A regarding a single company or real asset, as is usually the case with an initial investment by a private equity fund. In fact, whilst its effects will be long-lasting, the decisions taken in the first three to six months of implementing this plan will significantly influence the direction and velocity of travel, not to mention the morale of the employees and the culture of the new company. Private equity funds can then develop and execute several (often tens) of bolt-on acquisitions, adding scale, scope, and much else to the starting platform. For this, apart from strategic considerations on the changing competitive positioning of the company, they also add value through their experience and professional approach to M&A. These may be things the previous entrepreneur did not have the time or skills to do alone.

- In a final stage, work needs to be done to fully execute the merger and bring the M&A cycle to its natural end; that is, getting back to business as usual (BAU), but in a very different form: allowing the profitability, growth, and other intangible changes that, following an organic, incremental path could have taken years, if not decades, to be fully realized. In truth, while a merger can allow these inorganic quantum leaps to happen because of the consolidation of the businesses and the realization of multifaceted related synergies, mergers also become good excuses to challenge the status quo and accelerate long overdue transformations and evolution—sometimes even pursuing a turnaround of the acquirer that would be politically unfeasible in normal times; realizing a "mergearound," or what we have called (in the case of banks) a "bankaround"—deleveraging the balance sheet, reducing the maturity mismatch, increasing liquidity, cutting costs and risks, addressing redundancies in people, real estate, IT systems and applications, and eliminating other central support functions.

In our experience, whilst defining the right strategy and identifying the right deal are obviously critical prerequisites to avoiding disasters and setting the basis for future value creation, they entail no immediate accretion on the dividends being paid to new and old shareholders (assuming shares are traded at their fair price and no value is migrated because of the idiosyncratic negotiation and funding structure of the deal). But once the strategy has defined the synergies and the potential path toward transformation and evolution that can truly create incremental value, a 3x multiplication effect can be addressed in the preparation and execution of the deal, and a 9x can happen in executing the plan and in delivering the promised synergies. Finally, a 20x can derive in the long term by the full change that was initially pursued through inorganic means—by changing the newly combined entity and delivering on the creation of a long-term value for shareholders, stakeholders, and the wider society and ecosystem alike (including our environment and Mother Earth).

2 Private Markets: The Opportunity for Sustainable Values Creation

2.1 Too much equity chasing fewer and fewer opportunities?

The new macroeconomic context, with higher interest rates coming after almost a decade of loose monetary policies and a near zero cost of financing, has made deal-making more difficult and costly to finance with debt (and has reduced the capacity of private equity players to raise new money as equity), and also, given the stock of investment already realized, has created a backlog of portfolio companies already invested in and ready to be sold by private equity funds. As a result, several companies are just waiting in line to exit, as sponsor-to-sponsor deals (one private equity firm selling to another) have also been put on hold for the same reasons. Apart from these tactical issues, which may last until a new interest rate regime change happens, a more fundamental question has been posed by market participants and policymakers, given the high growth rates experienced by private equity since the early 2000s, which brought their "dry powder" (the capital raised by private equity players but not yet invested) to around $13 trillion (Preqin). Are private equity players a force to reckon with and sometimes to fear, with regard to financial risks, social and environmental disdain, and even compliance risk implications—if they are not well understood, managed, and strictly regulated? Another fundamental question ("Is private equity now managing too much capital for the fewer and fewer remaining opportunities?"—hence leading to potential asset bubbles, unprofitable or value-destructing deals, and ruthless behaviors in a more and more competitive market) has gained traction and sympathy from many stakeholders; partially because of the very high returns realized in the past by successful players, which were usually more able to take advantage of the loose lending policies of banks and of other information asymmetries happening in the market (so goes the argument of contrarians). And whose active management skills were not necessarily strong enough to truly create 'alpha' companies, even though they drove portfolio companies toward value creation and yield growth for most of their stakeholders.

In order to answer to this *vexata quaestio* in an analytic and impartial way, it is useful to break down it into several subquestions, regarding, for example, the extension of the investable universe, the attainable financial sources and related potential uses, the resilience of private equity investments in diverse macroeconomic contexts, their ability to provide an "industrial alpha" that can deliver on top of a "financial (mostly speculative) alpha" linked to market dislocations and inefficiencies, and so on. An even more important question would then regard the ability of private equity to deliver on the promise of sustainable values for the long term, which are (partly) economic in nature, with a critical contribution expected on green transformation. As a start, global data suggests that the investable universe of private markets (including, in this definition, apart from corporates, real estate and infrastructure real assets and other natural resources such as farmland or timberland). This universe, amounting to around $620 trillion in 2021, up from $160 trillion in 2000 (McKinsey & Company), is still largely untapped by professional capital pools managed in a private way (i.e. neither invested through public stock markets nor state owned), and has grown over time at a rate that is higher than the global gross domestic product (GDP) (loose monetary policies and resulting inflationary pressures may also have contributed to this). Secular trends are instead suggesting the financialization of those real assets and their more productive management by professional third parties (e.g. real estate is typically better managed at scale by a professional asset manager—which can manage thousands of units—than by its individual owner).

2.2 Too many private assets with less and less equity to invest in them?

This private market investable universe is also much larger and underinvested than the public market one, suggesting that the "too much capital chasing too few assets" may actually work the other way around (in Italy, as an example, the overall investable universe has been estimated by us at around €13 trillion, with a total market capitalization of the Euronext Italian Stock Exchange (excluding financial services) at around €0.6 trillion—or 5% of the total). Also, the equity capital required for corporates and other real assets to grow and transform (in particular, to adapt to the greener requirements needed to fight climate change) is an enormous amount and cannot be credibly addressed by the public markets only (for Italy, we have estimated an equity gap of around €500 billion for corporates and a similar one for real estate and infrastructure—almost twice as much the current market capitalization and around one third of the current stock of the already excessive public debt). Hence, not only are the potential uses from capital already raised by the private equity industry wide-ranging, but the potential further funds that could be tapped and made available for investments in the real economy are huge and mostly unexplored. In fact, the capital-funding universe of private markets is fragmented, underdeveloped, and mostly underinvested with regard to this specific asset class, with secular trends driving democratization (through "retailization," i.e., making these kinds of investment opportunities available to individuals and families—not only to ultra-rich and wealthy individuals, but also to the affluent, and, potentially, in some intermediate ways, to mass market ones). Among private markets (including real estate, infrastructure, natural resources, and direct credit or "private debt" as well), private equity—as an already large and mainstream asset class for institutional investors—appears to be of potential interest to households already exposed to real estate risk (as they own their home) and to fixed-income products, including government bonds (with infrastructure or direct credit proposing risk/return profiles similar to these).

Private equity could therefore enhance the risk-adjusted return of a portfolio of individual or family savings, adding diversification and resilience against inflation as well—as the underlying corporates and real assets tend to reprice along the nominal increase of prices, hence defending the purchasing power of savings. Because of this, the "dry powder" of the private equity industry is expected to grow from $13 trillion (2023) to $26 trillion (2026), according to Preqin, with greater competition and shareholders' activism expected because of this. Are private equity players then becoming (for good or bad reasons) the new "masters of the universe," as they grow into financial powerhouses with an increased ability to potentially impact sustainability in a big way? And could they also become a leading force at the geopolitical level, with regard to the development of the economies of nations and of leading regional blocs? US players are leading the pack at the global level and across asset classes, from private equity to venture capital, from real estate to infrastructure, with a very fragmented market of few at-scale players and a much larger wealth of under-scaled, likely inefficient, mid-market players acting across Europe, and with mostly state-sponsored or state-linked entities in China. It is thus worth considering the implications private equity and the real asset market structure stage of development (or underdevelopment) could bring to a country, and to the global ecosystem at large.

2.3 "Alpha" in private equity (and real assets)

If there is still a vast and largely untouched universe of investable assets, and an equally large pool of mostly untapped capital for private equity to raise and use to invest and transform these, then a critical question looms large. Assuming in the future these two demand- and supply-side opportunities are addressed and met, with a much larger pool of private capital raised by private equity and an equally large portfolio of real assets invested, would this be a good thing, or not? Also, would this be a positive thing for investors, asset and wealth managers, and for the other multiple stakeholders, including the employees and customers of the invested companies, the client and end users of the infrastructure and real estate assets, and the environment? In order to answer the first question, we need to consider past returns of private equity funds spanning different asset classes and investment strategies, comparing these to their historical volatility and to the losses that were experienced by their investors. A number of analyses we developed, using the past performances of private capital funds investing in corporates and real estate, as presented in other works,[1] have in fact shown that not only returns were higher than so-called liquid equity investments (investments in shares of companies listed on regulated stock markets), but that their

---

[1] Claudio Scardovi, *Speranza e Capitale* (EGEA 2021); Claudio Scardovi, *Investire Bene in Italia* (EGEA 2023).

volatility was also relatively low and was comparable to other safe assets, such as corporate and government bonds. More specifically, on a universe of 422 funds analyzed, just 41 (less than 10%) lost some of the capital invested, with an average loss limited to 26% for funds investing in corporates (and with lower losses for infrastructure and real estate investments), and with limited volatility measured throughout the fund investment life.

Of course, this limited volatility is also due to the way and frequency the NAV of private equity investments is calculated. Still, the very small number of funds that lost money, and the limited amount they lost in that scenario, show that the implied risk of private investments is much lower than is commonly understood. This may be due to the investors' expertise in M&A and in their "buying low and selling high" prowess, and to the greater amount of leverage they tend to use in the process. This should be driven by the more effective and efficient governance the new financial owner tends to impose on the target company from Day 1, after they take control of the portfolio company; and to the more focused and active management approach they tend to instill in their portfolio companies, to increase their EBITDA from the ground up, cutting costs and transforming the IT and operations of the company, increasing its sales effectiveness and its overall revenues through innovation and M&A, and reallocating its limited (equity and debt) financial resources toward their optimal and most productive end use. In short, there seems to be significant "alpha" to be gained in private equity, for institutional investors and retail as well, as long as they have the patience to hold the investment for the long term and the ability to keep cool during market turmoil and downturns. The relative illiquidity of these investment products, which cannot be sold freely in a short timeframe and have a limited discount, is certainly a risk factor that should be considered, as should an implied opportunity cost when gauging the overall profitability equation. But the extra pains appear to be worthwhile, with greater than expected returns for this "illiquidity" effect. There are also ways to limit any issues, through liquidity window mechanisms, the floatation of funds on regulated stock markets, and the development of a larger and more profound secondary market, where invested portfolios are continuously sold over the counter.

2.4 Opportunities for asset and wealth managers

For investors to become interested in private equity at scale, there needs to be significant payoff for asset managers and wealth managers as well. In fact, the latter need to develop the product suite that can address the pent-up demand of institutional and, maybe more importantly, retail investors. Investment strategies also need to profile and target the most promising assets and value creation opportunities, which, leaving aside the financial rocket science engineering and overleverage of the past, can be reached by focusing on creating alpha through the better, active management of companies and the synergies that a value accretive M&A can generate. If this kind of alpha is achieved, this can ultimately increase the productivity of the overall economy and create a larger payoff for stakeholders to share. From an asset management perspective, many at-scale North American private equity players already exist, whilst Europe is still better characterized by a coterie of small to mid-size players punching well below the weight of their American counterparts. For the US player opportunity therefore comes from consolidation, as smaller players disappear or just focus on super-niche asset classes and investment thesis, and mid-sized players merge together or are acquired and integrated by major players. Hence, a significant value creation opportunity can develop and be reaped through M&A in the alternative asset management market, as has happened already, in a similar way, in the traditional, long-only, asset management space.

Actually, consolidation is also expected among larger players in the United States, with the minimum critical mass of AUM (assets under management) shifting from around $10 billion to 20, 30, 50, or even 100 billion, with some minimal extension in geographical coverage and scope (most of the biggest and most successful players already play across the Western bloc and some globally, albeit with a degree of more recent retrenching from places like Russia and China). Whilst consolidation can happen among private equity players and can create value through synergies in capital-raising, deployment, funnels of origination opportunities as first investments, and add-ons, and for the build-up of the alternative asset managers' capabilities as operating partners, an even larger opportunity appears to regard traditional, long-only asset managers—now mostly focused on liquid, regulated markets, with a mix of actively managed funds and passive beta-tracking ones—highly. From a wealth management perspective, the opportunities from private equity and real assets are therefore at least twofold. On one side, private equity and real asset investing can allow investment opportunities for the remainder and much larger investable universe that is available, aside from money market products, bonds, and listed equities, to be pursued. A wider and deeper portfolio of available products can then allow financial advisors to suggest and offer greater portfolio diversification and a range of new products that, because of their inherent illiquidity and less competitive trading, can offer higher expected IRR, often with a less than proportional increase in their risk profile. In short, wealth managers can to do a better job for their clients if they are able to offer corporate buyouts, through professionally managed and well-diversified private equity funds, and real estate development and other tactical opportunities, via financial products that have these as their investment underlyings, further covering the opposite hedges of the investable universe with high-risk/high-return venture capital and low-risk/low-return infrastructure.

On the other side, as these products are more complex to source, select, and sell, and they also offer higher expected IRR, their distribution to private investors can allow for higher margins, in terms of both upfront and running fees gained through their investment period, which is rarely less than five to seven years. Hence, as for asset managers, for wealth managers the fee income coming from private equity and real asset investment products distribution appears to be sustainably higher and have lower volatility in the mid-term, as the savings invested in these products tend to be locked in for a few years (this is also a shortcoming, as this longer investment period usually limits the share of the products that can be allocated to retail clients and makes their sale much more difficult, requiring significant post-sale effort in communicating the performances, the trends, and the expected quantity and timing of payouts). Given the starting point of private investors (with, on average, 3–5% of savings allocated to private equity, versus the suggested optimal allocation for long-term investors of 30–50%), the growth opportunities in private markets are also huge, with wealth managers potentially playing a catalyst role in the education, promotion, and post-sales management of this asset class. This short-term opportunity for wealth managers catering to ultra-high net worth individuals or otherwise fairly wealthy private banking clients, could also develop into a mid- to long-term opportunity for retail banks serving affluent and even mass market clients, as these sophisticated products become industrialized, with structuring potentially allowing for minimum ticket investments, single drawdowns (instead of multiple capital calls, not manageable for a large number of investors with minimal capital committed), some limited liquidity features, and so on. Indeed, this "democratization" through "retailization" opportunity could be a very interesting one to pursue at scale, if the private equity industry and market opportunity want to truly become pervasive and keep growing and, more importantly, leave a profound and permanent mark on investment management and on sustainability as well.

2.5 Opportunities for insurance companies

For alternative asset managers pursuing private equity strategies and real asset investments, at the end of the day capital is almost everything. You may easily become forgotten if your investment strategy does not pay off or, worse, loses money. But eventually money attracts new money, or at least provides asset managers with more opportunities to pursue big deals and monetize, through their carried interest, a relevant portion of the financial wealth being created (as their percentage performance attribution is almost fixed at market standards, they can get more money if they increase the volume of capital invested, with limits only set by the availability of sources and deployment opportunities). Capital-raising is therefore key in deciding which investment manager gets the chance to invest big time and, fund after fund, has the ability to keep investing with new money in the future, investment cycle after investment cycle, with larger deals bringing larger capital gains for them (in monetary terms, even if the IRR may be the same as smaller ones). There are, however, several quite different forms of capital, and the more enticing for private equity and real asset investors is the "permanent" one, that is, a pot of capital that is allocated for very long periods of time, sometimes even with no stated end date (as is typical for the capital allocated to companies). Funds with no end date are also called "evergreen" or "eternal" capital. The dream of alternative asset managers is therefore to have, year after year, access to new flows of money with very long durations or, ideally, with a permanent or evergreen/eternal nature. This is exactly the typical capital that life insurance companies and pension funds want, which tends to grow year after year as they keep rolling forward long-term liabilities (the income they commit to provide to their policyholders or subscribers). These are funded by the premia or savings paid to its pool of policyholders or employees. The new funds that keep flowing in year after year fund a liquid pool of finance (the "float") that needs then to be invested wisely to achieve higher IRR in the long term and to also match the typically long-term horizons of their liabilities. What better match then than for insurers and pension funds to commit some of their funds to private equity and real asset players, ideally selecting a large number of the best performers across multiple investment strategies and asset classes, and diversifying away the risk that some of these "best" could lose their magic touch in the future?

However, what if a private equity player is taking over an insurance company, not as a typical investment trade and with a limited holding period ahead of the investment, but as a source of competitive advantage for getting more and more capital to manage, and of the best quality (the very long term, or permanent, type)? This is exactly what has happened in the last decade, with an acceleration to today. The three global top players, Blackstone, Apollo, and KKR, have in fact bought insurers or taken minority stakes in them in exchange for managing their assets, and smaller private equity firms are following suit.[2] The insurers they acquired were not intended as portfolio investments to be sold for profit; rather, they were valued for their extensive balance sheets, which provide a cheap, accessible, and highly attractive source of funding due to their long-term durations. The insurance companies they bought, in turn, are expecting to make higher profits from the private equity investment strategies pursued, to fund their future payouts and the annuities sold to policyholders and pensioners. Through their new owners, they can knowledgeably move their portfolios along the efficient frontier and toward the higher yielding private market investments in which the former specialize—so goes their reasoning, at least. As such investments have long-term durations (in contrast to banks), the long-term duration of the insurance companies' assets can match them and pursue a higher IRR.

2.6 A new, emerging, systemic risk?

This strategy brings, however, several risks for insurance companies and pension funds and to society as a whole, as the companies and funds are typically perceived as "systemic" in nature, and bound to be saved by taxpayers' money should anything go wrong. For a start, in a crisis, insurance policyholders could just panic and flee as they seek to get some of their savings back, even at a cost. A bank-run-like meltdown could occur if asset durations are excessively stretched and liquidity buffers are inadequate to meet customers' withdrawal requests. Such a crisis, similar to what happened with Eurovita in Italy in 2023 (owned by a private equity firm), could

---

[2] "The risk to global finance from private equity's insurance binge," *The Economist*, January 25, 2024.

be managed through coordinated efforts among remaining market players to prevent contagion. However, the rising prominence of private equity and real assets—amounting to around $13 trillion in assets under management, with major firms like Blackstone, Apollo, and KKR accounting for nearly $2.5 trillion—could trigger a global crisis if something were to go wrong. This risk extends beyond the clients of life insurance and pension funds; private equity funds, often referred to as 'shadow banks' due to their lighter regulatory oversight compared to traditional banks, are also heavily leveraged by banks. This interconnectedness means that any failures within private equity could potentially affect lenders as well.

In short, private equity big players are buying with insurers' money, and via insurance companies they previously bought and now control on an unprecedented scale, and also raising questions in terms of governance (e.g. are the policyholders of the life insurer better off if their money is allocated to just one alternative asset manager instead of a very high number of different ones?). The ensuing concentration of risk could in fact also mean that certain investments are made more in the asset manager general partners' interest, and less in the clients' one, as these general partners are also controlling the decision-making of the insurer. All in all, life insurers owned by investment firms amassed, at the end of 2023, assets of nearly $800 billion. For most of them, these assets have (not surprisingly) increased their share of allocated capital to private equity and specifically to the one owning most of their shares. Hence, there are all kind of reasons to suggest a closer monitoring and a deeper regulation of these crossholdings, and investment strategies should be carefully mixed and executed, with the long-term needs of policyholders and pensioners at their heart. Still, the logic of such tie-ups and intertwined alliances seems strong, and destined to become stronger and stronger as developed nations becomes older (the average age of their citizens increases and does the ratio of pensioners to workers) and a retirement crisis appears to be looming in the horizon. Defined-benefit pensions, where firms guarantee incomes for retirees, have been in decline for decades. Annuities instead allow individuals to plan for the future, without requiring the insurer or pension fund to commit necessarily to a minimum guarantee that would almost certainly require a significant investment in fixed-income investment products. The business of annuities, particularly under specific demographic assumptions, can create a 'float' of investable capital that appears to be permanent. This ongoing pool of capital can be more effectively managed through investments in private markets, which are often less liquid but can offer higher returns. By entrusting these investments to properly incentivized professional alternative asset managers, financial institutions can optimize their strategies and achieve better outcomes for their clients. These managers are motivated to align their interests with those of the investors, ensuring that the capital is deployed strategically to maximize growth while managing risk. But what if the insurers themselves bought private equity houses and not vice versa? Using them as in-house alternative investment platforms, as they are already doing for most of their liquid asset portfolios? Main insurance companies, with the scale and reach to manage this successfully, could then derive significant value for their policyholders and shareholders as well, with better risk-adjusted returns and larger fees, not to mention the greater control they could exert on the investment process—from the initial decision to invest to the following management and final exit—and on their related risks.

2.7 What it takes to become "master of the universe"

As we discussed, private equity and real assets are not only bringing with them a significant opportunity for the investable companies and other real assets (the investable universe) and for the investable pot of money (from institutional investors and from private clients and even retail ones). But, also, they are providing a chance for growth for more traditional financial service players (such as asset managers, wealth managers, retail and commercial banks, and even insurance companies). The growth in revenues can come from increasing volumes of AUM and higher margins, then translating into higher fee income. Because of this rerating opportunity, several traditional players are now integrating these kinds of offerings into their business and operating models, with a view to serving their clients better and making their shareholders wealthier. In fact, most of the large, traditional financial service players are already managing or gathering and advising huge quantities of savings, with multiple forms of permanent capital naturally being created by their investment processes. As they have so far allocated a very limited share of this capital to private equity and real asset investments, they have significant room to maneuver and great margins of improvement to deliver better value creation to their customers, shareholders, and—as we will discuss later—to their other stakeholders, including their employees, and communities and territories of reference, not to mention the environment. For them, or for the largest pure players already successfully competing in the global markets, a number of prerequisites ("qualifiers") need then to be taken into account, and a further number of competitive drivers or unique selling propositions ("winners") need to be considered also. For them to develop into a new (or remain as) "master of the universe" (MOTU), we have come up with four qualifiers and (at least) two winners (not to mention the ability to truly create "alpha"):

Qualifiers for developing into a MOTU:

- product innovation;
- consolidation and scale;
- democratization and digitalization;
- global reach for capital sourcing and deployment.

Key winners for truly becoming a MOTU:

- Access to permanent/evergreen capital, through longer term, patient capital supplied by insurance companies, pension funds, endowments, and sovereign wealth funds.

- Access to private wealth through a financial advisor or bank networks, to tap into the vast saving pools of private clients and promote the democratization of the industry.

This is not, of course, an exhaustive list of competitive drivers as these tend to change fast, following diverse market conditions and the changing behaviors and preferences of end investors. As these platforms keep growing, other "competitive invariances" will emerge with—we hope—the ability to truly deliver sustainable value creation and become the "next alpha" to target and make a difference, to leave a mark and make a more profound and long-lasting impact on economies, societies, and environment. It is not a small challenge. And the time to deliver is short.

2.8 Real estate opportunities for private markets

Our analysis indicates that private equity investments in corporations have significant potential for growth, considering the vast investable universe still available. The influx of private capital that these firms can attract may ultimately allow them to capitalize on numerous opportunities. This potential is further enhanced by changes in governance that can result from having a unique financial owner, who brings a distinct perspective and strategic direction. This shift in governance can create new avenues for value creation and operational improvements, ultimately benefiting the companies involved. This means that private capital could truly spur corporates' growth and transformation through M&A. In fact, as we discussed in the previous chapter, serial acquisition (or bolt-on M&A) can be used to accelerate the build-up of economies of scope and scale, and as a driver of innovation and change for the original company—to build bigger and better "platforms." For serial acquisitions to happen, having a financial shareholder very much focused on making these happen appears to be a competitive advantage, as financial capabilities are a requirement for executing this "bolt-on" strategy in such a way as to accelerate EBITDA growth and optimize exit multiples. However, corporates are neither the largest investable asset, in terms of baseline, within the many private market opportunities now available, nor do they appear to be the most exciting in terms of growth. Certainly, venture capital is also of interest, as it invests in startups and companies in their earlier stages of development, and usually pursue the adoption and go-to-market element of innovative technologies. Venture capital is, however, a fairly high-risk/high-return business, with an overall lower percentage of capital allocated to it by institutional and retail investors. As such, it appears today as a subsector of the alternative asset management industry, characterized by volatility and (at this point of the cycle) limited growth.

Real estate is instead a much larger opportunity, as the baseline is several times bigger, estimated at around €200 trillion globally. Private equity can be invested into real estate assets that are already rented and in no or limited need of refurbishment and repositioning—following a strategy of investing into "core" or "core-plus" assets. Greater "alpha" can, however, be gained by investing in real estate assets that need some repositioning, following a "value add" strategy, with greater risk/returns ahead. The more interesting opportunity to discuss, given the topic of this handbook, is, however, "opportunistic" investments in real estate as an asset class, which may include the repossession of a hard asset from the borrowing counterpart of NPLs, or new developments—at green- or brownfield stage. These opportunities may also address megatrends such as "urbanization" (with most of the global population expected to live in big cities by 2050), "digitization" (the development of "smart cities," where big data and connectivity are on offer and act as the fuel of AI-powered analytics that can manage the city in a more effective and efficient way, and offer extra value added to its residents and end users), and "green conversion" (the need to make cities more sustainable, with lower CO_2 emissions, to help fight climate change). We will thus discuss real estate and describe its potential development trends and the opportunity of "urban regeneration" investments, not to mention its evolution "as a service" business.

2.9 Real estate as an investable asset

As we discussed, the universe of investable private assets is vast and largely untapped. As part of this, real estate stands by far as the largest asset class, with a total stock of around $200 trillion[3]—even larger than the sum of all equities and bonds. Leaving aside the fact that a large chunk of this is directly owned by its end users, often families and individuals as householders, most of the owners of the remainder are just looking for ways to make their assets financially investable, in the easiest and cheapest way, fostering the transparency and liquidity of a market that has also been known for the opposite: opacity and illiquidity. Actually, most of the stock owned by the end users could also become financially investable should the long-term trend of renting ("rent generation") develop, toward a steady state where we use our home and benefit from the associated, well-diversified, and customized services offered by professional third parties (or "real estate service platforms"), without actually owning that home, which could be invested in and owned by long-term investors, such as insurance companies, pension funds, and endowments pursuing other secular trends ("build to rent/buy to rent"). At the same time, having monetized our single ticket investment in our home (that, on average and for main European countries, stands as a 50–60% of our overall individual savings), we could have the opportunity to reinvest that sum into real estate, through investment funds with greater diversification and granularity and with a professional approach to investment selection and management. Hence, if real estate can be fully developed into a financial asset that can be easily added to or subtracted from the overall investment portfolio of an individual or institutional investors, it could greatly contribute to the optimization of the investors' overall risk/return profile, as it would add diversification and decorrelation vis-à-vis the other asset classes in the portfolio and an obvious hedge against

---

[3] *The Economist*, www.economist.com.

inflation. It would therefore extend the range of the portfolio optimization opportunities coming from private markets (i.e. private equity and other real assets), with great benefits to the investor, as shown in Table 2.1.

Of course, the investment cycle in the real estate sector is very much driven by the economic cycle and by the macroeconomic environment of reference. In turn, given its relevance, it can influence most other industrial sectors and the end consumers' behaviors (the value of real estate drives a form of "monetary illusion" that impacts consumption patterns). It is also closely intertwined with the banking system, with balance sheet and profit-and-loss interrelations that are often deep, complex, and continuously evolving. Most of the banking crisis of the past, for example, partly originated in the burst of real estate bubbles and the following "vicious loops" that developed: as real estate lost value, banks had to crystalize accounting losses and had to decrease their leverage because of their lower regulatory capital; and as they reduced their lending to real estate this kept losing value, leading to further "fire sales" and further losses for banks. As investment activity in real estate is even more profoundly influenced by the availability of lending, the other opportunity for real estate coming from private markets is represented by credit funds, which can complement the lending supply coming from banks and, as they are not as strictly regulated as the former, can better absorb the downside volatility of the real estate assets they finance. Multiple strategies are then available to invest in this asset class, with opportunistic ones that have been able to decorrelate better from the macroeconomic cycle and with a much higher resilience shown through crisis by trophy assets (best buildings based in prime locations). The real estate sector is also being impacted by radical transformation and by a wide range of disruption factors: from digitization and the ever increasing use of structured and unstructured big data, captured by the Internet of Things (IoT) and then analyzed by machine learning and AI algorithms; to green transformation and the ever increasing need to turn buildings and entire cities into net-zero CO_2 contributors to fight and contrast climate change; to demographic and social changes, as developed nations become characterized by smaller and more dynamic families, greater mobility and longevity, with older citizens and higher ratios of pensioners to workers.

All these change agents can then offer opportunities for private equity to be deployed in the sector with a significant impact and a clear strategy to create incremental value—not only better economic returns but also positive payoffs in social and environmental dimensions. For example, digitization allows the pursuit of smart cities and smart buildings where investments in data center, connectivity, and other high-tech infrastructure need to be made, adding value to the overall built environment and developing the nature of real estate "as a service." With greater necessity to rent more and own less, alongside a new "buy to let/buy to rent" investment strategy emerging as a global opportunity and as a key driver of this servitization of real estate, individuals and families, by selecting to own less directly, in terms of "first/second home," end up freeing a significant share of their own savings and financial resources that can be reallocated elsewhere, although not necessarily away from real estate as an asset class. As already mentioned, we could end up deciding to rent our

2 Private Markets: The Opportunity for Sustainable Values Creation

Table 2.1 Real estate as a financial asset for portfolio management

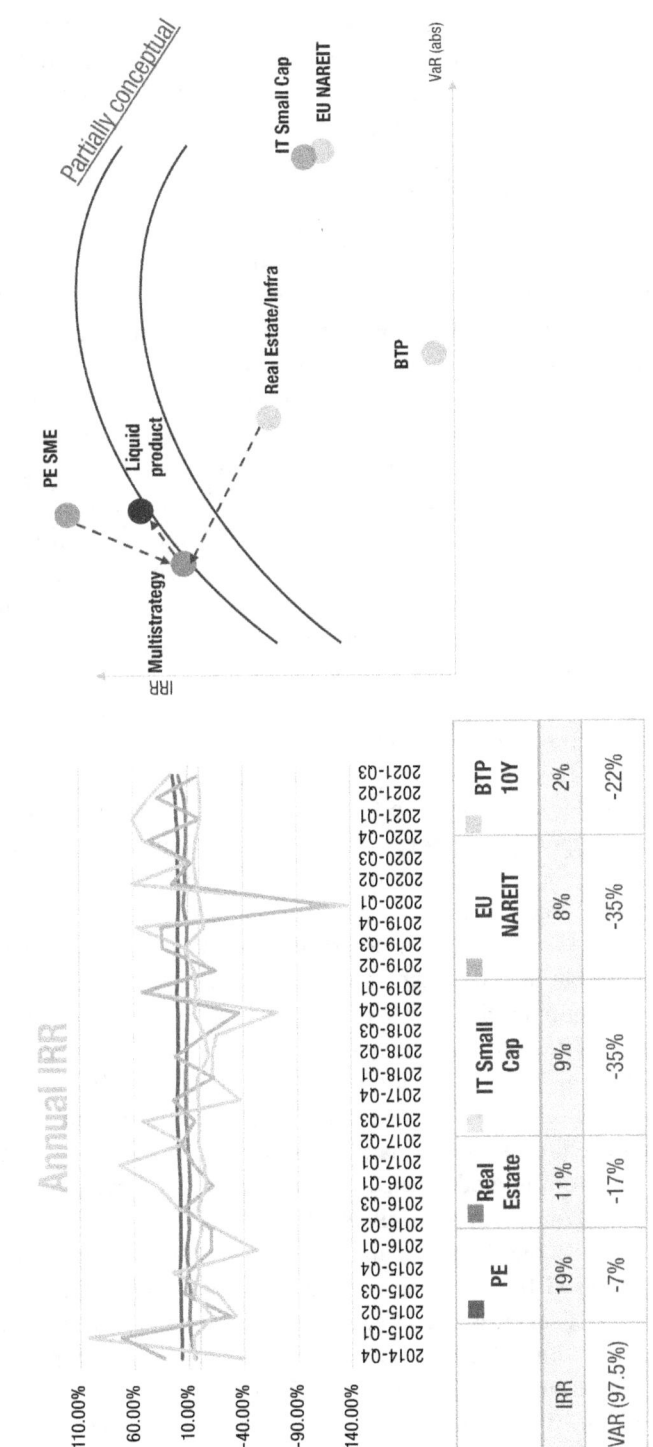

home, divesting from a single asset with an high concentration of risk and limited efficiencies in terms of maintenance costs and no income produced, and invest in one or more well-diversified real estate funds, pursuing different investment strategies and with a professional, active management approach to their underlyings—to also realize operational cost efficiencies and the optimization of the yield these can attain and pay back to their investors.

This financial trend could also be seen acting consistently and in parallel to the "shared economy" one, where individuals tend to own directly to a lesser extent, and rely more and more on shared assets and services to increase their productivity and reduce their overall CO_2 footprint whilst increasing their own personal utility. The opportunity of redeploying the financial savings of citizens currently invested in their own real estate is also paving the way toward the regeneration of these assets, often in serious need of refurbishment, restructuring, redesign, and potential conversion to different end uses and requiring extensive upgrades in their energy efficiency that in Europe is now also required by law, following the approval and implementation of the so-called Greenhouse Legislation. All this transformation will require significant amounts of equity capital and new debt financing as well, but could lead to a higher yield and enhanced productivity for a stock in which we usually invest around half of our national savings—inefficiently, as we own a single, poorly managed asset. On top of the economic value creation opportunity, a greater social sustainability should also follow, spurred by the rent economy that is making housing more available to everybody, through the greater digitization and connectivity that is supporting inclusion and favored as well by city redesigns that prevent the "gentrification" of certain prime locations and the formation of neglected suburbs. New designs for cities can also support a greater environmental sustainability as well, as decarbonization is accelerated not just through the energy efficiencies achieved at buildings level, but also via the accompanying investments made in the renewable energy infrastructure and in the overall transportation system (aiming to produce less CO_2 to move us around, but also to make us move around less, through, for example, the concept of the "15-minute city"—where we can reach everything we need in a walk of not more than fifteen minutes), not to mention the better management of clean water and waste. It is also worth mentioning that new ways of living could present an investment opportunity for private capital keen to invest in real asset and in the transformation of real estate as a financial asset class and as a fungible "product" where the value add from related services ("real estate as a service") becomes more and more important. For example, business designs for student housing, or silver housing or hospitality (second homes managed as a hotel or as shared assets that can be rented when not used by the direct owner), are becoming more and more common, with facilities and services specifically designed for their targeted end users (from house maintenance and cleaning, to safety and security for people and things, to first aid and lifestyle-supporting services such as baby- and dogsitting, etc.), not to mention the creation of shared facilities such as gyms and swimming pools, spas, meeting and business centers, entertainment facilities, green spaces, and so on.

2 Private Markets: The Opportunity for Sustainable Values Creation   37

Table 2.2 Urban regeneration: main regulatory drivers

Urban regeneration can be the next big-big thing, for bad or good, if done sustainably

CHANGES IN THE BUY-SIDE TARGET PROPOSITION	CHANGES IN THE SELL-SIDE TARGET PROPOSITION
SFDR - Sustainable Finance Disclosure Regulation Regulation (EU) 2019/2088 Article 8: products that promote, inter alia, environmental or social characteristics (or a combination thereof), even if these are not their primary objective; Article 9: products that have sustainable investment objectives	**EPBD - Energy Performance of Building Directive** *under approval* **Jan. 2030**: all buildings within the regulatory perimeter will have to achieve energy class E; **Jan. 2033**: *all buildings within the regulatory perimeter must achieve energy class D*; **Jan. 2050**: achievement of the Carbon Neutrality target for the European built heritage
- **Effective from 2021** and for all financial products - Interesting for **institutional investors** - Already visible effect on **capital allocation** - Preference for real estate with high **ESG standards** - **Value differentials** between ESG and non-ESG properties - **ESG as a driver** for value creation	- Focus on **real estate** and **energy efficiency** - **Quantitative approach** with data needs - Effects **on the entire real estate sector** - Requires large **amounts of capital** for redevelopment - Affects **all types of owners** (also public administrations and households)
OBJECTIVES: - provide transparency with regard to sustainability impacts - facilitate comparison between different investment options - channel capital flows toward sustainable investments The regulation provides for **pre-contractual and periodic disclosure requirements** and introduces a classification of financial products	**Objectives:** - Defining a common methodology for calculating energy consumption - Improvement of energy efficiency - Redevelopment obligations within set deadlines The law is aimed at accelerating the **redevelopment of the building** stock by introducing more stringent energy efficiency requirements

In conclusion, because of the several meta trends discussed, investing in real estate, as the largest financially investable asset class globally, could become more exciting in the future, with significant potential for sustainable values creation. As a summary, and as an "umbrella brand" of these many multifaceted opportunities, urban regeneration could become the next big-big thing in real estate investing and (given the sheer size of the required investments) in private markets. The ESG angle of this would also be very important and impact both buy- and sell-side propositions. As detailed in Table 2.2, on the investors' (or "buy") side, several regulations, notably the SFDR (Sustainability Financial Directive on Reporting), will require funds pursuing total sustainability objectives in accordance with Articles 8 and 9 of the legislation: to control, monitor, and report the objectives pursued and achieved. On the current owner and end users' (or "sell") side, other regulations, starting with the EPBD (Energy Performance of Buildings) will require an acceleration in our transition toward net zero, needing huge amounts of capital (equity and debt) to turn these assets "from brown to green" and, at that point, opening up the opportunity for a fuller redesign of their proposition that could include other disrupting factors discussed, such as digitization, social inclusion, segmented end-user proposition, shared economy, and the overall trend toward "real estate as a service."

2.10 Infrastructure opportunities for private markets

Infrastructure is the other, very significant, emerging opportunity for private equity and real asset managers and investors, as the world is on the cusp of an "infrastructure revolution" (in the words of Larry Fink, the CEO of BlackRock, the largest asset manager globally; BlackRock recently bought Global Infrastructure Partners, the third-largest investor in infrastructure). Not only have infrastructure funds risen fivefold to $1.3 trillion (Preqin) since 2014, but pension funds and sovereign wealth funds keep asking for more opportunities to invest, as they are attracted by the lower but much more stable returns expected by this asset class. The opportunity on the demand side is also huge, for a few reasons. On one side, as public debt has risen consistently across the globe, states have been using existing infrastructure to deleverage, by partially privatizing and selling this. They are also seeking new private capital to refurbish and develop further infrastructure, often through PPP (public–private partnership) structures. On the other side, three megatrends are asking steadily for more new infrastructure, with an accelerated timeline to completion. First, the world needs to meet its climate goals, with some $8 trillion that needs to be invested over the 2020–2030 decade in renewable energy such as solar and wind, as well as batteries to store this and transmission lines to transport it. Other infrastructure investments will then be needed in hydrogen facilities, to produce carbon-free fuel for planes and ships, as well as for carbon sequestration (where CO_2 is extracted from the atmosphere and sequestered safely below the earth). Second, the world is moving toward an almost unstoppable digitization, as smart megacities are followed by others and AI becomes a dominant force in almost every industry, as well as in our everyday lives. The software that is needed to run AI and reap the benefits of digitization needs, however, huge physical assets, from fiber-optic cables and 5G networks to data centers, ideally not physically far from the location of our end use—to reduce lag time and increase security. Third, deglobalization—a byproduct of geopolitical tensions, trade wars, and regional conflicts—implies significant changes and geographical relocation of entire supply chains (the move of sensible manufacturing from China to India and South Korea, or the repatriation of critical industries such as chip-making are just recent examples).

Governments of heavily indebted states may be more willing to consider private capital investors to rise to the challenge of change of these megatrends, but these assets remain strategic and of an acutely sensible nature, as they determine the nature of many public goods that are eventually delivered to voting citizens. For this reason, and given the macroeconomic environment described in the first chapter, with more costly and less easily available debt, the growth and success of infrastructure investing should not be taken for granted. Long gone are the times where huge leverage (made possible by the physical nature of the collateral, its extended lifetime, and the steady stream of revenue) was making most of the recipe of winning big time in infrastructure. A similar approach to the active management of corporates' portfolio companies is thus being pursued by most sophisticated investors, which are trying to add value throughout the life of their investments through operational efficiency and commercial effectiveness, and not just through financial engineering and hyper-leverage. As infrastructure becomes a larger and larger engine of growth and wealth creation for the global economy and specifically for the "global south" (in greater need of basic infrastructure and a laggard on digital infrastructure), the contribution of private capital to this asset class and to the economy is therefore becoming of the utmost importance. As is already its contributions to green transformation (through renewable energy and others) and to social inclusion (through connectivity and enhanced, easier, and cheaper mobility, allowing people easier access to location-based opportunities), both key drivers of urban regeneration and of smart, sustainable cities.

Finally, it is worth mentioning the increased interest of private equity investments in natural resources, such as land, forests, and water. With a growing global population (now approaching almost 8 billion people), and subject to the negative effect of the anthropogenic, post-Industrial Revolution influence of humans, these natural resources are becoming scarcer and scarcer and therefore more and more critical, notwithstanding advances in innovative technologies, such as genetics, precision agriculture, and other biotech developments. Private equity investments are therefore growing in farmland, timberland (wood is used for industrial production but trees are now becoming more valuable for CO_2 capture and sequestration, and, therefore, they can be monetized through green certificates and sold to third parties), and even fish-farming. As an asset class, natural resources are addressing the need of states to deleverage and find new sources of capital that can fund land preservation, fish and stock repopulation, or reforestation programs, introducing new and more effective ways to scale the businesses and share the investments that can make these assets more profitable and productive, on top of becoming more sustainable. In the event of more negative climate change scenarios, useful natural assets could also become scarcer and scarcer, with inundation taking back to the ocean entire regions or the accelerated depopulation of fishes caused by pollution and acid waters, not to mention devastation of entire forests caused by extreme winds, fires created by scorching temperatures, and the like. In short, there is a business opportunity for alternative asset managers, of diversification for investors and a greater chance of survival for humankind, by limiting the negative impacts on the planet introduced by our Anthropocene era.

2.11 Closing the funding gap for green transformation

After a few years of great interest (mostly from 2019) on everything related to ESG, private equity and real asset "sustainable investing" appeared as just another incarnation of the drive and widespread support to use finance to contribute to the development of a better world and, specifically, to fight and mitigate climate change. From an asset management perspective, the tide is now apparently turning, with sales of climate-focused mutual funds (one of the most simple and retail investor-focused investment products) falling by 75% in 2023 versus 2021 ($38 billion of new money versus a record of $151 billion in 2021). This has happened not only because of the challenges coming from a high interest rate environment, but also from the poor performances achieved (versus "browner" investments, which have done quite well, specifically in the dirty oil and gas sectors and after the beginning of the Ukrainian War). The (so far) mostly United States-centered political campaign against "woke" investments is also not boding well for ESG.[4] The slowdown in private capital-funded money comes at a crucial time for climate finance, as the world experienced in 2023 the hottest year on record, with extreme weather, droughts, wildfires, and flooding. In fact, from a demand-side perspective, estimates developed by the Climate Policy Initiative think-tank are suggesting there is a needed increase in these funds at least fivefold, from a total of $1.3 trillion in 2021–2022 (including bank lending), which should be provided as soon as possible, to avoid the worst effects of climate change. A significant step up in funding must then come from a mix of public and private initiatives, and from private capital and bank lending—for the global economy to be able to face the challenge of change and ensure the world is on track to achieve some kind of sustainability—with ultimate aims that extend well above the monetary one. While the asset/wealth management industry (including private equity across all asset classes) has appeared so far unable to cope with these targets, the banking industry has not seemed to fare any better. In fact, a joint report by the ECB and the European Systemic Risk Board on the impact of climate change on the European Union

---

[4] Attracta Mooney and Sally Hickey, "Sales of climate-focused mutual funds fall 75% in two years," *Financial Times*, February 28, 2024.

(EU) financial system (December 2023) points out that the main European banks are significantly exposed to high-emitting firms and households, with the result that future climate risks, as a consequence, are underpriced and underinsured. More specifically, the share of high-emitting sectors in bank lending is around 75% higher than its equivalent share in economic activity, meaning that these sectors are overrepresented in banks' loans. Similarly, 60–80% of all mortgage lending in the euro area is at present allocated to high-emitting households, with the Greenhouse Legislation trying to address this in the mid- to long term—but also requiring a lot of capital to execute this.

A recent ECB report has also been assessing the (mis)alignment between banks' financing and EU climate objectives, and it highlights significant risks in the transition to a decarbonized economy. The report analyzed ninety-five significant institutions in the euro area banking sector and evaluates transition risks across fifteen technologies in six key sectors, which account for about 70% of CO_2 emissions, using the PACTA (Paris Agreement Capital Transition Assessment) methodology, a forward-looking analysis based on corporate production plans with a five-year forward-looking horizon. The report proposes a robust macroprudential strategy that focuses not only on the banking sector but also on the end borrowers, addressing risks in non-bank financial intermediaries. It then examines how a strong economic dependence on natural ecosystems could exacerbate climate-related financial stability risks (related to the risk that most of the lending of European banks is to companies and assets destined to become "stranded," hence, out of business). These financial stability risks are also coming on top of the transition and physical ones that are already driven by climate change and that also impact the creditworthiness of banks' borrowers. In greater detail, over 75% of bank loans and 30% of insurer investments in corporate bonds and equity are in economic sectors that are heavily reliant on at least one ecosystem service, with dependence on services relating to surface and groundwater, mass stabilization and erosion control, flood and storm protection. On average, euro area bank loans appear therefore overweighted relative to the economy in more emission-intensive (or "brown") sectors. This bank lending "tilt"[5] toward higher emission-intensive sectors results mainly from lending to the transportation, energy, and agricultural sectors. Systemic risk buffers or risk concentration limits have also been suggested to address climate change-related financial stability risks in a more targeted and scalable manner. A working paper by researchers at the ECB has also recently examined the relationship between banks' environmental disclosures and their lending activities—and similar conclusions could be potentially extended to asset and wealth management.

Based on this working paper, it appears that, counterintuitively, EU banks with more extensive environmental disclosures extend more credit to "brown" borrowers,

---

[5] The carbon tilt is the ratio between loan-weighted emission intensity and GVA (gross value added)—or weighted emission intensity. Changes over time come from changes in the emission intensity of each sector as well as in the share of loans or share of GVA of the respective sector, and from lending shifts to carbon-intensive sectors (relative to the change in GVA).

indicating a disconnect between their public environmental goals and lending practices. Maybe banks (and asset managers) with greater exposure to brown industries are under greater pressure to disclose their environmental strategies and plans for decarbonization? Or the amount of environmental disclosure correlates also with higher environmental ratings, provided by external rating agencies but not yet fully correlating with higher actual funding contribution to green transformation? No matter the causes, on average, high environmental disclosure banks have recently extended about 4% more (new) loans to firms in brown industries compared to other banks. And banks with significant environmental disclosures often continue lending to high-emission firms, which typically don't reduce emissions or set voluntary targets. This could indicate a form of "zombie lending," where banks continue to finance firms that may not be financially sustainable or environmentally friendly, in order to keep the borrowers alive and to avoid realizing losses on their balance sheets. Also, these banks may simply be hesitant to lend to young firms in brown industries, which could potentially drive innovation in cleaner technologies through R&D. As a result, banks may lack motivation to accurately report their environmental policies in line with their lending practices, as these disclosures barely impact their reputation and ESG rating anyway. In short, we are living in a conundrum where, on one side, lots of capital seems available to pursue green transformation across most asset classes. On the other side, these transformations are many, urgent, and critically required, but appear unable to attract the required mix of equity and debt, notwithstanding public policies support and moral suasion from most developed countries, media coverage, and the widespread interest of the general public. Hence, we find a supply/demand-side mismatch not dissimilar to what we discussed in the beginning with reference to private equity and real assets, with great potential on both sides of the equation and a unique opportunity if only alternative asset managers are able to find a solution to this conundrum.

2.12 M&A, private equity, and real assets for green transformation

In order to meet the Paris Agreement targets, a significant portion of the world's fossil fuel reserves would need to become "stranded." The risk of these assets becoming obsolete is primarily politically determined through regulatory actions but can also be influenced by technological changes or sudden price shifts. As a result of this, global and, most notably (because of more stringent regulations), European financial institutions face credit and liquidity risks due to their lending and investment activities in fossil fuel businesses. In fact, despite the Paris Agreement of 2015, banks' financing to brown sectors in 2020 still exceeded 2016 levels (with a 15% increase from 2006 to 2014), whilst debt financing for fossil fuel companies has grown significantly in the last two decades, with an estimated annual increase of 15% from 2006 to 2014. In short, on an aggregate exposure level, banks have maintained most of (or increased) their exposure to the fossil fuel sector, with continued investments despite known risks, albeit with unknown timelines. And notwithstanding the FSDR (Financial Services Regulatory Directive), the lack of transparency has remained high, with deficient disclosure about the value of fossil fuel assets and their related systemic risks. As an example, current disclosure initiatives and net-zero commitments do not specify actions for the fossil fuel sector. From a regulatory point of view, the ongoing debate on new regulations and disclosure requirements is trying to target the banks' fossil fuel exposure to enhance transparency, control systemic risks, and steer banks toward sustainability—but it is not fully addressing the potential systemic impact coming from the "stranded assets' risk," with a large number of corporates and real assets that could become stranded due to shifts in market dynamics and regulations. Whilst, on one side, current regulatory capital charges and credit allocation policies are hindering banks' green investments and credit reallocation "from brown to green" initiatives; on the other side, patterns in bank and shadow bank players in credit flows to the fossil fuel sector indicate potential shifts toward opaque financing methods (i.e. brown companies and assets keep getting funding through less or unregulated investment vehicles). This appears particularly relevant for a few sectors, from oil and gas to coal, to power generation to automotive, steel, and cement.

Given this huge challenge, and the direction and velocity of travel that appear both wrong, could M&A, private equity, and real asset investing contribute to sorting this out for the common good? And what kind of contribution could alternative asset managers give to close the supply/demand-side mismatch discussed? A relatively recent experience could offer some interesting food for thought. In fact, the 2008 global financial crisis led to an almost unprecedented rise in financially NPLs that almost broke the global financial system. Since then, the alternative assets management industry has been characterized by the growth of NPL workouts, investment funds, and secondary markets. The emergence of a new industry subsectors, product sets, and market segments have greatly contributed to addressing the issue, which is now almost completely solved. Government-sponsored, taxpayer-funded "bad banks" worked as a costly backstop solution, but it was ultimately due to the merits of private markets, with some support from states (e.g. as with the Italian GACS (Garanzia Cartolarizzazione Sofferenze or Non-Performing Loan Securitization Guarantee)—a financial insurance guarantee provided by the state on the senior tranches of securitized NPL portfolios) that private equity players were able to address the issue. What if the focus of private markets and private equity and real asset investors could shift, during the next five to fifteen years, from (financially) non-performing assets to environmentally non-performing ones—that is, from financial assets and their reference hard assets (companies, real estate, infrastructure), which will certainly become "stranded" (e.g. destined to be run down), albeit with uncertainty on the "when" and the "how," due to regulations, macroeconomic policies, and geopolitical dynamics? Indeed, that could provide an invaluable contribution to addressing the funding gap described and the climate change issue at hand, and stand as the ultimate proof of the sustainable values that M&A, private equity, and real asset investors can create and share with the wider community.

2.13 M&A, private equity, and real assets: transforming stranded assets

Talks at the highest level of policymakers, regulators, and business communities are already underway on an hypothetical "climate bad bank," set up at either national or EU level, as a public, public and private, or just private entity, with policies aimed at supporting the creation of a secondary market for the safe and certain decommissioning of stranded assets. The idea of a climate bad bank is also being discussed as a potential backstop solution should something go wrong—for example, with the expected loss from oil and gas stranded assets sinking most of the banking system. Such systemic ideas and potential initiatives are certainly relevant and could work as an accelerator and multiplier of the economic forces we need to unleash to address the issue. Notwithstanding, we believe that a private market-based answer is duly needed and requires the emergence of new subsectors in the alternative asset management industry—leveraging the capabilities and potential opportunities that could come through M&A and with the involvement of private equity and real asset investors. State-led and private market-led initiatives should then address the many failures that are now preventing the matching of supply and demand of capital to drive stranded assets' transformation from brown to green, to achieve environmental sustainability whilst at the same time avoiding sinking the banking system. In fact, there are at least two main market failures to address:

- *First market failure*: The "traditional" asset management industry and the traditional lenders approach that, using the ESG lens, are pursuing (at best) a "1–0" approach. If the borrower is green (1) it can be financed, with limited contribution to green conversion and with the potential creation of potential "green bubbles," if an imbalance between supply and demand ensues. If the borrower is "brown" (0), it can be financed until the law says otherwise and it will then become uninvestable, hence "stranded" and "non-performing," potentially causing a systemic bank failure. Alternatively, these assets could be funded by private lenders that are not subject to policymakers' and regulators' scrutiny, leading to arbitrage opportunities and further opacity (the financial crisis is avoided, but not the climate one).
- *Second market failure*: The "alternative" asset management industry (including private equity and real asset investors) that, using the IRR lens, are looking at holding periods of three to five years and at NPV (net present value) calculations that make the terminal values (TVs) immaterial fast enough in the future and therefore quickly forgotten. In fact, in our experience, scenario analysis in private market investment opportunities shows how an economically self-sustainable conversion of brown assets usually requires eight to fifteen years holding period on average, with an incentive to pass the "hot potato" around and postpone green conversion investments—and arbitrage away any ESG-forced seller in the meantime. Hence, IRR and NPV calculation methodologies would need to be revised to incentivize and support the long-term realization of sustainable values creation by alternative asset managers, spurring as a consequence their reallocation of the

capital invested in the green transformation that could avoid companies and real assets becoming stranded, and, at the same time, prevent a banking crisis and the rapid deterioration of our environment.

Similarly to what happened with the 2008 "financially" NPL (or FNPL), a private markets-based end game could then see the creation of specialized subsectors within the alternative asset management industry, with investment and workout platforms managing private capital funds where "environmentally" NPL (ENPL) are contributed or sold by banks and by relevant borrowers (e.g. transportation, energy companies, agriculture) and invested by long-term investors that could be better holders because of the longer holding periods. For this to happen, several roadblocks would need to be considered and removed—at least two require immediate attention:

A first, sell-side, roadblock would consider the profit and loss (P&L) impact on ceding banks and borrowers, as these loans and assets are still mostly marked at full value, with limited regulatory capital charge (and limited impact on the ESG rating of companies because of what we previously discussed). Hence, at present there is little or no incentive for banks to pursue a true sale.

A second roadblock for buy-side investors is the perception that expected returns may be low and associated with significant transformation risk. This concern stems from the long-term nature of transformation initiatives, which typically require a time horizon of eight to fifteen years or more. As a result, these investors may view the prospects for achieving satisfactory returns as uncertain. To effectively navigate this challenge, there is a need for new financial models that can accommodate the extended timeline and complexity of transformation projects. Additionally, a comprehensive set of incentives is necessary to motivate decision-making and execution plans that align with the long-term goals of the business. In this context, recognizing the importance of these new approaches and incentives is crucial for attracting long-term investors and successfully implementing transformation strategies.

2.14 Permanent capital: a link between illiquid assets and liquid markets

Some potential solutions could be considered to overcome most of the roadblocks, with the direct involvement of private equity and real asset investors and active managers, and with a critical contribution coming from creative M&A and financial structuring. For example, banks could retain the ownership of their ENPL exposures and work them out whilst still retaining them on their balance sheets, hence avoiding immediate accounting loss recognition on their profit-and-loss statements. Alternatively, they could contribute exposures to a third-party fund at nominal value, entailing some potential derecognition from Day 1. Some forms of state-backed financial guarantees or tax waivers could also be introduced to support the creation of this new secondary market by reducing the risk of the incremental funding needed to drive the green transformation, hence enlarging the pool of potential investors, including retail ones, looking for low-risk/low-return income over the long run. Some form of permanent capital fund could be considered as well, to support longer term business plans and investing through direct credit products, which could enjoy seniority in repayments versus the loans already extended, or could be "covered" and guaranteed by part of the assets being financed. A comprehensive definition of KPI (including some gauging returns on natural resources and environmental sustainability as well) could be introduced to promote a different incentive structure and diverse market mechanisms, in order to address the previous free market's failures and overcome some of the old paradigms of IRR and NPV.

A first option would then be for European main banks to set up their own green transformation-funding allocated pot, to support green transformation—but that would hardly be enough to close the gap, and likely suboptimal from a governance standpoint, as banks are already involved in multiple relationships with sellers and would tend to focus on a number of goals—with the environmental one likely not becoming one of their first priorities. A second, alternative or complementary, option would be to provide financing for the conversion of brown assets through flexible debt capital (senior debt, with state financial and/or asset-backed guarantees) on top of the current banks' financing, hence avoiding further capital charges—addressing the market via a permanent capital structure that would work through private markets and in a more lightly regulated way (as it does not introduce any systemic risk as banks do, because of their deposit-gathering activity and close interlinkages with other banks). Such a permanent capital structure would be better able to finance the transformation and pursue the stated environmental goals beyond the typical holding periods of private equity funds, and to reach their prospective breakeven. Such a permanent capital investment vehicle could raise funds from institutional investors and from private clients, with main European banks in the role of asset gatherers. The fund could then provide liquidity window features and pay dividends (from the direct credit underwritten) and eventually also be floated on the stock market. In this way, the opportunities coming from investing in the illiquidity world—the world of private markets—could be linked with the larger and more efficient pools of capital invested in regulated liquid stock markets—the world of public markets. Aside from the investment management company managing the fund/investment vehicle (AMCO), a specialized service company (Serco) could offer advisory and operational services to drive and support the conversion, with third parties involved in the stage-by-stage certification of the achieved green conversion as required by contractual requirements and potentially linked to the cost of debt or to some financial guarantee or tax incentive structure provided by the state. With the ideal, synergistic union of the best of private and public markets, and of the opportunities coming from illiquid investable uses and liquid investing sources, a strong move toward pursuing sustainable values creation, with critical targets as well, would be at hand—if all this is driven by a clear mission, an ambitious vision, and a sharp strategy. With these driving M&A, private equity, and real assets as tools and means, we can look toward a better future.

3 Worth It? Delivering Sustainable Alpha in Private Equity

3.1 The past: was it true glory?

Has private equity, the burgeoning industry now managing about $2.49 trillion of "dry powder,"[1] been creating "alpha" for its limited investors, truly contributing to make them comparatively wealthier? Alongside their general partners, who have certainly benefited from the "2/20" golden rule, have they strong incentive not only to outperform this rule, but also to take more and more extreme risks as well? "Flipping a coin and destroying the world, if you get tails, as long as the world improves by more than double, if it gets heads," were the words of former Crypto King and CEO of FTX Sam Bankman-Fried.[2] More importantly, is private equity positioned to generate further "alpha" in the future, as the industry is rebounding and expected to double its AUM between 2021 and 2026, reaching the $26 trillion watermark, as predicted by Preqin?[3] In short, have the many spectacular investments and the few disastrous ones reported in the media over the past few decades been generating, on a weighted average basis, excess returns earned on an investment above the benchmark return, when adjusted for risk? In fact, the best "alternative" asset managers (i.e. the general managers of private equity funds, first and foremost) have a mission to generate "alpha" by adding some diversification to their portfolios to reduce unsystematic risk. Because of that, they can rationally justify their asymmetric appropriation of 20% of the gains achieved above the hurdle rate (heads), even if they do not lose anything if a bad outcome (tails) ensues, as they get 2% of the AUM no matter what.

If we take the risk-weighted returns generated by public regulated stock markets (e.g. the returns of their indexes, such as Standard & Poor's 500 or the Euronext 100), rather than the traditional 7–8% indicated in their investment policies ("no-matter-what-the inflation-is"), as their true hurdle rates to compare and see if they create alpha, the answer may not be as clear-cut as expected. This is partly due to the relative opacity of this industry—spurred on by its limited regulation and light oversight.

---

[1] "Private equity dry powder swells to record high amid sluggish dealmaking," *S&P Global*, July 20, 2023.

[2] According to Caroline Ellison's testimony in court and as reported by the *Financial Times* and other media.

[3] "Alternative investments lose steam as fundraising slows down," *Financial Times*, August 29, 2023.

Figure 3.1 **Private equity, true glory?**

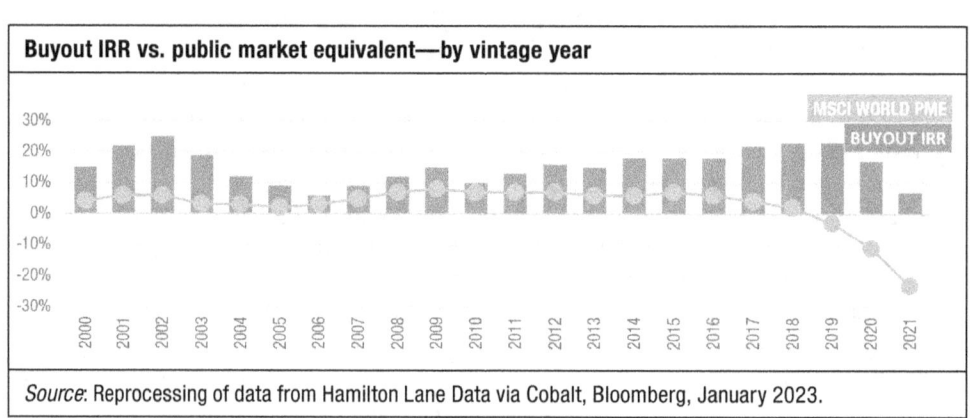

as indicated in Figure 3.1, academic and professional research is mixed and their results appear significantly influenced by at least a couple of reasons, and counting:

- First, the returns to the limited investors must be calculated net of management fees (the 2%) and performance fees (the 20% "carried interest" on any gain realized over and above the hurdle rate), taking into consideration the hidden opportunity cost of keeping the committed (but not yet invested) capital quickly available for the next capital call (IRR of investments are calculated based on the cash invested and divested, which are called "just in time").
- Second, returns—as stated in the definition of "alpha"—must be risk-weighted, for example, using their standard deviation as a proxy for value at risk. It is fortu-

nate for the industry that the volatility of a stock market index is usually calculated using daily data points (and with "marked-to-market" values) based on highly liquid transaction markets, whereas that of private equity is at best calculated on a quarterly basis (and with "marked-to-model" NAV fair values). Finally, should private equity confirm its "gross alpha" creation—as its detractors argue—netted against an "illiquidity discount" that investors should consider when committing their savings for long periods (on average seven to nine years), with little chance of getting them back earlier in case of need, with a 20%-plus discount, and no certainty on the "if and when" of the cash-in (liquidity facilities and secondary markets are currently providing these liquidity options).

Still, according to our own research, as shown in Figure 3.2, there is value in the risk-adjusted performance of private equity if we consider the past ex post returns in Europe realized by over 400 funds in the last decade, not to mention the diversification that they certainly add to investment portfolios that, for the average European saver (be they an institutional pension fund, an insurance company, an endowment, or an household), are heavily skewed toward government bonds and real estate (as used asset), with some limited exposure to stock markets. In short, according to our analysis, private equity appears to have strongly outperformed any other asset class and therefore created "alpha" (to be split between limited and general partners and not considering any "illiquidity discount," but also not considering any "diversification premium"). Given the low weight invested by, for example, Italian savers (less than 1% for private banking clients), would it then be worthwhile for savers to consider the private equity option more and "flip its coin" more often—no questions asked?

Assuming private equity has indeed overperformed in the past, it is important to analyze the type of "alpha" it generated and the methods used (Figure 3.3). The absolute size of this "alpha" can vary significantly, and the ways it has been achieved may not always reflect sustainable value creation. Academic and professional research on "relative alpha" attribution, using simple regression analysis, indicates that this outperformance was primarily driven by a few key factors:

- Adding leverage, using the company as collateral. This can create market value either because targets were underleveraged, or—more likely—the targets were already operating with significant leverage., with the further leverage added migrating de facto value from bank lenders to equity limited investors.
- Achieving financial synergies by M&A (a larger company has a better chance to attract investors and at higher multiples. This is partly due to the hyper-scaled size effects of the replicating portfolios invested by passive funds that tend to buy whatever falls into the market index).
- Addressing cost synergies, cost reductions in areas such as procurement and HR, along with decreased amortization from new capital expenditures, can temporarily boost EBITDA. However, this approach can lead to a rebound effect in the mid- to long term.

- Pursuing distinctive competitive advantages, consolidating players across the value chain can lead to quasi-dominant positions, allowing for the renegotiation of contractual obligations with stakeholders. This can extract additional value but may also raise concerns about fair competition.

Figure 3.2   **Portfolios' frontier: efficient?**

Performance and risk of private market funds vs. market indices (2014 Q4–2021 Q3)			
Private equity funds		**Real estate funds**	
N. of European PE funds	400	N. of European PE funds	111
Average annual return	18.9%	Average annual return	11.2%
Standard deviation	20.6%	Standard deviation	13.5%
VaR (confidence level 97.5%)	−7.1%	VaR (confidence level 97.5%)	−17.2%
FTSE Italy Small Cap Index		FTSE Italy Small Cap Index	
Average annual return	8.7%	Average annual return	8.1%
Standard deviation	50.7%	Standard deviation	34.9%
VaR (confidence level 97.5%)	−34.9%	VaR (confidence level 97.5%)	−35.2%

Source: Claudio Scardovi, *Investire bene in Italia*, EGEA 2023.

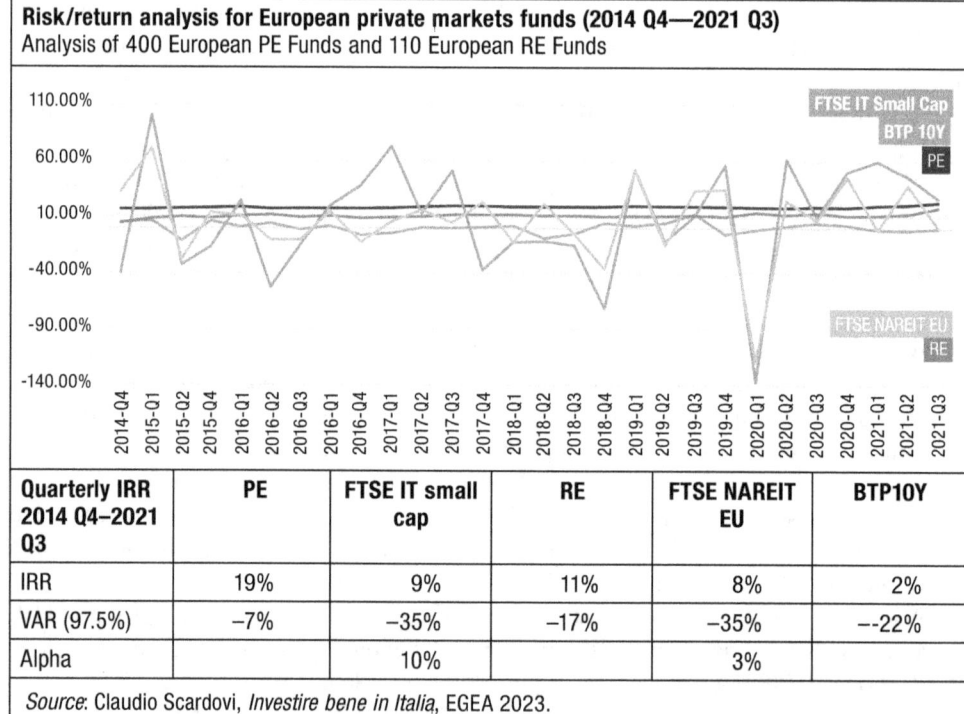

Quarterly IRR 2014 Q4–2021 Q3	PE	FTSE IT small cap	RE	FTSE NAREIT EU	BTP10Y
IRR	19%	9%	11%	8%	2%
VAR (97.5%)	−7%	−35%	−17%	−35%	−−22%
Alpha		10%		3%	

Source: Claudio Scardovi, *Investire bene in Italia*, EGEA 2023.

3 Worth It? Delivering Sustainable Alpha in Private Equity

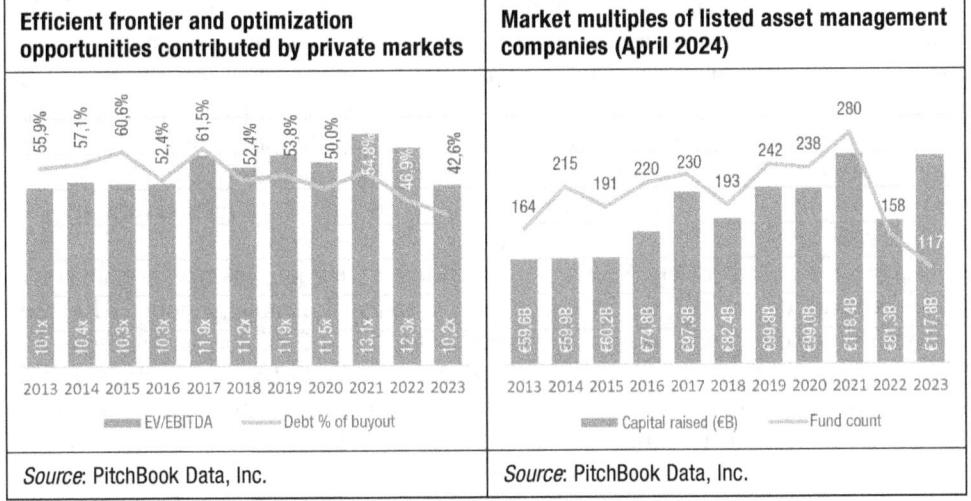

Median PE buyout EV/EBITDA multiple and average share of debt in buyouts	Private equity fundraising activity			
	Investment company	EBITDA mult.	P/E mult.	Revenues mult.
	3i Group	3.7x	6.6x	3.6x
	Apollo	9.6x	14.8x	1.9x
	BlackRock	16.3x	19.1x	8x
	Blackstone	50.8x	26.2x	22.6X
	Bridgepoint	10.6x	15.2x	26.3x
	Carlyle Group	N/A	1.9x	11.9x
	EQT	28x	25.4x	15.8x
	KKR & Co.	71x	21.1x	9.4x
Source: Claudio Scardovi, Investire bene in Italia, EGEA 2023.	Source: Refinitiv, April 2024.			

Figure 3.3 EU private equity: investment activities

Efficient frontier and optimization opportunities contributed by private markets	Market multiples of listed asset management companies (April 2024)
bar/line chart with EV/EBITDA and Debt % of buyout, 2013–2023	*bar/line chart with Capital raised (€B) and Fund count, 2013–2023*
Source: PitchBook Data, Inc.	Source: PitchBook Data, Inc.

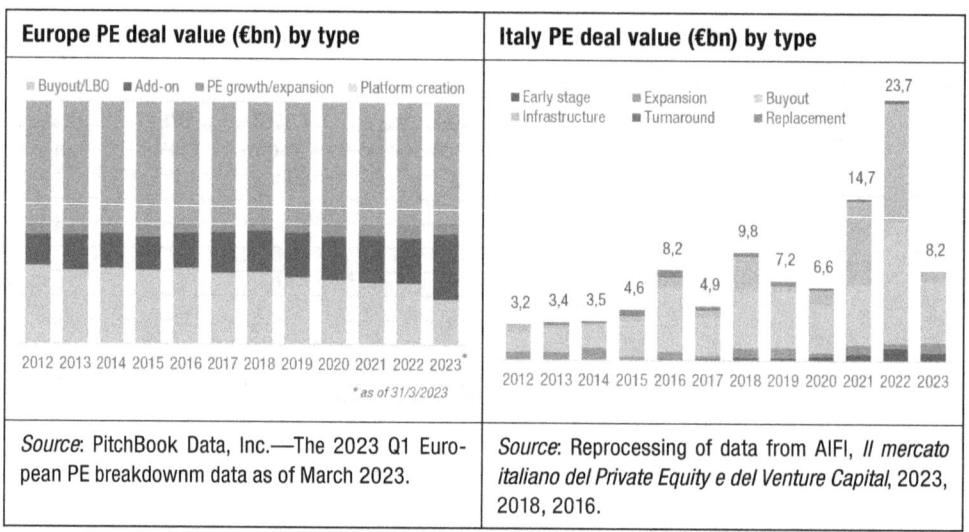

Source: PitchBook Data, Inc.—The 2023 Q1 European PE breakdownm data as of March 2023.

Source: Reprocessing of data from AIFI, *Il mercato italiano del Private Equity e del Venture Capital*, 2023, 2018, 2016.

3.2 The future: are there reasons to worry?

In any case, as often remarked upon in academic research and regulatory documents (such as the hardly ever read by anybody KID—key information document), "future, positive performances are not warranted by past ones." Not only does the longest streak of "heads" not increase the future probability of getting another one, but, also, a number of exogenous factors may be suggesting that the "golden age" of private equity's "super-returns" (SuperReturn being the name of one of the most famous jamboree events of the industry) is coming to an end. In fact, several reasons suggest this.

As the amount of "dry powder" keeps growing, with countless new private equity funds popping up and the big American ones such as Blackstone, Apollo, KKR, and Carlyle (but also the big European one such as EQT and CVC) becoming larger and larger, a first question relates to the competition in the industry. Is "too much capital chasing too few assets?" And is the industry ripe for consolidation and polarization, with few big, generalist winners and a few remaining super-niche specialists? In fact, based on Figure 3.4, even assuming double-digit growth in private markets (including private equity but also real estate, infrastructure, and natural capital), the investable universe appears quite large, suggesting a long run ahead for this asset class. A well-structured consolidation among main players could thus strengthen the overall industry and benefit investors as well.

Does the industry's sheer size mean it's becoming too powerful and noticeable enough to suggest heavier regulation with consequential supervisory burdens? Is it now too big to deliver "alpha" (by mathematical definition, a larger and larger asset class approaches the impossibility of delivering "alpha" as it becomes an essential part of the market "beta"—i.e. its relative contribution to the weighted average of all investable assets classes grows so much that whatever "super-return" is able to achieve in absolute terms it becomes "beta" in relative ones). Also, as private equity bets rise in size it becomes more difficult to deploy these as simple, financial arbitrage opportunities. In fact, some deeper regulation and wider supervision could help the industry improve its transparency and fairness to limited investors, opening the door to much awaited "democratization" (i.e. the opportunity for retail investors to access this, so far, exclusive asset class). Finally, with its still quite low weight relative to the investable funds and assets (Figure 3.4), there appears to be ample room to deliver "alpha" to end investors.

As the macroeconomic environment has been changing radically (with less debt available at a much higher cost) and the geopolitical context becomes more uncertain and therefore risky (from deglobalization and decoupling trends, to regional wars potentially expanding into global ones, to the threats posed by climate change), are there enough good opportunities to make up for the increased opportunity cost of capital? Will the largely untested, never fully proved, private equity value proposition of "delivering alpha in good and bad times" be convincing enough to keep attracting new capital and best talents, which provide the high-octane energy required for the industry to grow? In fact, the lack of accessible debt financing and higher cost of debt has become the latest at-scale opportunity for private equity, which extended and diversified its product sets into direct credit. And it appears that private equity does deliver better "alpha" during testing times, when public markets tend to malfunction and overreact to negative news.

Ultimately, assuming some "alpha" was indeed created in the past by private equity, what kind of value and how sustainable was that? How much of this was "value creation" or else just "migration"—from lenders to super-wealthy equity investors, given the typical overleverage of the industry and its asymmetric payoff; and from workers to superrich managers and investors, given the typical overreliance of the industry on cost-cutting aimed at boosting the exit EBITDA—as exit transaction prices are often based on an EBITDA multiple calculation? Even assuming the economic value created was sustainable, has private equity strategy also being pursuing other values, that is, social and environmental—aimed at delivering psychophysical well-being to a large number of people—and not just a stash of cash to the usual privileged 1%? Was ESG merely a passing trend, now facing backlash and something companies are eager to move away from as quickly as possible? In fact, whilst future worries are not necessarily implying undemanding "alpha" performances, a significant opportunity for private equity to pursue sustainable economic value creation and other sustainability goals is long overdue and could be fast approaching.

In short, for the private equity industry, whilst past performances were not always unquestionably positive, and the future looks full of sensible worries, there are plenty of reasons to believe in it as a strong, secular turbine that can ignite growth, innovation, wealth, and well-being.

Certainly, new structural factors are posing new questions and require new solutions for the players that want to qualify as winners and deliver true "alpha" along with sustainable values creation.

Figure 3.4   Reasons to worry? Or optimism to gain?

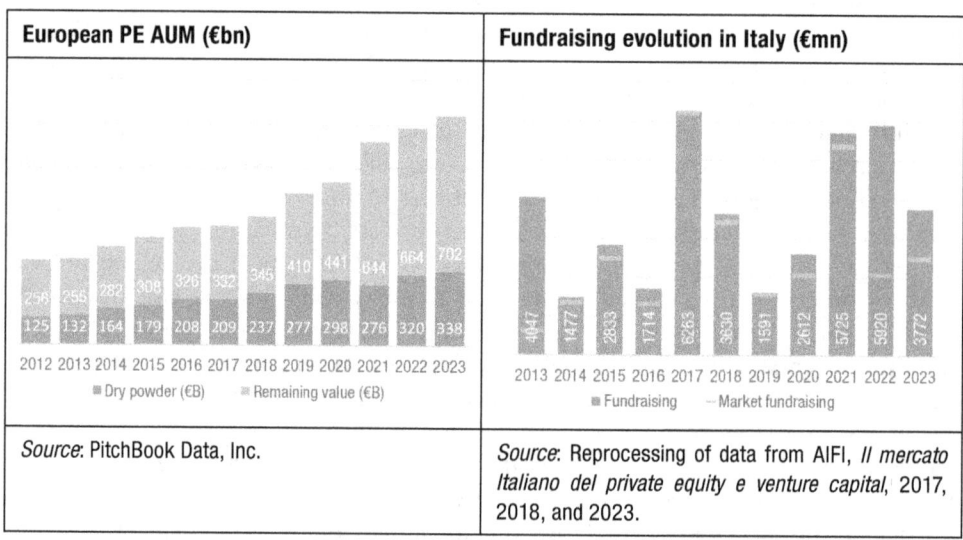

AUM and Market capitalization		
Investment company	AUM	Market cap.
BlackRock	10,009	119
Blackstone	1040	159
Apollo Global Management	651	65
KKR & Co.	553*	89
Carlyle Group	426	17
EQT	141	40
Bridgepoint	52	3
3i Group	8	35

Source: Refinitiv, data as of April 8, 2024.
* KKR AUM as of end of 2023 (from KKR Investor Day, April 2024).

In short, to paraphrase Gustave Flaubert, the past may be constraining us, and our future is worrying—that's why, to ensure private equity becomes more and more successful, and a real force for good, we need to act now, with optimism, transforming the industry to avoid the otherwise unavoidable leveling of its performance. Eventually, as the saying goes, "pessimists may look smarter, but optimists make money in the long run." There has never been a better moment to be an optimist in private equity (Figure 3.5).

Figure 3.5 Long-term rationale and solutions

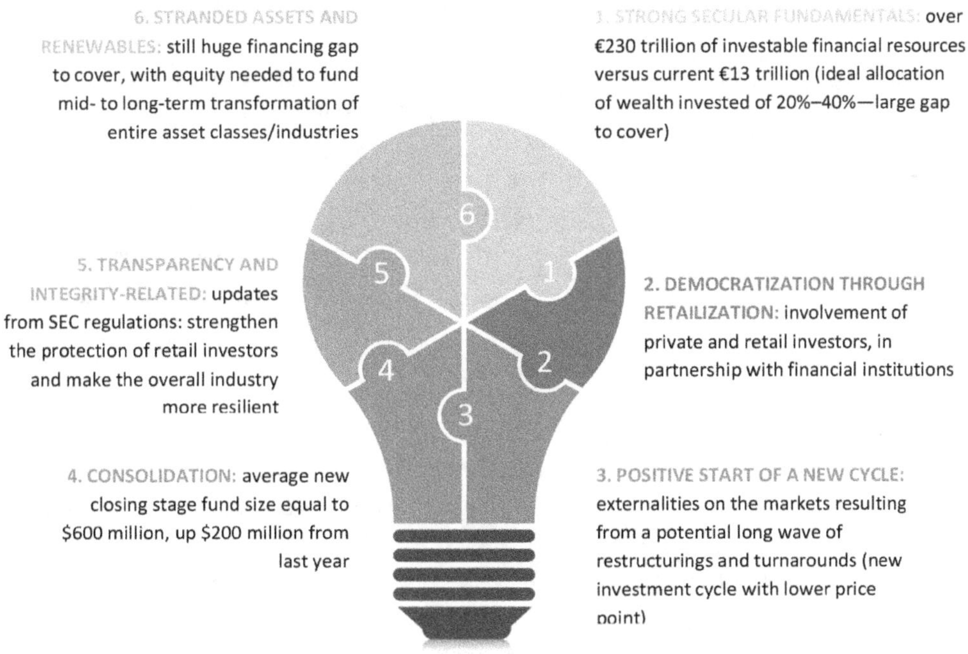

6. STRANDED ASSETS AND RENEWABLES: still huge financing gap to cover, with equity needed to fund mid- to long-term transformation of entire asset classes/industries

1. STRONG SECULAR FUNDAMENTALS: over €230 trillion of investable financial resources versus current €13 trillion (ideal allocation of wealth invested of 20%–40%—large gap to cover)

5. TRANSPARENCY AND INTEGRITY-RELATED: updates from SEC regulations: strengthen the protection of retail investors and make the overall industry more resilient

2. DEMOCRATIZATION THROUGH RETAILIZATION: involvement of private and retail investors, in partnership with financial institutions

4. CONSOLIDATION: average new closing stage fund size equal to $600 million, up $200 million from last year

3. POSITIVE START OF A NEW CYCLE: externalities on the markets resulting from a potential long wave of restructurings and turnarounds (new investment cycle with lower price point)

3.3 Designing a "smart beta" strategy in private equity

Based on our analysis, private equity has indeed generated "alpha" in the past. However, this performance has not been unanimous and has often relied on strategies such as leveraging information asymmetry, using traditional financial techniques, and operating in relatively undeveloped markets with limited competition. Consequently, much of the "alpha" embedded in its current business model may face erosion due to evolving macroeconomic and geopolitical conditions, which introduce unprecedented challenges and headwinds. The base case for private equity in the next decade is therefore one of a "great leveling trap"—with the "alpha" Holy Grail harder and harder to find. A "betization" meta trend could characterize the world of asset management, as passive investments become more and more dominant and driven by indexes—hence, with the largest companies included in them getting bigger, as they are invested in almost by default, and the small and medium-sized enterprises (SME) remaining out of the big money flows and subscale almost as a consequence. The investment selection of best SME, and their active management once invested, is in fact a crucial function performed by private equity, as it ensures that a Darwinian "survival of the fittest" contributes to a market-based mechanism of

Figure 3.6 **Meta (not meme) investment themes to fight the betization of the industry**

Alpha denotes the **abnormal returns** stemming from non-market origins, as PE operations, typically deduced by assessing the overperformance or underperformance of the investment **relative to a specified public market benchmark**.

ALPHA AND BETA IN PE INVESTMENTS

Beta denotes the **systematic risk** of a specific investment. A contemporary interpretation of this metric is **Smart Beta**, also known as strategic beta, which encompasses **various investment factors** such as momentum and quality.

MEME — Refers to an **investment strategy** that follows what concepts **spread rapidly among industry professionals**. It may encapsulate shared insights, humor, or cultural references within the **peers of private equity community**.

Refers to an **investment strategy** that follows **overarching trends** that influence the industry as a whole. These meta themes may include broader economic factors, technological advancements, shifts in consumer behavior, or global market dynamics **that impact the overall landscape of private equity**. — **META**

META THEMES

 01 TECHNOLOGICAL DISRUPTION: Innovative technologies coming to maturity and leading to breakthroughs in value creation across industries and sectors

 **02 CONSUMER TRENDS AND PREFERENCES:** Structural changes in demand and supply acting as catalysts for new competition dynamics across value chains

 03 CULTURAL AND DEMOGRAPHIC SHIFTS: Other structural changes in the fabric of society (e.g. demographics, urbanization, social behaviors)

 04 MACROECONOMIC DISLOCATIONS: and other exogenous risk factors leading to market dislocations and value migrations

 05 REGULATORY CHANGES: 'Geopolitical and industrial policies changes' impacting on global and local market structures and trade/finance corridors

 06 LONG-TERM ECONOMIC RESILIENCE: Existential challenges ahead linked to sustainability and their impact on short-mid-long-term economic value creation

 07 CYBERSECURITY AND DATA PRIVACY: Recognize the increasing importance of cybersecurity and data privacy in an increasingly digital world

 **08 EDUCATION AND LIFELONG LEARNING:** Explore opportunities in the education sector, including online learning platforms, vocational training, and lifelong learning initiatives

 **09 DIVERSITY AND INCLUSION:** Fostering innovation and resilience within industries, enhancing corporate governance, and driving sustainable economic growth

 10 HEALTH & WELLNESS: Consider the growing focus on health and wellness, including trends in preventive healthcare, personalized medicine, and wellness tourism

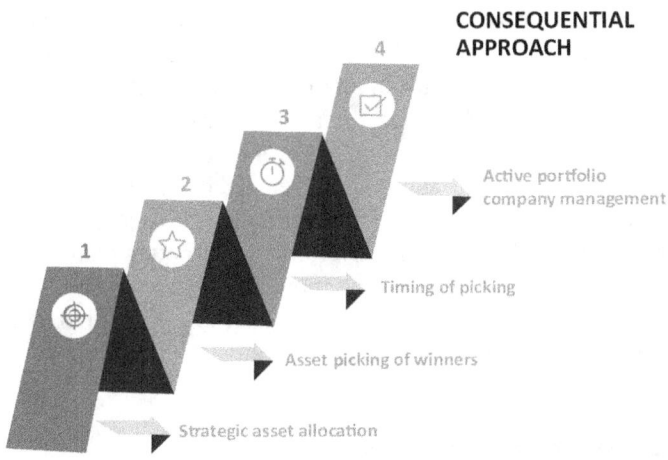

Source: Adapted from Oleg Gredil, Barry E. Griffiths, and Rüdiger Stucke, "Benchmarking private equity: the direct alpha method," *SSRN*, 2014 and Morningstar, "What is smart beta?". Available at: Investing Definitions | Morningstar, June 2021.

optimal allocation of any kind of scarce resource—capital included—and to the Schumpeterian "destructive innovation" that follows, dynamically readjusting the composition of the indexes. As this applies to companies as well as sectors and countries, we argue that a significant opportunity to overperform in the future will come from "smart beta" strategic asset allocation, based on emerging "competitive invariances" coming from meta (and not meme) investment themes (Figure 3.6).

That is, for generalist private equity players, correct positioning on the meta trends and investment thesis that, on average, will create more value in the future (regardless of the dispersion between winners and losers), will become a more significant, and better appreciated, competitive advantage. Positioning into "electric-batteries vehicles" and out of "combustion-engine vehicles" within the car manufacturing sector could be a good example of a "smart beta" positioning that could have been done in the past, as "alpha" creation was not assured anyway (many producers of the former went bust and a few of the latter are still doing fine and progressively reconverting), but it could made easier to get successfully through the successive asset and time pickings, leading to a better performing investment. A greater focus on strategic asset allocation and on the selection of long-term meta investment themes—today almost absent in mid-market private equity—could not only drive "smart beta" positioning, making sure the index is almost certainly beaten, albeit just by a little, but could also decrease the opportunity cost of capital, increasing chances to create value. We can then define "smart beta" as the strategic, selective positioning targeted by design by "alpha" platforms as they try to anticipate economic cycles and value migrations that are going to happen across sectors, subsectors, phases of the value chain, technologies, and geographies.

As beta aims to maximize diversification (and can be easily invested through indexes by passive funds, but only including companies already traded in stock markets), "smart beta" can offer further diversification originating from private SMEs with a unique approach—repositioning the asset allocation in advance of new value creation or migration waves. By lowering its overall risk profile, a "smart beta" approach could also make private equity more easily investable by retail savers and hence more democratic and inclusive. This could also be used as a counterargument to its "illiquidity discount," as a more diversified and better planned private equity "smart beta" investment portfolio could be more easily invested by secondary funds, building their own larger "smart beta" portfolio (as the sum of shares of many, independent funds), or even floated on the stock market.

Figure 3.7   **Mid-market fund investments in Europe**

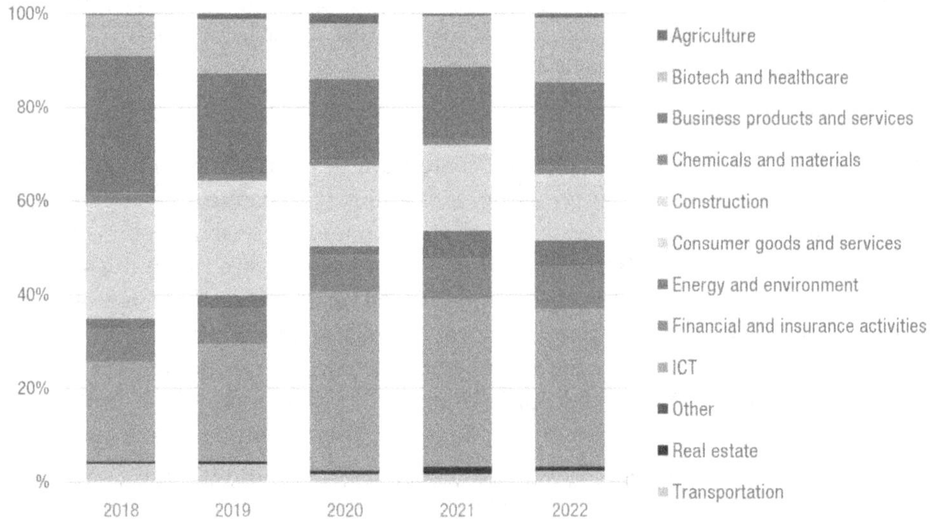

Source: Invest Europe, *Mid-Market Private Equity—Europe's Engine for Growth*, October 2023.

3.4 Developing an "alpha platform" in private equity

Over the last few years almost everything has been changing, with several factors potentially impacting private equity's future performances and competitive positioning. Increased macroeconomic volatility has led first to inflation and then to less (and more expensive) debt available, followed by geopolitical decoupling, supply-chain ruptures, regional war escalations, and climate change risks—all of which has been eroding most of the "alpha" traditionally supported by leverage. Also, an inherent trade-off between the increased calls to adopt an ESG playbook and the backlash promoted by its detractors has made the lives of private investors more difficult, with ESG-conscious investors asking for more sustainability goals, but at the same time not being ready to give away any expected extra return. Not only is cost-cutting—another traditional "alpha" booster—becoming more difficult to execute as it is less socially acceptable, but ESG frameworks have also become more expensive to manage. If all this was not enough, significant delays (if not roadblocks) in the exit of invested portfolio companies (circa 28,000 at the end of 2023) have hampered the traditional capital "raise–to deploy–to distribute–to raise again" cycle. Forced longer holding periods are then leading to higher "illiquidity discounts," reduced IRR (because of the higher time-value-of-money discount effect), and hence lower "alpha" (if any).

Regarding raising capital, the reduced funds available for reinvestment have been feeding fewer and fewer players, with institutional investors concentrating their bets on the "big names" of the street. Whilst greater amounts of capital managed by fewer players make more difficult for them to maximize IRR (as a percentage) and therefore "alpha," for their general managers there is a huge incentive to push for larger and larger deals, as their carried interest is driven by IRR (as a percentage, over and above its "hurdle rate") multiplied by the capital employed (as volume). How much easier is it for them to then increase volume, make up for the percentage lost, and get the same carried interest in euros! In fact, the implicit incentive to do bigger and bigger deals, often involving companies already public, can simply further erode the true "alpha" delivered by the industry and limit its contribution to the "survival of the fittest" SME and its related "creative destruction." Asymmetric payoffs can also lead to an incentive to increase risks, as little correlation links the risk-adjusted returns track record of the alternative asset manager and its ability to raise further capital (that is raised just by the "big names").

How, then, could private equity, as an industry and as a business model, be transformed to regain its competitive allure and its ability to deliver true and sustainable "alpha"—to its limited investors and (more widely) to its stakeholders? Certainly, greater transparency around fees and governance, a cunning strategic asset allocation focused on "smart beta," and a better aligned incentive model for general managers to focus on sustainable "alpha" could all help. However, the proof of concept of the "alpha" creation capabilities of private equity should come from its active management of portfolio companies. If a private equity company is proving to be a better owner and manager, truly accretive value should naturally follow along the holding period. Even in cases of forced longer periods of "holding," that should just mean greater opportunity to create even higher "alpha." In fact, companies' active management can create "relative alpha" across multiple dimensions, not just by adding debt and cutting costs. The track record relevance of the operating partners (the "portfolio companies' shadow managers") should then be equal to one of the investment partners (the "deal makers—buying and selling"). They could include a well-balanced mix of professional experiences, technical skills, and vertical sectorial depth. As private equity can demonstrate its replicable prowess in "alpha" creation by managing companies better, it should also be able to attract more patient capital with a lower opportunity cost. As the "alpha" gets embedded in the "alpha platform" processes and managerial approaches, private equity should also be able to better attract entrepreneurs as potential sellers and partners, as they would see a financial partner with a deep industrial understanding and potentially better suited to run their company over their next growth cycle. An "alpha platform" active on its portfolio companies' management would then focus on accelerating growth, increasing its margins, and augmenting its innovation—almost in parallel. A greater "platformization" of the most critical services provided would then lead to their faster and more extensive adoption, with a long-term goal of delivering "private equity as a service"—with active management as a winner and financial capital (a mere commodity) as a qualifier. Ultimately, should this pursuit include other non-economical values as well, the private equity "alpha platform-as-a service" could help its invested portfolio companies to develop into even better best sustainable companies.

3.5 A "decalogue" to drive sustainable values creation

Whilst it is fundamental for private equity to get "smart beta" meta trends and their related investment thesis right, groundbreaking truly sustainable values creation, including but not limited to financial and economic targets, must be defined and addressed at the portfolio company's level. In fact, the acid test of any "alpha platform" ultimately relates to its ability to deliver "alpha," no matter what the sector or economic cycle it's in. Being a strong asset and time picker is certainly a qualifying trait in private equity, but whilst this is a dominant characteristic of successful investors in stock markets, for financial sponsors (the industry parlance for private equity players) their winning attribute is the ability to better govern and manage the invested company—demonstrating they are its best owner for the upcoming holding period.

In fact, no matter what the many technicalities differentiating private and public markets, the most unique and special proposition of private equity is its ability to command (in the case of majority investments) or strongly influence (in the case of minorities) and initiate the transformation that is required for a company to innovate, develop, and grow profitably.

To reach these strategic targets, "old tricks" (load the debt, cut the costs, inflate the EBITDA on the final "sprint") are no longer good enough. And the main value creation strategy should not rest on the hypothesis of being able to "buy low and sell high" (always a good starting point, assuming a world of stupid people). If the economic value that will be delivered is sustainable in its pattern and also strives for other socially and environmentally sensible goals, private equity will have become not just an almost unstoppable industry, but a force for good as well.

With this ambition in mind, we focus now on the description of a partial, ever changing (subject to constraints) decalogue of drivers to actively manage portfolio companies and evolve them into better and stronger ones, hopefully along with their ecosystems (Figure 3.8):

Figure 3.8   **MASA: make alpha sustainable again**

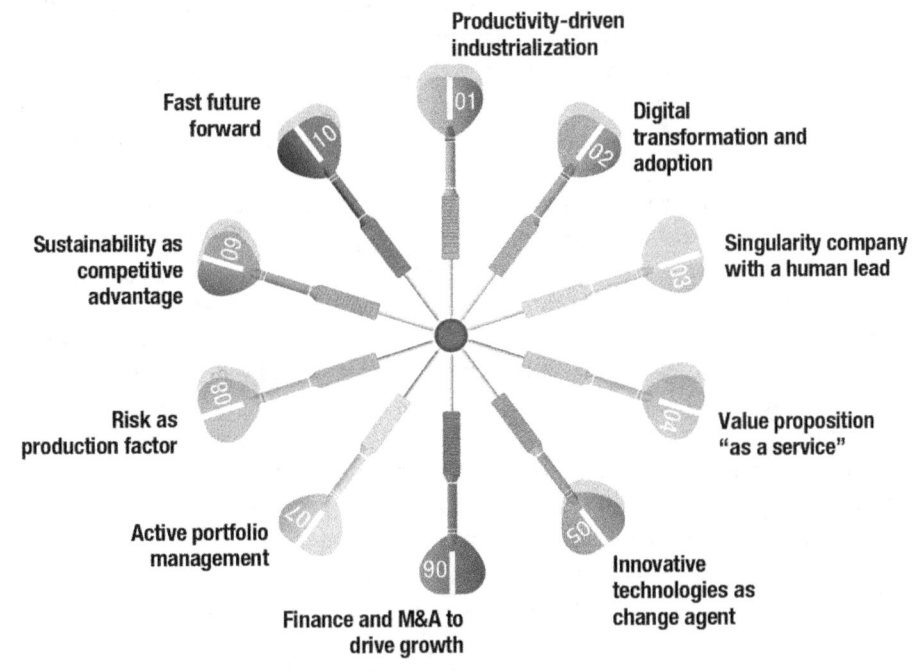

Source: Image from "Worth It? Delivering Sustainable Alpha in Private Equity," Report published by Deloitte in May 2024.

- *Productivity-driven industrialization*: Cost outs on HR, purchasing, and other expenses, and as reduced amortization on new investments, have been one of the most fashionable strategies pursued by private equity to achieve short-term EBITDA improvements (or "sprints," executed when the fund is just about to exit its investments). As such, they have often backlashed, with unhappy employees and uncommitted suppliers leading to cost structures' "bungee jumping," and with reduced investments (including in advertising and marketing) leading to lower growth and eroded margins. A new emphasis on "industrialization" should instead target real productivity enhancement, doing more with less, and taking care of all non-renewable resources used. An optimal industrialization should start with the design of the target operating model and reconsider all required capabilities and processes as front-to-back, starting with customers.
- *Digital transformation and adoption*: For all the mind-numbing talk on digital transformation, its required investments and hyper-scaled expected return on investment (ROI), not much has yet been done by SME. When pursued, large IT investments have often been implemented inconsequentially, leading to (at best) more efficient/effective ways of doing the usual things. Cloud-based solutions

adoption can instead lead to the overhaul of large technology stacks and the decommissioning of legacy applications. It can also allow SME to pursue large-scale changes that were once the exclusive preserve of large corporates with huge IT budgets. In fact, agility and the flexible adoption of new digital apps and technologies, as they come to market and mature, are becoming a source of competitive advantage, especially when leading to new ways of doing things in order to deliver innovative value propositions and change the business model in the process.

- *Singularity company with a human lead*: AI, particularly Generative AI, has generated a lot of hype, often overshadowing the significant scientific progress made in the field and the limited number of practical applications that are already available for small and medium enterprises (SMEs). These applications, while few, are both interesting and potentially highly rewarding. To bring this to fruition, a limited number of cases can be identified and promoted by the financial sponsor for initial testing before, if successful, full-scale adoption. With humans in the lead, almost any capability could be augmented, from planning, to risk management, to production and marketing. Whilst a "singularity moment" dominated by an artificial general intelligence (AGI) is still some way off, singularity-minded companies could already benefit from a better general (artificial and human) intelligence of doing things, to deliver the best value to their best customers.
- *Value proposition "as a service"*: Decades of discussion have centered on the long-term transitions from farming and agriculture to industrial manufacturing, and then to the service sector. This structural shift is believed to have resulted in increased wealth for the most innovative nations. A new trend is now making these broad sectors more and more codependent, with intertwined destinies. As farming, cars, and even real estate become mostly about data, software, and the related services that can be provided by specialized third parties, so service companies need natural resources, hardware products, and a built environment to fully deliver on their promises. For SME operating in any of these, their strategic option is to focus on their core competitive advantage and let other strategic parties synergically operate the remains, to then focus jointly on the ultimate and resulting value proposition delivered "as a service" to the final customers.
- *Innovative technologies as change agent*: Innovative technologies are not the preserve of digital software and are not limited to AI or quantum computing. In fact, a vast array of such technologies is now maturing and ready for large-scale adoption, coming from disparate fields such as biotech and life sciences, genetics and longevity, precision materials, food and agriculture, renewable energy, communication transportation, and space economy, to name a few. Whilst large R&D investments have likely already been made by state-backed institutions or large corporates, a "fast and furious" adoption by SME could lead to transformative value generation and the development of some competitive hedge on the selected "application verticals." Therefore, innovative technologies, even if not created and developed in-house, can lead to discontinuities in the company's business model and even in its end purpose, truly acting as change agents.

- *Finance and M&A to drive growth*: Strategy should be informed by the company's mission and vision of the future it wants to achieve, with finance (and M&A) as tools to support its execution. Still, finance and M&A can play a critical role in identifying and executing organic (e.g. with capital investments required) and inorganic (e.g. involving M&A) options to drive sustained growth. A financial sponsor-led growth strategy could then consider an optimal mix of the two, adding more of an industrial focus to the typical "buy and build" M&A and leveraging more on the PMI to truly create an augmented, newly combined resulting entity. As "small is (not) beautiful (anymore)" and likely less efficient and effective, for SME great value can accrue from growth strategies that are ignited by the capital and M&A promoted by the financial sponsor—but they need a strategic rationale and industrial vision to make them work.
- *Active portfolio management*: Active portfolio management can add value, on a risk-adjusted basis, to a private equity at the fund and company level. At the fund level, the CFO of the financial sponsor can strategically allocate its investments, diversifying long-term bets and creating synergies among the value creation levers used across multiple portfolio companies (e.g. on the overall cost of funding or the pooled third parties' procurement). At the company level, the CFO can steer the optimal allocation of scarce resources within the internal marketplace of potential users (e.g. business units, service and product lines, distribution channels), thus leading to an optimal value creation. For a CFO to act as warden of the capital invested by the financial sponsor and as arbiter of the competitive marketplace using scarce and non-renewable resources, they need a fully integrated, standardized cockpit of relevant financial information.
- *Risk as production factor*: Any entrepreneurial activity entails uncertainty. Therefore, risks are the unavoidable and required "production factor" of any SME. Risks can eventually lead to superior returns—above the financial sponsor cost of capital and higher than the stock market index ones (hence, producing economic value added and "alpha"). Or they can potentially lead to losses in value—of the equity invested by the shareholders, the debt provided by lenders, the professional commitment paid by employees and business partners, and the natural resources supplied by the overall ecosystem (e.g. including clean air and water, fertile soil, nice environments, stable climates). A holistic understanding of risks and their pragmatic, proactive management can lead to the optimization of the wealth created by the company for its financial sponsors and well-being for other stakeholders—and is required for sustainable values creation.
- *Sustainability as competitive advantage*: A common interpretation of sustainability by private equity is one of "constraint." It is something private equity needs to have to raise capital and fulfill regulations, yet is also a cost that can hinder efficiency. It is, moreover, a set of further limits (often conflicting) that can delay or derail a company's IRR maximization strategy or set a cap on the fund capital-on-capital multiplication. In fact, there can be ways and instances where the SME pursuit of sustainability can support the creation of a more unique and com-

pelling competitive positioning, leading "consequently" (and not "notwithstanding") to higher economic performance and "alpha." For example, SME can bet on a structural shift driven by green transformation (e.g. solid state energy batteries), or change in sustainability-minded customers' behavior (e.g. controlled environment, regenerative agriculture produced food), and win big.
- *Fast-forward future*: Despite the never exhaustive and always changing "decalogue list" of drivers to support value creation and "alpha" generation, private equity can act as catalyst and accelerator of the SME that are willing to consider this as an option, rising to the challenge of change, to build their future and move fast. Financial sponsors can do this by evolving the governance of the invested company, professionalizing its organizational structure, and investing to develop on multiple fronts, from education to R&D, from technology to M&A. More importantly, they can bring and embed new and higher ambitions, aligning the incentives of multiple stakeholders toward a few, shared common goals. They can energize and inspire a passion for performance, bringing best practices and talent along with them. In summary, a key 'alpha' driver is the ability of SMEs to shorten their timelines and rapidly advance toward brighter futures.

3.6 Primary research: creating "alpha" in mid-market private equity in Italy

Deloitte conducted a survey among multiple private equity professionals, specifically focusing on the Italian mid-market, to gather insights into the sector's ability to generate "alpha" through investments. Thirty-two private equity houses participated in the survey (Figure 3.9).

Overall, respondents expressed confidence that the private equity industry has historically and will continue to outperform public markets in delivering "alpha." Eighty-one percent of interviewees agreed that this additional return was consistently generated through the cycle, while 75% maintained this would apply to future perspectives as well. To uphold its advantageous position, which, since 2004, was mainly driven by consolidation via bolt-on M&A as prevailing strategy (64% of answers) and manufacturing as leading sector (36%), the industry must not rely on blind optimism but rather stay attuned to emerging trends and influences. This awareness and adaptive response to both internal and external factors are crucial for maintaining expectations of future 'alpha' generation. External factors such as international conflicts, geopolitical decoupling, and deglobalization were identified by 44% and 31% of respondents, respectively. Coupled with internal drivers within industries—like intensified competition (33%) and a growing pool of uninvested capital, or 'dry powder' (also 44%)—these have emerged as key challenges facing the industry. Additionally, it was noted that, within the Italian landscape, the complexity of the current legislative framework may pose an underestimated challenge for investors assessing legal system risks, potentially influencing their preference for investment opportunities in other European countries.

Figure 3.9   Private Equity survey: target trends to support "alpha" in the next decade

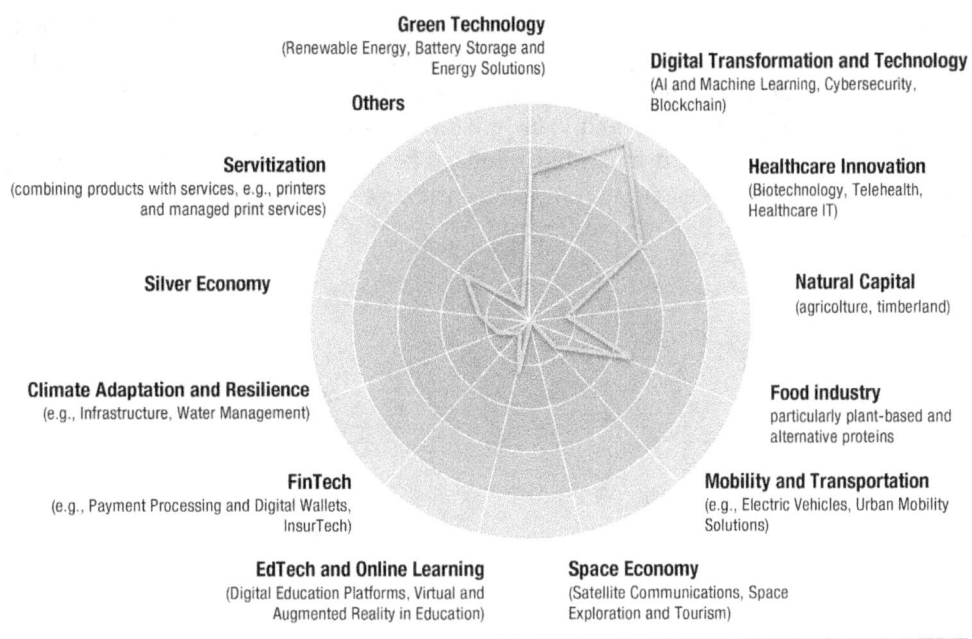

On the flip side, other exogenous factors, such as heightened consideration of private equity as an option (56% of answers) or the implementation of AI and Gen AI, and endogenous drivers, such as consolidation to establish a scalable platform through bolt-on M&A, chosen by nearly 70% of professionals, can serve instead as levers to sustain value creation. Among the comments that emerged in the survey, it was noted that the primary challenge in the Italian mid-cap market is the "dwarfism" of companies. Limited revenue restricts cash flow available for investments. Therefore, the foremost driver to enhance company growth is scaling it to a level where it can invest, attract top-tier human capital, and compete internationally. Consequently, private capital infusion can fuel growth and yield exceptional returns.

Forty-seven percent of respondents considered strategic allocation, both at the sector and investment thesis levels, as a key requirement to deliver "alpha" in the coming years. As argued by one of the interviewees, professionals investing in the private capital space accrue expertise over the years, leading to the understanding that focus is not only crucial as a thesis but also key to mitigate investment risk.

Two other critical factors mentioned are the leadership's capacity to manage the organization while adapting to ongoing changes and the sector's current trajectory. Successful investments frequently coincide with companies experiencing significant sector disruption, showcasing their ability to identify and capitalize on these changes effectively.

In conclusion, harnessing the substantial emerging competitive advantages underscored in the survey, including the digitization of businesses, strategic leveraging of M&A, and the industrialization of operational models (ranked as the top three favorable paths to succeed in the market), should be complemented by a forward-looking approach to sector-specific trends. This comprehensive strategy is essential for enhancing "alpha" generation. While underscoring the excellence of Italian manufacturing as a magnet for capital and value creation, insights from the experts involved in the survey point toward emerging trends. These trends indicate a pivot toward more innovative sectors such as digital transformation, technology, green technology, healthcare innovation, and the food industry.

Part II
Fundamentals of M&A, Private Equity, and Real Asset

by *Mario Ciunfrini*

4 The M&A Process

4.1 External growth strategies

4.1.1 Introduction

An M&A transaction is an intricate and costly undertaking that necessitates a substantial commitment of information, capital, and time. The existence of an almost codified M&A process yet different M&A professionals is a direct result of the unique nature of the M&A activity. This includes its infrequent occurrence, its transformative impact on a firm, and its profound effect on the lives of managers and owners, and, as a consequence, society as a whole.

These transactions involve competencies not typically developed within companies, require careful evaluation before a decision is taken, and must account for the differing agendas and goals of all the involved parties.

The overarching aim of the M&A process is to use all resources, including time, efficiently, in order to maximize the likelihood of closing the deal, which ultimately means determining an appropriate transaction price and a reduced transaction risk.

4.1.2 Players involved in an M&A transaction

- *Involved companies*: The companies involved in the transaction are the target company, which is being acquired, and the bidder company, which is doing the acquiring. "Involved companies" is a key definition in a complex transaction with large perimeters, which may or may not include certain subsidiaries, parent companies, business units, or some assets.
- *Shareholders of the acquiring company (bidder) and the acquired company (target)*: Individuals or entities that own shares in either the acquiring company or in the target company. They have a vested interest in the outcome of the transaction as it can significantly impact the value of their shares.
- *Advisors and experts*: Individuals or entities that play a key role in deal executions (and origination), providing both technical knowledge (legal, financial, business, etc.) and negotiation skills.
- *Banks and third-party financiers*: The financial institutions or other entities that provide the funds needed for the transaction. This could include banks providing loans or leasing companies providing equipment or other assets.

- *Other stakeholders*: Individuals or entities that may have an interest resulting from their relationship with the companies involved in the transaction. This could include customers and suppliers, employees, institutions, and the community at large. For example, customers and suppliers may be concerned about the continuity of business relationships, employees may be concerned about job security, and the community may be interested in the company's impact on the local economy or environment.
- *Bondholders*: Individuals or entities that hold the debt securities (bonds) of the companies involved in the transaction. The outcome of the transaction can affect the value of these bonds and the ability of the company to repay its debts.

4.1.3 Typologies of transactions

The different typologies of M&A transactions vary based on the outputs of the transaction itself, therefore on the characteristics of the new legal entity to be established.

Mergers:

- Merger by consolidation: This creates a new company from two or more merging companies that, as a consequence, will have the same legal identity. There are two main types of mergers: a merger by consolidation and a merger by absorption. With a merger by consolidation, a new company (called a NewCo) is formed from the merging companies. The NewCo will have a new legal and economic identity, and the previous companies will cease to exist legally.
- Merger by absorption: This involves one company absorbing one or more other companies. While the acquiring company will keep its legal identity, the absorbed companies will relinquish theirs.</BL>

Acquisitions:

- Acquisitions can be partial (minority or majority stake) or total. In a total acquisition, one company acquires another company, which will maintain its own legal autonomy.
- Acquisitions can be horizontal (companies operating in the same sector or market), vertical (companies involved in different stages of the value chain), or conglomerate (companies in unrelated sectors or markets).

Leveraged buyouts (LBOs):

This is a type of acquisition where a significant amount of debt financing is used. This is the typical transaction implemented by private equity funds. After an LBO, the target company will have a large amount of debt to finance the acquisition. If the promoters of the acquisition are the managers of the target company itself, it is called a management buyout "MBO." If the promoters are managers from other companies, it is called a management buy-in.

Strategic alliances and JVs:

These are medium- to long-term collaboration agreements between companies. They may involve creating a new JV company that receives specific assets (such as complementary products, equipment, technology, or know-how).

Companies entering a strategic alliance, typically competitors, maintain their independence but establish a mutually beneficial agreement to gain market leadership.

In a JV, the partners not only contribute assets but also agree on how to jointly reinvest profits and plan their short- and medium-term goals together. A JV allows a company to enter a new business by leveraging a partnership with a company that already operates in that sector.

Acquisitions of business units:

This process involves buying assets or an entire business unit from the seller. An example can be buying a product line or a brand, an entire manufacturing division in a certain country, a customer segment, a technology or Intellectual property, a distribution channel, or a financial asset. The main reasons why this process is pursued are to obtain a strategic expansion into new markets, regions, or new product lines, enabling strategic growth and making the bidder more competitive.

Spin-off:

This is a process where a company (the parent company) separates a portion of its business unit and transfers it to a newly formed company (the spin-off company). In exchange for this transfer, the parent company receives shares issued by the spin-off company. These shares are then typically distributed to the parent company's shareholders. A spin-off can be total, where the parent company ceases to exist, or partial, where only parts of the assets are transferred, allowing the parent company to remain operational.

Split-off:

This involves a company (the parent company) dividing its assets among two or more existing or newly created companies. In a split-off, the parent company assigns all or part of its assets to these companies and distributes the corresponding shares to its shareholders. The shareholders then exchange their shares in the parent company with shares in the new entities. The parent company may dissolve without liquidation or continue its operations. The key difference with a spin-off (where the parent company cedes part of its asset to NewCo) is that, in a split-off, the change in asset ownership occurs directly with the shareholders, not with the parent company.

Equity carve-out:

This is a particular type of spin-off. The parent company sells a portion of its subsidiary's equity to the public while retaining ownership and control of the remaining shares. In other words, the parent company aims to obtain financial resources from the stock market through the sale of a business unit (spun off into a company vehicle), intended to be listed through an IPO.

Turnaround:

This is a corporate restructuring operation performed to restore profitability to a company that is in a financial/operational crisis that could lead to insolvency.

In addition to the necessary financial resources, investors participating in the restructuring also bring specific professional skills.

4.2 The M&A process

In this chapter, we will go into detail of the M&A process, touching base with other types of transactions, as they are very often closely related.

An M&A transaction takes place between two parties, an acquirer and a seller, or the buy-side and sell-side, as they per the technical terms. The perspectives of the buy-side and sell-side in an M&A transaction can indeed be quite different, yet complementary.

From the buy-side (investors') perspective, the focus is identifying a suitable target that aligns with the strategic goals, such as expanding into new markets, obtaining new clients, acquiring new technologies, or achieving economies of scale. The buyer needs to conduct different analyses to understand the target's business model, financial health, and potential risks. The buyer also needs to arrange financing for the acquisition and negotiate a fair price.

On the sell-side, the goal is to present the company in the most favorable manner in order to attract potential buyers and maximize the sale price. This involves preparing detailed information about the company's operations, financials, and prospects. The seller also needs to manage the bidding process (with the help of M&A professional advisors) to ensure a competitive sale process and negotiate the best terms and conditions for the shareholders. Despite these differences, both sides are working toward a common goal: to close a deal that brings value to their respective stakeholders. This complementary dynamic is what makes M&A transactions challenging, exciting, and sometimes difficult.

4.2.1 The buy-side process

The process has a flexible but defined structure:

1. Define the strategy and scope
   a. Establish the objectives of the contract, both in terms of ideal business characteristics of the target (size, industry, location, value chain positioning, client portfolio, product portfolio) and desired timing, keeping in mind both industry trends and financial/debt-related constraints.

2. Research and selection of the target(s)
   a. Identify potential targets through a market analysis, often partnering with a financial advisor, which will typically filter companies based on KPIs or industry, size, and geography or will consult industry experts.
   b. Rank and select a shortlist of targets based on publicly available data.
3. Approach selection and documents preparation
   a. Deep analysis of the chosen targets.
   b. Approach selection consists of the preparation of a document "approach letter" that describes how the bidder communicates with its potential targets. This concise document typically outlines the following information provided by the bidder:
      i. Profile of the acquiring company, a section that provides an overview of the acquiring company, including its background, financial strength, and industry expertise.
      ii. Strategic motivations for the proposed transaction.
      iii. Prospects offered to the target company with the acquisition.
      iv. Prospects offered to the shareholders of the target company.
      v. Formal steps to be taken for the completion of the transaction.
   c. Based on the reactions of potential targets, a shortlist of companies that have positively responded to the initial investment solicitation, expressing interest in continuing the process based on the sharing of some minimum objectives, is compiled.
   d. For the initiation of the following phases, a non-disclosure agreement (NDA) between the parties is prepared. This agreement imposes strict confidentiality constraints on the information that will be transmitted by the target company. The purpose of the NDA is to agree on a limited time period (generally between one and three years) during which it is not possible to disclose the received information to third parties and to use it only for purposes strictly related to the proposed transaction. After the signing of the NDA, the target's advisor prepares and shares the corporate information memorandum (often referred to as info memo, CIM, or IM). The information memorandum plays a crucial role in facilitating informed decision-making among potential bidders and establishing a strong foundation for successful negotiations. Key components of an information memorandum are:
      i. Market analysis: A thorough assessment of the target company's primary market, including its dynamics, opportunities, and potential threats.
      ii. Product/service portfolio analysis: A detailed examination of the target company's product or service offerings, highlighting their strengths, weaknesses, and competitive positioning within the market.
      iii. Shareholders and organizational structure analysis: A comprehensive overview of the target company's shareholders composition, organizational structure, and any affiliated or subsidiary entities and identification of key management personnel and their respective roles within the organization.

      iv. Asset analysis: A detailed assessment of the target company's key assets, including tangible and intangible assets, their value, and their contribution to the overall business operations.
      v. Financial analysis: A thorough evaluation of the target company's financial performance, including historical and projected revenue, profitability, cash flow generation, and overall financial health.
4. Negotiation
   a. First "real" contacts with the management and shareholders of the targets and start of negotiations.
   b. Signing a letter of intent (LOI). The LOI usually contains:
      i. Confirmation of interest from the bidder to continue negotiations.
      ii. Explicit mention of a price considered acceptable by the parties, provided that the assumptions made in the initial analyses prove to be correct.
      iii. Description of the due diligence process (often attaching a due diligence checklist prepared by the appointed M&A professional advisors).
      iv. Identification of an approximate timeline for the completion of the process.
      v. Identification of any suspensive or obstructive conditions for the completion of the operation.
   c. Identification of the next steps and potential timeline up to closing. Planning the process up to closing.
   d. Signing of non-binding offer (NBO). Such a document is constructed in the form of a real purchase offer, with the aim of sharing the essential conditions of the agreement between the parties that could be subsequently signed. The reason why this document is not binding is that the acquiring party requires due diligence to be carried out on the target in order to confirm its assumptions and thus make its binding offer.
5. Due diligence
   a. Due diligence is operated by an internal team or an external pool of consultants and experts (M&A professionals). Topics covered by due diligence usually include:
      i. financial
      ii. fiscal
      iii. legal
      iv. business
      v. other specific topics (insurance, environmental, real estate, etc.).
6. Closing
   a. Final negotiation of contracts.
   b. Signing of the sales and purchase agreement (SPA). This document usually contains:
      i. Scope of the SPA: This outlines what the agreement covers, essentially the terms and conditions of the sale.
      ii. Target's description: This is a detailed overview of the target company, including the core business and its structure.

iii. Condition precedents: These are conditions that must be met before the transaction can proceed.
iv. Interim period: The time between when the agreement is signed and when the deal is closed.
v. Price determination: The price is often determined using a "locked box" mechanism, where the purchase price is fixed based on the target's economic performance at a specific date prior to the transaction, with minor or no adjustments for subsequent cash flows. Alternatively, other price adjustment methods may be used, where the purchase price is modified based on the target's actual chosen item (such as net working capital) at closing compared to a predetermined benchmark.
vi. Earnout clauses: These make part of the purchase price dependent on the company's future performance.
vii. Escrow clauses: These refer to provisions that outline that certain funds or assets will be held by a neutral third party (the escrow agent) until certain conditions are met or certain obligations are fulfilled by the parties involved in the transaction. These involve a third-party holding assets until certain conditions are met.
viii. Bank or parent company guarantee: This provides additional security to the seller.
ix. Transfer modalities: This details how the transfer of ownership will take place.
x. Change of the corporate bodies: This refers to any changes in the company's management or board of directors.
xi. Covenants: These are contractual promises made by the seller to protect the buyer (and vice versa), such as maintaining current operations or not taking on new debt.
xii. Responsibilities: The obligations that each party has under the agreement, such as conducting due diligence or obtaining necessary approvals.
xiii. Legal warranties: Assurances given by the seller about the target company, such as the accuracy of financial statements or the compliance with laws. If a warranty is false, the buyer may seek damages.
xiv. Issue of guarantees and repayment of shareholders loans at closing: This addresses the repayment of any loans the shareholders have made to the company.
xv. Business warranties and legal warranties: These protect the buyer from potential risks and liabilities.
xvi. Disclosure schedule: This lists exceptions to the seller's warranties.
xvii. Indemnity clause: This specifies the compensation to be paid if certain specified losses occur after the transaction.

c. Closing, the first date at which the deal is effective once the interim period is over. At closing, the payment can be completed either via:

i. Cash—the most immediate and straightforward form of payment.
ii. Stock—the acquiring company issues its own shares to the shareholders of the target company, instead of paying cash. The number of shares issued is determined based on the valuation of both companies. The advantage of stock payment is that it allows the acquiring company to make acquisitions without depleting its cash reserves. However, it also means that the shareholders of the target company will become shareholders of the acquiring company, which may affect the control and decision-making of the acquiring company.
iii. Assets—a form of payment where the acquiring company pays for the target company using its own assets rather than cash or stock. These assets can be tangible (such as property or equipment), intangible (such as patents or trademarks), or financial (such as securities or shares in a subsidiary). The advantage of asset payment is that it allows the acquiring company to make acquisitions without depleting its cash reserves or diluting its stock. However, it requires a careful valuation of the assets being used as payment to ensure fairness in the transaction. It's also important to note that transferring assets could have tax implications and may require regulatory approval.
iv. Deferral/value bridging—this involves a portion of the purchase price being paid at a future date. Deferred payments can be structured in various ways, such as earnouts, seller notes, or escrow arrangements. The advantage of deferred payment is that it can bridge the gap between the buyer's and seller's valuation of the target company. For example, if the buyer and seller cannot agree on the value of the target company, they can agree on a lower purchase price "now," with the agreement that additional payments will be made in the future if the target company achieves certain financial targets (earnouts) or certain non-financial results.
v. A combination of the above.

The length of the entire process depends on the size of the operations and on how many actors are involved. At times, however, transactions fail to culminate but instead remain stuck in intermediate processes for several years, ultimately resulting in their non-completion.

4.2.2 The sell-side process

For a sell-side process, the seller typically appoints a financial advisor to prepare the needed documents and handle the negotiation steps. The process then unfolds in different ways, depending on whether it is a competitive auction, a private transaction, or a listed deal.

4.2.2.1 Competitive auction

Typically, the structure for a competitive auction is defined as follows:

1. Defining the strategy and preparing the documents:
    a. The management declares its objectives for the deal, both in terms of value and timing.
    b. The advisor starts the industry analysis in order to understand the position of the seller in its value chain.
    c. The advisor coordinates with the seller management in order to collect the information needed to prepare the set of documents.
    d. The set of documents prepared is composed by the information memorandum, the blind-profile "teaser," and the NDA.
2. First contact with buyers, NDA, and teaser:
    a. A longlist is cut down to a shortlist of potential buyers, who are subsequently contacted by the advisor.
    b. The advisor sends a blind teaser that provides some general information without disclosing the name of the target.
    c. Interested potential buyers ask for NDA in order to proceed with the negotiation.
3. Information memorandum and management presentation:
    a. The information memorandum is handed over to buyers (after signing the NDA).
    b. Management presentations are (usually) organized to answer questions arising from potential investors.
4. Choice of the bidder(s):
    a. Analysis of the bidders and choice of the best offer(s).
    b. This phase, given its competitive nature, is also referred to as the "beauty contest."
5. Negotiation:
    a. Collection and valuation of the LOI(s).
    b. Signing of the NBO with the chosen bidders.
6. Due diligence and closing:
    a. Due diligence is operated; if claims are not arisen or are resolved, the process continues.
    b. Binding offer.
    c. Final negotiation of contracts.
    d. Signing of the SPA.
    e. Closing.

As in the case of buy-side, if negotiations fail with the selected targets, the process can resume at stage 2 to identify new bidders.

4.2.2.2 Private transaction

A private transaction unfolds as a simplified variant of a competitive auction. The seller might engage an advisor from the initial stages, but, regardless, the negotiations are conducted solely between the seller and a single prospective buyer. The preliminary stages are discretionary, as the bidder, already familiar with the seller, may bypass and skip them and proceed directly to the LOI, perform the due diligence, and close the deal.

4.2.2.3 Private transaction

A listed deal, however, adds layers of complexity to the base structure of a deal. Additional steps to include are:

- Regulatory requirements: Listed companies are subject to stringent regulatory requirements. They must comply with securities laws and regulations, which often necessitate public disclosure of the transaction. This includes filing necessary documents with regulatory bodies like the Securities and Exchange Commission (SEC) in the USA, or equivalent bodies in other countries.
- Shareholder approval: The company must obtain approval from its shareholders before proceeding with the transaction. This typically involves a vote at a shareholders' meeting. The details of the proposed transaction, including the price and terms, are provided to the shareholders, who then vote on whether to approve the transaction.
- Tender offer: In some cases, the acquiring company may choose to make a tender offer directly to the shareholders of the target company. A tender offer is a public bid aimed to buy a significant portion of the target company's shares, usually at a premium to the current market price. Shareholders can choose whether to sell their shares at the offered price.
- Fairness opinion (FO): This is a financial advisor's valuation as to whether the price to be paid/received in the transaction is fair under the client's shareholders' point of view. It is grounded in a thorough analysis and offers an impartial view on the financial appropriateness of a transaction. It does not represent the advisor's valuation of the target, nor does it pass judgment on the deal's validity for the client or its shareholders. It should be transparent, succinct, and effective, but it must evaluate:
  – the sufficiency of the valuation inputs
  – the plausibility of the forecasts used
  – the appropriateness of the valuation methods employed
  – the valuation's sensitivity to risk factors.
  FOs are sought by boards and board committees to gain a holistic understanding of a transaction's financial aspects and to demonstrate prudence in decision-making. Given that board members have fiduciary duties to act based on informed decisions and in the company's (and/or its shareholders') best interest, a FO aids

board members in fulfilling these fiduciary duties while enhancing board decision-making.

Requesting a FO may be mandated by debt covenants or regulations, or it may be a best practice in cases of:
- M&A deals of substantial value and/or involving related party transactions.
- M&A deals involving non-cash considerations such as stock, seller financing, earnouts, and options.
- M&A deals involving a target in the early development stage or in a different industry, or that brings significant synergies.

- Delisting: This means the shares will no longer be publicly traded, which can have significant implications for shareholders. This is the case with private equity transactions.

4.2.2.4 Special purpose vehicle

SPVs play a crucial role in M&A. They are separate legal entities created by a parent company to isolate financial risks. In the context of M&A, SPVs are often used to facilitate transactions without exposing the entire business to the associated risks. For instance, an acquiring company might establish an SPV to purchase the target company. In this way, if the acquired company underperforms or has hidden liabilities, the financial risks are contained within the SPV and do not affect the parent company directly. Moreover, SPVs can also be used to transfer assets, manage tax obligations more efficiently, or to improve the financial appearance of the parent company by keeping certain liabilities off the parent company's balance sheet.

Two examples of commonly used SPVs in the context of M&A are:

- *Special purpose acquisition companies (SPACs)*: SPACs are companies with no commercial operations that are established solely to raise capital through an IPO for the purpose of acquiring an existing company. Also known as "blank check companies," SPACs have been around for decades. In recent years, they have become more popular, attracting big-name underwriters and investors, and raising a record amount of IPO money.
- *BidCo*: This is a type of SPV used in LBOs and stands for "bid company." The BidCo is set up by the private equity fund to acquire the target company; in this case it is used to shoulder the debt used to finance the acquisition. Once the acquisition is complete, the BidCo becomes the parent company of the acquired business. It is also possible to do a reverse merger of the acquired company into the BidCo, resulting in a company holding the debt used to purchase itself. This structure aims to isolate risks and may have tax advantages.
- *JV vehicles*: When two or more companies want to undertake a specific business venture together, they often set up an SPV as a JV vehicle. This allows them to pool resources for the venture while keeping the financial risk separate from their main businesses.

4.2.3 Post-closing considerations

4.2.3.1 Earnouts

Earnouts are a type of deferred payment in M&A transactions where a portion of the purchase price is contingent on the target company achieving certain milestones post-acquisition. These milestones can be:

- Event-based earnouts: These are tied to the occurrences of specific events post-acquisition. For example, an event-based earnout could be structured around the target company securing a key patent or launching a new product within a certain timeframe or even around the permanence of the manager in the company for a given number of years. If the event occurs, the sellers receive an additional payment. If not, the earnout is not paid.
- Performance-based earnouts: These are tied to the financial performance of the target company post-acquisition. For example, a performance-based earnout could be structured around the target company achieving certain EBITDA targets. If the targets are met or exceeded, the sellers receive an additional payment. If the targets are not met, the earnout payment is reduced or not paid at all. In numbers:
  - Buyer and seller agree on a 10x valuation on EBITDA in year t.
  - The buyer believes EBITDA at the end of year t will be $80 million.
  - The seller believes EBITDA at the end of year t will be $100 million.
  - Buyer and seller agree that the buyer pays $800 million now ($80 million x 10), and an additional $200 million if the overperformance is achieved.

The concept of earnout may also apply to the period following the transaction, as a way for the seller to participate to the company upside. As hinted before, the options for setting the clauses are limitless.

4.2.3.2 Net working capital adjustments

The purchase agreement often includes a provision for adjusting the purchase price based on the target company's net working capital (current assets minus current liabilities) at the time of closing. If the actual net working capital is less than the estimated amount, the purchase price may be reduced accordingly.

For example, Company A is acquiring Company B. In the purchase agreement, they agree that the target net working capital, which is defined as current assets minus current liabilities, should be $500,000 at closing.

1. At closing: At the time of closing, the actual net working capital of Company B is calculated to be $450,000.
2. Post-closing adjustment: Since the actual net working capital ($450,000) is less than the target net working capital ($500,000), there is a shortfall of $50,000.

3. Result: According to the terms of the purchase agreement, Company A would be entitled to a reduction in the purchase price of $50,000 to make up for this shortfall.

4.2.3.3 Cash adjustments

Similarly to net working capital, the purchase price may also be adjusted based on the target company's cash balance at closing. If the actual cash balance is less than the estimated amount, the purchase price may be reduced.

In some deals, buyers prefer to acquire a "cash-free" company. This means that the seller, prior to the closing, would distribute excess cash to its shareholders in the form of a special dividend. This could be for various reasons, such as the buyer not wanting to pay for the cash or the buyer wanting to ensure that the purchase price mainly reflects the operating business and not the cash on the balance sheet.

The distribution is structured as follows:

1. Pre-closing: The buyer and seller agree that the target company will have zero cash at closing. The seller then declares a dividend to distribute the excess cash to its shareholders before closing.
2. At closing: The buyer verifies that the target company's cash balance is zero. If there is cash left in the target company, the purchase price would be adjusted downwards by the amount of remaining cash.
3. Post-closing adjustment: After closing, the buyer may perform a more detailed review of the target company's financials. If it turns out that there was cash in the target company at closing, the buyer would be entitled to a post-closing adjustment, reducing the purchase price by the amount of cash found.

4.2.4 Other considerations

- *Integration planning*: Once the transaction is finalized, the acquirer's focus shifts to assimilating the acquired company into its existing operations. This process may involve the consolidation of various systems and procedures, necessitating meticulous planning and execution to avoid disruption. A crucial part of this process is aligning the corporate cultures of the two entities, which is vital for maintaining employee morale and retention. Another key aspect is the management of human resources issues that could arise from the M&A process, which includes clearly communicating any changes in roles, responsibilities, or terms of employment to the people of both companies. The management of human resources is also key in order to avoid "culture clash" events.
- *Tax considerations*: The tax consequences of the acquisition can be intricate and substantial. The acquirer needs to comprehend how the purchase price will be treated for tax purposes, as this can influence the company's taxable income and cash flow. The tax attributes of the acquired company, such as net operating losses or tax credits, can also significantly impact the acquirer's tax liability.

- *Legal and regulatory compliance*: The merged entity is required to comply with all the applicable laws and regulations. This includes anti-trust laws that prohibit anti-competitive behavior, securities regulations that govern public companies and securities transactions, and industry-specific regulations that can vary greatly depending on the sector. Moreover, governments may have the power to scrutinize transactions involving "strategic" industrial sectors, with the authority to impose conditions on such transactions or even veto them if they pose a threat to national economy or to the labor market of a specific area.
- *Post-closing indemnities*: The purchase agreement may stipulate indemnities from the seller for certain liabilities of the acquired company. These indemnities safeguard the buyer from financial loss if those liabilities materialize after closing. The management of these indemnities post-closing can involve making claims under the indemnities if necessary, or offsetting indemnity claims against deferred consideration or other payments owed to the seller. To quote some of the commonest topics, indemnities can be related to tax audits, breach of representations and warranties, environmental damages, employment irregularities, and intellectual property rights legal claims. All of these potential indemnities should be identified during the due diligence process.

5 Introduction to Valuation

5.1 Introduction

If we start with the premise that every asset has both a price and a value, then valuation serves as the method to discern the disparity between the two. Accepting this premise, valuation becomes crucial when aiming to purchase assets for less than their true worth, which is the widely accepted definition of a rational investment.

However, historical financial episodes such as the tulip mania of the 17th century, the booming stock market of the 1920s, the Dot-Com bubble, and the 2007–2008 financial crisis illustrate that this principle is sometimes misunderstood or outright ignored. These financial collapses have empirically shown that when investors begin to value assets based solely on what others are willing to pay, prices are often dramatically realigned.

With this foundation laid, financial analysts, as delineated by Professor Damodaran,[1] bifurcate into two factions:

> At one end are those who believe that valuation, done right, is a hard science, where there is little room for analyst views or human error. At the other are those who feel that valuation is more of an art, where savvy analysts can manipulate the numbers to generate whatever result they want. The truth does lies somewhere in the middle (...)

It is important to keep in mind that, whichever your philosophy is, all valuations are biased to some degree, and most valuations are (even ever so slightly) wrong. This is a result of confirmation bias (choosing the result closer to what we thought was the value before looking at the numbers) and uncertainty, as well as lack of information (think about valuing US financial institutions in 2007) that could lead to the formation of an estimation error.

This chapter is dedicated to acquiring the basic tools for valuing companies and other real assets, using both intrinsic and relative approaches.

---

[1] *Damodaran on Valuation, Security analysis for investment and corporate finance*, second edition. Aswath Damodaran, pag. 2.

5.2 The two valuation approaches

In intrinsic valuation, the value of an asset is determined by its future cash flows, growth, and risk. The greater and more certain the cash flows, and the faster they grow, the higher the valuation of the asset.

In contrast, relative valuation assesses an asset value by comparing it to similar assets. Specifically, when valuing companies, this approach involves selecting a "peer group" of comparable businesses and examining their values as a benchmark.

While neither approach is inherently superior to the other, the intrinsic valuation method is theoretically more precise. However, relative valuation often yields a more pragmatic valuation and is generally easier to apply in practice.

We will dive into the details of when one is preferred over the other later in this chapter.

5.3 The toolbox of valuation

5.3.1 The time value of money

The idea that €1 today has a higher value than €1 tomorrow is straightforward and easy to grasp, but there are several explanations for this concept:

- Immediate consumption is preferred over delayed consumption by rational subjects.
- A promise of future cash flow is inherently less reliable than actual "cash in hand," as there is always the risk of non-delivery.
- The impact of inflation and deflation can alter the value of money in the future, introducing additional uncertainty to future cash flows.

To quantify how much less "€1 tomorrow" is worth today, we need to consider its present value.

The variable to consider when calculating present value is the discount rate, which reflects the magnitude of the uncertainty of receiving the cash flow. The discount rate is also defined as cost of capital in the context of company valuation. It is important to note, however, that it is not a monetary cost but essentially an opportunity cost. It represents the return that investors could expect to earn on investments of comparable risk. If a project or investment cannot generate a return greater than the cost of capital, the company should invest this capital elsewhere, or return it to investors, who could then invest it in other opportunities of comparable risk.

In valuation, we estimate the present value of two types of cash flows:

- Simple cash flow

$$\frac{\text{Cash flow in the future period (t)}}{(1 + \text{discount rate})^t}$$

where:
- t: the time period (usually measured in years) for which the cash flow occurs.

This formula is employed to estimate the present value of a sequence of predetermined cash flows. For instance, consider the cash flows generated from a five-year business plan.

- Growing perpetuity

$$\frac{\text{Cash flow in current period} \times (1 + \text{growth rate})}{(\text{Discount rate} - \text{growth rate})}$$

This formula is used to determine the present value of a sequence of perpetually growing cash flows. For example, think of the cash flows occurring from year 6 onwards in the previously mentioned business plan.
Let's consider a scenario where we have a business plan with the following cash flow projections:

- Years 1 to 5: $100,000 per year ("Step 1").

- Year 6 onwards: growing perpetuity with an initial cash flow of $150,000 and a growth rate of 3% ("Step 2").</BL>
We will discount these cash flows using a discount rate of 5%.

Step 1: Calculating the present value (PV) of simple cash flows for years 1 to 5:

$$PV \text{ years 1 to 5} = \frac{100.000}{(1.05)^1} + \frac{100.000}{(1.05)^2} + \frac{100.000}{(1.05)^3} + \frac{100.000}{(1.05)^4} + \frac{100.000}{(1.05)^5}$$

$$= 95.238{,}10 + 90.702{,}95 + 86.383{,}76 + 82.270{,}25 + 78.352{,}62$$

$$\cong €432.947{,}67$$

Step 2: Calculating the PV of the growing perpetuity starting from year 6:

$$PV \text{ years 6 to } \infty = \frac{150.000 \times (1 + 3\%)}{5\% - 3\%}$$

$$= \frac{154.500}{2\%}$$

$$= €7.725.000$$

So, the total present value of the cash flows from this business plan would be approximately €6,485,687.30 (equal to the sum of "PV years 1 to 5" and "PV years 6 to ∞").

5.3.1.1 Accounting basics

In this section, we will go through the basic financial statements knowledge necessary to understand valuation.

Income statement:

As far as income statement is concerned, the main lines are:

Revenue (sales)

– Operating expenses (salaries, rent, utilities, etc.)

= EBITDA

– Depreciation and amortization (D&A)

= EBIT (earnings before interest and tax)

– Interest expense

= EBT (earnings before tax)

– Taxes

= Net income

Depreciation and amortization (D&A) are accounting methods for allocating the cost of tangible and intangible assets respectively; both are used in accounting to reduce a company's taxable income since they are both considered non-cash expenses. Since these expenses are subtracted to obtain the net income, but are essentially non-cash, they are added back into the cash flow.

EBITDA is a crucial metric that gauges a company's operational performance. It is frequently the optimal indicator as it allows for an assessment of a firm's financial performance, excluding elements such as financing decisions and tax environments. These elements are often swayed by external factors and can result in fluctuating outcomes in the lines beneath EBITDA (i.e. EBIT, EBT, and net income). As we will explore, EBITDA serves as the initial point for both intrinsic and relative valuation.

Balance sheet:

The balance sheet, on the other hand, is composed as follows:

Assets = liabilities + shareholders' equity

Assets are resources owned by the company that can provide future economic benefits. Assets are split into current assets and non-current assets.

5 Introduction to Valuation

Liabilities are the company's debts or obligations. Liabilities are divided into current liabilities and non-current liabilities.

Shareholders' equity represents the amount of money that would be returned to shareholders if all the company's assets were liquidated and all its debts repaid. It primarily includes common stock, retained earnings, and treasury stock.

Cash flow statement:

The income statement and balance sheet combined, shown as follows, allow us to reclassify the cash flow statement.

The main components of the cash flow statement are:

Operating activities:

This section reflects how much cash is generated from a company's core business operations. It starts with net income and then reverses out all non-cash items (like D&A) and adjusts for changes in working capital.

Net income

+ D&A

+/− Changes in working capital (current assets − current liabilities)

= **Cash flow from operating activities**

Current assets are all the assets of a company that are expected to be sold or used during the course of the core business operations over the next year. They can be easily converted into cash or used to pay current liabilities and include accounts receivable, inventory, and prepaid expenses.

Current liabilities are the company's debts or obligations that are due to be paid to creditors within one year and include accounts payable, accrued liabilities, and unearned revenues.

Working capital is the difference between current assets and current liabilities and it is a measure of the company's ability to meet its short-term obligations. A reduction in working capital equals a cash generation, as it means cash has been collected from current assets and/or cash has been saved from current liabilities and vice versa.

Note that cash and cash equivalent, usually part of currents assets, are not included when calculating working capital (which is referred to also as net working capital). The same considerations can be made for short-term financial debts, which you could find in current liabilities and should not be included in working capital calculations, as it is already included in net debt, as we will discuss later in this chapter.

Investing activities:

This shows the cash invested in long-term assets (like property, plant, and equipment) and cash received from divesting these assets.

– *Purchase of assets (capital expenditure or CAPEX)*

+ *Proceeds from sale of assets*

= **Cash flow from investing activities**

CAPEX refers to the fund employed by the company to acquire, upgrade, or maintain physical assets. Examples are property, plant, and equipment, or even technology or new business ventures.

Financing activities:

This shows the cash received from issuing debt or equity and cash spent on repaying debt, paying interest, and distributing dividends.

+ *Proceeds from issuing debt or equity*

– *Repayment of debt*

– *Dividends paid*

= **Cash flow from financing activities**

When a company issues new debt (e.g. a bond) or equity (e.g. new shares in an IPO or a seasoned offering) it results in a cash inflow for the company.

When a company repays a tranche of its debt principal (the interest portion is not considered in this line), pays dividends, or realizes shares buybacks this results in a cash outflow for the company.

Finally, the cash flows from these three activities are added together to get the total change in cash:

+/– *Cash flow from operating activities*

+/– *Cash flow from investing activities*

+/– *Cash flow from financing activities*

= **Change in cash**

This change is then added to the company's cash balance at the beginning of the period to arrive at the cash balance at the end of the period.

5.4 Risk and return: CAPM and discount rates

From the perspective of the investor, risk can be defined as the volatility in the return of the purchased asset. The two main types of risks that affect a company's value are as follows:

- Market risk (or systematic risk) refers to the risk that affects all companies and securities in the market. Such risk cannot be eliminated through diversification. It includes factors such as interest rates, inflation, political instability, and economic recessions.

- Firm-specific risk (or unsystematic risk) refers to the uncertainties and potential problems that affect a specific company or industry. Such risk includes factors like management decisions, product recalls, labor issues, and other events that characterize a particular company or its industry.

A rational equity investor will always demand a return for the risk they are facing.

The capital asset pricing model (CAPM) is widely used by banks worldwide and calculates the expected return of a generic security as the sum of the return of a risk-free government bond and a premium representing the systematic risk of the security in relation to the entire market (MRP, market risk premium), multiplied by a proxy of the company's risk relative to the market (beta):

$$\text{Expected return of equity} = \text{Risk-free rate (Rf)} + \text{Beta } (\beta) \times \text{Market risk premium (MRP)}$$

- The risk-free rate can be considered as the average return of ten-year government bonds to represent the long-term time horizon. Both domestic bonds and international bonds from leading economies in the same macroeconomic area with a country-specific premium can be applied (example: Italy's ten years bond or Germany's ten's years bond plus a risk premium for Italy).
- The MRP used in practice is generally estimated from empirical external sources, such as those developed by Aswath Damodaran of New York University or by Pablo Fernández of the Instituto de Estudios Superiores de la Empresa (IESE).[2]
- The beta (β) expresses the systematic risk of a company operating in a certain sector and is equal to the ratio between the covariance between a security and the market and the variance of the market. A beta >1 indicates that the company is more exposed to market risk than the average company, while a beta <1 indicates that the company is less exposed to market risk than the average company. It is important to note that beta must be calculated using leverage, that is, the ratio of onerous indebtedness, of the company being valued. The level of indebtedness (or leverage) gives origin to the distinction between:
  - Unlevered beta (asset beta): This is the beta of a company without considering its financial leverage. It only reflects the risk of the company's assets and operations. Unlevered beta is used to compare companies that have different capital structures.
  - Levered beta (equity beta): This is the beta that includes the financial risk associated with the company's debt, that is, it takes into account the company's capital structure. Levered beta is typically higher than unlevered beta because debt increases the company's risk.

Beta unlevered can be calculated with the Hamada formula:

---

[2] https://pages.stern.nyu.edu/~adamodar/; https://papers.ssrn.com/sol3/papers.cfm?abstract_id=4407839.

$$Unlevered\ beta = \frac{Levered\ beta}{(1 + (1 - Tax\ rate) \times \frac{Debt}{Equity}}$$

In practice, once the average beta unlevered of the peer group has been calculated, the company's specific leverage can be applied using the inverse formula allowing us to find the beta levered of our subject of valuation.

CAPM is a relatively simple and very popular model but has its limitations. Some valuations could consider multifactor models (in which the market risk is broken down into various components, each with its specific risk) and proxy models (which look at characteristics like size or price-to-book value of equity ratio). However, for the purpose of this book, we will consider the previously described standard CAPM.

5.5 Deriving value with intrinsic valuation

5.5.1 The weighted average cost of capital

The discount rate used for the purpose of intrinsic valuation is the weighted average cost of capital or WACC.
   WACC is calculated as:

$$WACC = \frac{D}{D+E} \times Kd \times (1-t) + \frac{E}{D+E} \times Ke$$

where:
- D, E: market value of debt and equity respectively.
- Kd: cost of debt. It can be calculated as the effective cost of debt or can be estimated as the sum of risk-free rate (typically ten years' government bonds) and a spread that encapsulates the specific credit risk of the company.
- t: effective tax rate. Since debt is tax deductible the effective cost of debt has to be considered net of taxes; this deduction is the origin of the so-called tax shield.
- Ke: cost of equity, as defined in Chapter 4 and calculated with CAPM.

5.5.2 Discounting cash flows

When approaching a valuation there are two alternatives:

- Valuing the entire business or enterprise valuation.
- Valuing the equity (which stands for valuing the business net of debt) or equity valuation.

The difference lies in the cash flows considered and the discount rate used.

5.5.2.1 Enterprise valuation

This method provides an estimate of the enterprise value (EV), obtained based on intermediate elements, starting from the operational cash flows (FCFO) discounted at the WACC.

FCFO is defined as follows:

EBIT x (1-tax rate)

+ D&A

− Changes in working capital

− CAPEX

= FCFO

And the formula for EV is:

$$PV \text{ of } FCFOs = \sum_{t=1}^{\infty} \frac{FCFO_t}{(1 + WACC)^t}$$

where:
- t: the time period (usually measured in years) for which the cash flow occurs.

5.5.2.2 Equity valuation

This method identifies the value of the equity capital, from which the EV can be traced back with the reverse path to the previous one, starting from the cash flows for the shareholders (FCFE), discounted at the cost of levered capital.

FCFE is defined as follows:

EBIT x (1-t)

+ D&A

− Changes in working capital

− CAPEX

= FCFO

+ Proceeds from issuing debt

− Repayment of debt

= FCFE

$$PV \text{ of } FCFOs = \sum_{t=1}^{\infty} \frac{FCFE_t}{(1 + Ke)^t}$$

where:
- Ke: cost of levered equity capital
- t: the time period (usually measured in years) for which the cash flow occurs.

While deriving FCFO and FCFE, income taxes contribute to both: from the perspective of the entire company, the result before financial charges and taxes (EBIT) generates figurative taxes (usually higher than total income taxes), while the underlying income components, primarily passive interests, create a tax shield, reducing the taxable base.

5.5.3 Estimation of future cash flows

Future cash flows should be estimated until it is believed that the company and the cash flows do not reach stability. From a practical point of view, a maximum period of five years and a minimum period of three are usually preferred, in order to reduce the impact on the value of the so-called TV, which we will analyze in the next paragraphs.

5.5.4 The growth rate

Since valuation is an exercise of future forecast, using historical growth rate is inconsistent and could mislead the valuation into undervaluing or overvaluing.

Intuitively, growth is linked to how much a company invests. Consequently, to get a snapshot of a company future growth potential, we have to look at the two financial ratios that express investments:

- Reinvestment rate: A ratio that captures what portion of net operating profit after taxes (NOPAT) is invested both in current and fixed assets, or, in other words, the proportion of income reinvested into the company and not used to pay dividends.

$$NOPAT = EBIT \times (1 - tax\ rate)$$

$$Reinvestment\ rate = \frac{\Delta\ Working\ capital + \Delta\ Fixed\ assets}{NOPAT}$$

- Return on invested capital (ROIC): A financial ratio equal to the NOPAT divided by the invested capital, which is a measure of how efficiently a company uses its capital to generate profits.

$$Invested\ capital = Working\ capital + Fixed\ assets$$

$$ROIC = \frac{NOPAT}{Invested\ capital}$$

Finally, the formula for the computation of the growth rate is:

$$Growth\ rate\ (g) = Reinvestment\ rate \times ROIC$$

It is important to keep in mind that the growth rate should match the company's life-cycle phase and be aligned to that.

A young company in the growth phase should grow more than the economy and a mature company can grow at a rate similar to the economy's rate of growth, while a distressed/declining company is unable to grow at all or has a negative rate.

5.5.5 The TV

Assuming a company will remain in business for an indefinite number of years, the TV represents the portion of the enterprise value that cannot be derived by discounting future cash flows. As previously mentioned, cash flow forecasting is typically done for a certain number of years, a timespan that is relatively short compared to the lifespan of a company.

The trade-off here is clear: the larger the value of n (the number of years of cash flow forecasting), the more complex and less reliable the model becomes, as it is unrealistic to assume that we can accurately forecast numerous future cash flows. Conversely, if we decrease n, the portion of value accounted for by the TV becomes larger, oversimplifying the model and leading to a larger estimation error.

To calculate the TV, assuming n is the last year of cash flow forecasting, the growing annuity formula we discussed a few paragraphs earlier is:

$$Terminal\ value\ (TV) = \frac{Cash\ flow\ in\ year\ n \times (1 + g)}{Discount\ rate - g}$$

5.5.6 Net debt and other elements of the equity bridge

Net debt is a financial metric that gauges a company's capacity to settle all its obligations if they were to become due immediately. It juxtaposes a company's total liabilities with its liquid assets. Essentially, net debt is the residual debt that would persist after a company has utilized all its liquid assets to pay off as much debt as possible.

The formula to compute net debt is:

Net debt = Short-term debt + Long-term debt − Cash and cash equivalents

where:
- Short-term debt encompasses liabilities due within a year, such as short-term bank loans, and lease payments.
- Long-term debt includes liabilities with a maturity date exceeding the year, like bonds, lease payments, and term loans.
- Cash and cash equivalents are the company's most liquid assets, which can be swiftly converted into cash. These comprise marketable securities, treasury bills, and cash in bank accounts.

Net debt serves as an indicator of a business's capability to settle all its liabilities if they were to become due simultaneously on the date of calculation, using only its readily available cash and highly liquid assets. Net debt is not considered in the equity value, because equity value is designed to measure the value of the equity, therefore excluding debt but including cash and cash equivalents. This is because cash and cash equivalents can be used to pay down a portion of the debt. Therefore, when calculating equity value, we subtract net debt from EV.

Net debt could either be positive, meaning that total debt exceeds cash and thus EV is higher than equity value, or negative, meaning the opposite.

The same treatment as that given to net debt is reserved for other items that constitute the so-called equity bridge.

These items are:
- Preferred stock: Preferred stock is a class of equity securities that holds a higher claim on the company's assets and earnings than common stock. Preferred shareholders typically receive dividends before common shareholders and have a superior claim on assets and earnings in the event of liquidation. However, preferred shareholders generally do not enjoy voting rights.
- Minority interests: Also known as non-controlling interest, this refers to an ownership stake of less than 50% in a company. This often occurs in subsidiaries where the parent company owns more than 50% of the voting shares. Minority interests come with certain rights for the stakeholder, such as participation in sales and certain audit rights.

Now, why aren't these included in the equity value?
- Preferred stock: Preferred stock is not included in the equity value calculation because it holds a higher claim on the company's assets and earnings than common stock. In the event of liquidation, preferred shareholders are paid before common shareholders. Therefore, when calculating equity value, preferred stock is treated separately to reflect its distinct characteristics and claims.
- Minority interests: These are not included in the equity value calculation because they represent ownership by outside investors, not the parent company. When calculating equity value, we are interested in the value attributable to the shareholders of the parent company. Therefore, minority interests, which belong to outside investors, are excluded.

5.5.7 Drawing conclusions: the two-step discounted cash flow

To summarize, the discounted cash flow (DCF) valuation is performed as follows:

1. Forecast the cash flows of a business in two stages:
   a. Forecast period: near term, often three to ten years, for which we forecast the operating performance of the business for each year. The result can be either

FCFO or FCFE depending on whether we are doing an asset valuation or an equity valuation.
   b. Terminal period: the entire period after the forecast period. We assume at this terminal stage that cash flows grow indefinitely at a lower rate than the forecast period.
2. Find the discount rate or cost of capital:
   a. WACC in case of an asset valuation;
   b. Ke in case of an equity valuation.
3. Calculate the stable growth rate with reinvestment rate and return on capital invested.
4. Find the EV; let's suppose a forecast period of five years for the sake of this example:

$$EV = PV \text{ of cash flows in the forecast period} + PV \text{ of } TV$$

$$EV = \sum_{t=1}^{\infty} \frac{Cash\ flow_t}{(1 + Discount\ rate)^5} + \frac{\frac{Cash\ flow\ in\ year\ 5 \times (1 + g)}{Discount\ rate - g}}{(1 + Discount\ rate)^5}$$

5. Find the equity value by applying the equity bridge concept:
   EV
   − Net debt
   − Preferred stock
   − Minority interests
   = Equity value

5.5.8 Deriving value with multiples

As previously mentioned, relative valuation is a method that compares a company's financial indicators with those of similar "peers." This method relies on the assumption that similar companies should have similar valuations. However, it is important to note that relative valuation does not consider the qualitative differences among companies, such as management or competitive position. Therefore, it should be adjusted for differences or used in combination with other valuation methods to obtain a more accurate estimate of a company's value.

5.5.8.1 Commonly used multiples

Similar to intrinsic valuation, multiples refer either to an asset valuation or an equity valuation.

Table 5.1   **Equity side multiples versus Asset side multiples**

Equity-side multiples	Asset-side multiples
Price/earnings (net income)	EV/EBITDA
Price/book value of equity	EV/FCFO
Price/sales	EV/sales

Equity value and EV can be computed by multiplying the multiple for the item found at the denominator. For example, multiplying the EBITDA of Company A for the EV/EBITDA multiple will result in the EV, while multiplying the net income for the P/E (price/earnings) ratio will result in the equity value (Table 5.1).

These multiples are driven by the following fundamental determinants:

Table 5.2   **Fundamental determinants driving multiples**

Multiples	Fundamental determinants
P/E (Price/Earnings)	Expected growth (↑), payout ratio (↑), risk (↓)
Price-to-book equity	Expected growth (↑), payout ratio (↑), risk (↓), Return On Equity (ROE) (↑)
Price-to-sales	Expected growth (↑), payout (↑), risk (↓), net margin (↑)
EV to EBITDA	Expected growth (↑), reinvestment rate (↓), risk (↓), Return On Invested Capital (ROIC) (↑), tax rate (↓)
EV to sales	Expected growth (↑), reinvestment rate (↓), risk (↓), operating margin (↑)

Source: Adapted from Aswath Damodaran, *The Little Book of Valuation* (Wiley 2011).

It is important to understand the drivers behind each multiple, in order to understand the difference that may arise among comparable companies. For example, when looking at a company with a low Price-to-Earnings ratio, where the expected growth is not significantly lower than their peers', we may be experiencing an undervalued company. This result may be experienced both with listed companies, whose valuation can be seen at any time in the stock market, and private companies, whose valuations arise from precedent transactions analysis. We will explore the differences between these two valuation methods next.

5.5.8.2 Market multiples versus transaction multiples

There are two ways to select multiples, potentially leading to very different results:

Market multiples: Also known as trading multiples, these are derived from the current market prices of publicly traded companies. They are used to value a company by comparing it to similar companies in the market. These multiples are based on the premise that similar companies would have similar valuation ratios.

5 Introduction to Valuation

The main factors to account for in choosing comparable companies with this method are:

- similar reference industrial or commercial activity
- similar size (in terms of turnover)
- similar operating margin
- similar financial structure (especially for equity-side multiples, as we will see)
- similar country, both of headquarters and sales breakdown.

The multiples must be consistent also in terms of over which timespan they're computed:

- Actual multiples consider the income value of the last available annual balance sheet.
- Trailing multiples consider Last Twelve Months (LTM) metrics, or annual values given by the sum of the last four quarterly values.
- Forward multiples consider the average estimates of analysts for the prospective value.

Transaction multiples: However, transaction multiples are derived from the prices paid in actual transactions of companies, usually in M&A. These multiples reflect the price that a buyer is willing to pay for a company in a real-world transaction. Transaction multiples can provide a more accurate valuation as they consider the synergies, strategic value, the control premium, and other factors specific to the transaction.

In the choice of transactions, the goal is to select operations that have activities and financial characteristics comparable to the transaction considered:

- Transactions related to the same business sector of reference.
- Transactions in nearby geographical areas.
- Acquired share: majority or minority.
- Rationale of the transactions and financial profile of the acquired activities: economies of scale, growth, synergies, diversification.
- Times: the more recent the data, the more relevant, particularly in cyclical industries.
- Size of the transaction: transactions of a similar size to the company being valued are generally more relevant.
- Typology of the buyer: financial versus industrial.

In order to identify the preferred method, we will analyze the pros and cons of each one:

Transaction multiples: These are derived from the price paid in actual transactions (such as M&A) for companies similar to the one being valued.

Pros:

- Real transactions: These are based on real-world transactions, which may reflect the true market value more accurately than theoretical market prices.
- Specific deals: They can capture the specifics of a deal that market multiples might not, such as synergies expected, the strategic value of the acquisition, or a control premium.
- Independence from market fluctuations: These are not affected by market fluctuations, excluding possible overvaluation or undervaluation due to the investors' confidence.

Cons:

- Availability: Relevant transaction data may not always be available, especially for private companies or unique transactions.
- Outdated information: Past transactions may not reflect the current market conditions.
- Deal specifics: The specifics of a deal that can cause the transaction multiple to be higher or lower than market multiples might not apply to the company being valued. Moreover, the specifics are often undisclosed and may account for high or low valuation.

Market multiples: These are derived from the market values of publicly traded companies that are similar to the one being valued (the so-called peer group).

Pros:

- Current information: This is based on current market prices and is therefore always up to date.
- Availability: Data for publicly traded companies is readily available.
- Benchmarking: This allows for easy comparison across a broad set of similar companies.

Cons:

- Market fluctuations: These can be heavily influenced by overall market fluctuations that may not reflect the fundamentals of the companies.
- Differences in companies: Publicly traded companies used for comparison may not be truly comparable to the company being valued due to differences in size, growth rates, risk profile, profitability, or other factors.

In practice, both transaction multiples and market multiples are often used in conjunction while valuing a company, providing a range of values that reflect both historical transactions and current market conditions. It is important to consider the context and use judgment when applying these multiples, trying to explain the reasons behind multiple inconsistences by recovering as much information as possible.

5 Introduction to Valuation

Finally, one last factor must be considered: statistical relevance. Descriptive statistics prove useful when analyzing multiples, as opposed to just using the simple mean. Median is already a much better indicator, but diving deep into standard error, skewness, and minimum and maximum values, and plotting a histogram are key to discovering potentially biased data.

5.6 Conclusions

Intrinsic and relative valuation will often give different results. The single biggest difference is whether you believe the market is efficient or is currently mispricing assets. Intrinsic valuation flattens out the assumptions on growth, considering a stable growth rate that smoothens inevitable market cycles. In practice, relative valuation is easier to perform and relies on simpler assumptions, limiting the space for human error in picking the assumptions of complex models. Having established this, the more comprehensive approach suggests performing both valuations and come up with a reasonable and justifiable estimate. For this purpose, the football field chart allows us to compare the results of the different valuation methods applied (Figure 5.1).

Figure 5.1   **An example of football field chart**

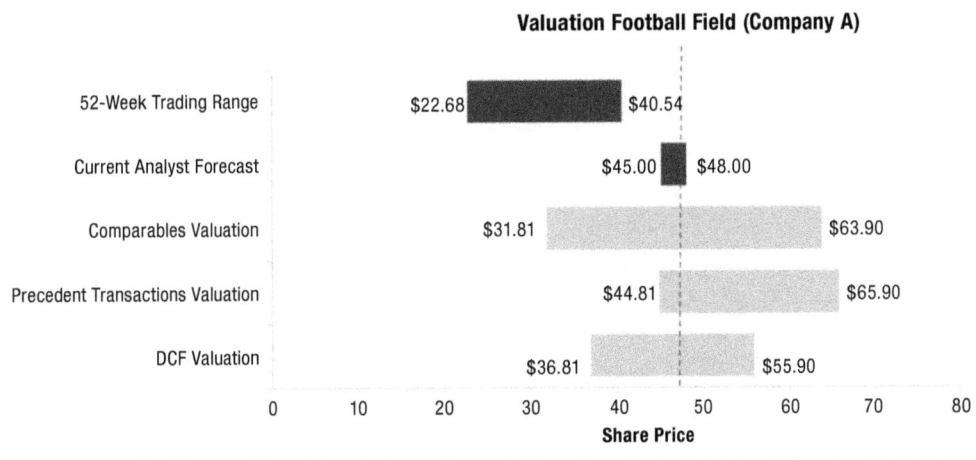

Source: https://corporatefinanceinstitute.com/resources/financial-modeling/football-field-chart-template/.

Part III
M&A and Private Equity in Practice

6 Legal and Tax Processes in M&A and Private Equity

by *Carlotta Robbiano* and *Daniele Cevolo*

6.1 Introduction to the legal side of M&A

The legal profiles within M&A transactions carried out by private equity firms are multiple and entail unique complexities. M&A activity involves a considerable amount of business strategy, enabling companies to achieve disparate objectives such as growth, diversification, and market expansion. Within this very broad sector, private equity firms play a pivotal role. Indeed, they often drive transactions through strategic investments in valuable companies, with the intent of realizing value through efficient management and subsequent specific exit strategies.

This chapter, which will analyze the main characteristics of M&A transactions from a legal perspective, does not claim to be exhaustive, given that the complexity of the subject matter would require a dedicated book. The chapter does, however, provide good food for thought and insight into the main legal dynamics that a private equity player faces when initiating an M&A transaction. Moreover, for the sake of clarity, it will not deal with the differences, albeit significant, between majority (or totalitarian) and minority acquisitions.

Finally, although this chapter focuses on M&A transactions carried out by private equity operators, its content may also apply—to some extent—to operators that do not belong to the category of private equity firms (e.g. industrial operators). Our approach has been a purchaser-oriented one.

6.1.1 The role of corporate lawyers in M&A transactions

M&A transactions in the private equity sector are complex processes that require meticulous planning, comprehensive due diligence, and strategic negotiation. These kinds of transactions involve a multitude of legal considerations that can have profound implications on the outcome and legality of deals.

For these reasons, the role of corporate lawyers is essential, as they provide the legal framework and guidance necessary to navigate corporate law and make the transaction a success. Corporate lawyers boasting solid expertise in M&A transactions are tasked with a multifaceted role that encompasses advisory, business acumen, and drafting/negotiation skills. They need to possess a deep understanding of the industry in which their clients operate as well as an intimate knowledge of the fundamentals of civil law and common law (as the case may be), and of, amongst others, corporate finance, corporate governance, anti-trust regulations, and employment law. Their expertise ensures that any given transaction complies with the applicable legal requirements and that their clients' interests are protected throughout the entire process, which may take weeks, months, or, in some cases, even longer.

During the initial stages, lawyers play a crucial role in structuring the deal, advising on the way in which the transaction can be carried out (e.g. share deal vs. asset deal, mergers, JVs, etc.) and, together with tax and financial advisors, assessing the risks and advantages associated with each option. Additionally, during the introductory phases, they also assist in drafting the preliminary documents (e.g. LOI, memorandum of understanding, term sheet), which outline the main understanding between the parties involved and set the foundation for a possible due diligence process.

During the legal due diligence phase, corporate lawyers meticulously review the target company's documents to identify potential risks and liabilities. They work closely with financial and tax advisors to ensure that the legal, financial, and tax aspects of the transaction are aligned. As one can imagine, this process is crucial in determining the valuation and structure of the deal.

Once the due diligence process is concluded, if the client elects to carry on the transaction the negotiation phase commences—a phase that can be considered the most critical of the whole deal. This is when the primary agreements, such as the share purchase agreements, asset purchase agreements, or investment agreements, containing all the terms and conditions of the deal, are drafted and negotiated. The lawyers must strike a balance between the need to protect their client's interests and that of reaching a mutually satisfactory agreement.

This chapter will mainly focus on share purchase agreements.

Lastly, corporate lawyers are responsible for the signing and closing phases as well as for the preparation and filing of all necessary documentation with regulatory authorities (if any) and, more generally, for ensuring that the transaction complies with all applicable laws and regulations.

6.1.2 Distinctiveness of M&A transactions in the private equity sector

M&A transactions within the private equity sector are distinct from those in other sectors due to the investment strategy and structure of private equity firms. Private equity firms typically acquire companies with the intention of implementing strategic changes to increase their value and obtain a high return by subsequently exiting the investment through either a sale or a public offering after a certain period. This investment horizon influences the structuring of the deal, often leading to more complex arrangements regarding governance, financing, and exit strategies.

M&A transactions in the private equity sector often involve leveraged finance usage, where the acquisition is financed through debt, which is then serviced by the target company's cash flow. This adds a layer of complexity, in terms of legal structure and negotiation of financing terms with the lender. Moreover, private equity deals often include incentive schemes for the management of portfolio companies, such as stock options or carried interest mechanisms, which require careful legal crafting to align the interests of private equity firms, the target company, and its management.

In conclusion, the legal support required in M&A transactions and, particularly, in the private equity sector, is extensive and versatile. Corporate lawyers play a critical role in guiding clients through the legal complexities of these deals, ensuring compliance and facilitating successful outcomes.

6.2 The legal process in M&A transactions

As briefly anticipated in the previous chapter, the legal process in M&A transactions is complex and involves multiple stages, ranging from preliminary agreements to post-closing integrations. This chapter aims to delve into the main characteristics of M&A processes with a particular emphasis on the private equity sector.

6.2.1 The LOI

The initial phase of an M&A transaction—without considering a relevant number of introductory conference calls and/or business meetings that have no formal value—typically involves the execution of one or more preliminary agreements, such as NDAs, letters of intent, memorandum of understanding, or term sheets, which serve as precursors to the subsequent phases and the definitive agreements.

The LOI (i.e. the most common type of preliminary agreement) outlines the basic terms and conditions of the proposed transaction and reflects the parties' intention to engage in negotiations in good faith. The main content of a LOI is characterized by the commercial terms and conditions on which the parties have already reached an agreement, the way in which the due diligence will be carried out (i.e. the areas of investigations and the timing), or some specific clauses concerning the confidentiality terms and the exclusivity period.

Leaving aside the confidentiality and exclusivity clauses, we deem it appropriate to point out that the Italian legal system does not identify a typical contractual case to which the LOI can be attributed. Therefore, the legal framework of the same must be sought in the actual will of the parties, and its binding force—if any—is strictly related to the actual content of such document.

Therefore, should the parties not wish to find themselves in relevant interpretative disputes, they should expressly specify whether they intend to give the LOI any binding force. As a general rule, the Italian legal system establishes that the parties, while negotiating an agreement, must act in good faith, this being a parameter of fundamental importance in assessing the behavior of the parties during the negotiation phase, and also in terms of possible precontractual liability.

In most cases, an LOI does not contain binding elements as it only sets out the intention of the parties to evaluate a certain transaction, without any commitment at that stage except for certain specific obligations that are normally marked as binding, such as confidentiality and exclusivity clauses.

6.2.1.1 Confidentiality clause

Confidentiality clauses typically protect sensitive information being disclosed during the negotiation process, preventing their misuse and unauthorized dissemination. Confidentiality clauses require the recipient of information to use any such data solely for the purpose of evaluating the potential transaction and prohibit the disclosure of such information to third parties without express prior consent. Breach of confidentiality can lead to legal remedies, including injunctions and damages, thereby underscoring the importance of these clauses in safeguarding proprietary information.

These clauses are also common in tender processes (as detailed further later in this chapter) as confidentiality obligations are assumed even before a LOI is signed. In fact, in that case, the seller's advisors will make an information memorandum available to third parties to express their interest and, in that context, a confidentiality agreement will also be made available for signature before any confidential information is shared.

6.2.1.2 Exclusivity clause

Exclusivity arrangements also play a crucial role in M&A transactions because these agreements, whether negotiated within a LOI or through independent documents, grant the potential purchaser an exclusivity period during which the seller cannot engage in negotiations with other third parties. Exclusivity provides a safeguard to the potential buyer, who will be investing significant resources—both in terms of time and cost—in due diligence exercises and deal structuring, by reducing the risk of a competing bid emerging.

For the seller, the granting of exclusivity can be a double-edged sword. While it can lead to a more focused and potentially faster negotiation with one party, it may also limit the seller's leverage by precluding simultaneous negotiations taking place with other interested parties.

The duration and terms of exclusivity are indeed points of negotiation, aimed at striking a balancing between the purchaser's need for protection and the seller's desire to retain some level of competitive tension.

6.2.2 Auction process versus one-to-one negotiation

The way in which a company is sold can profoundly influence the dynamics of the transaction. Consequently, sellers face a crucial initial series of inquiries: What is the optimal approach for selling the company? Should they opt for a broad auction, aiming to engage the widest pool of bidders? Should they pursue exclusive negotiations with a single potential purchaser?

In an auction process, the seller invites multiple potential purchasers to submit bids, creating a competitive environment that can maximize the sale price. This process is often preferred by private equity firms looking to divest equity or assets, as it represents the best mechanism for determining the market value and making the most valuable deal. It can also expedite the sale process, as normally the seller's advisors set the steps, the timing, and the framework of the negotiations.

Conversely, a one-to-one negotiation involves a bilateral discussion between the purchaser and the seller. This approach can offer more privacy and flexibility, allowing for tailored deal structuring and potentially fostering a cooperative atmosphere. However, without the competitive tension of an auction, the final price may not reflect the highest value the market is willing to pay.

6.2.2.1 Legal due diligence

In M&A transactions carried out by private equity operators, the due diligence process has significant importance and presents specific characteristics. During this process, in fact, the purchaser intends to acquire as much information as possible for the purposes of evaluating the company and determining its own actual interest in the deal.

As mentioned in Section 6.1, in fact, being supported by a lawyer who has extensive experience in the corporate and M&A sector is essential for the successful execution of an M&A transaction. A deep knowledge of the specific industry where the target operates is also crucial to circumstantiate the perimeter of the due diligence exercise and meet the client's needs.

Taking a step back, it is crucial that, in the preliminary phases, when the scope of work and the perimeter of the legal due diligence are being defined, a good lawyer advises the client on the issues that should be investigated and those that, given the characteristics of the transaction and/or the target itself, can be overlooked or minimized. This approach is known as a "tailor-made approach," as each transaction is unique and requires a different investigation based on the specific business of the target, its size, the industry in which it operates, and so on.

As a matter of fact, as anticipated previously, the due diligence process covers various areas of investigation, among which are tax due diligence, financial and accounting due diligence, business due diligence, and, last but not least, legal due diligence. The latter involves reviewing and analyzing the target company's legal affairs, including—among the principal matters—its corporate structure and ledgers, contracts, pending or potential litigations, intellectual properties, employment matters, and regulatory and anti-trust compliance. The wider the spectrum of activities to be analyzed, the greater the number of lawyers who will be involved, as each area needs to be addressed and investigated by a competent team.

The objective of the legal due diligence is to identify potential legal impediments that could affect the transaction's value or feasibility. The legal due diligence findings can influence the transaction's structure, pricing, and even the decision whether to proceed with the deal. For private equity firms, the due diligence process is not only about risk assessment, but also about identifying opportunities for value creation and operational improvements. Tailor-made legal due diligence allows the client to focus on the areas of greatest relevance to the specific transaction and to identify possible improvements to be put in place after the acquisition.

For instance, a legal due diligence involving a target operating in the direct-to-consumer sector, compared to one operating in business-to-business, will require greater attention to General Data Protection Regulation (GDPR)-related matters, as, on the one hand, the target will be involved in significant relationships with end users and will be required to comply with local and EU regulations regarding data protection use, storage, and so on. On the other hand, a business-to-business operating target will have much more limited GDPR impacts.

Again, in cases where the target is a manufacturing company, the environmental impacts will be significantly greater compared to a service company. A target company owning real estate assets will require a different approach to a company that only deals with leased properties.

The industry in which the target operates has also significant impacts on the type of contracts to be analyzed and the way in which they are analyzed, depending on whether the company operates in the industrial, automotive, beauty, or energy sector, and so on. Moreover, even within contracts of the same type (e.g. supply agreements, service agreements) different clauses may be analyzed and emphasized differently depending on the industry and operating sector.

Leaving aside operational methods for carrying out legal due diligence, which is not the subject of this chapter, here is a summary of the benefits that can be obtained through this exercise:

- Identification of any significant issues or risks affecting the target company that may discourage a potential buyer from continuing the negotiations.
- Gaining knowledge of the main characteristics, both current and prospective, of the target company's business.
- Determination of the relevant risk areas relating to the business of the target company, in order to negotiate representations and warranties more efficiently.

As a side note, while proper legal due diligence undoubtedly adds significant value to clients and enhances the chances of a successful conclusion of the transaction, it must be pointed out that only under limited circumstances can legal due diligence investigations replace safeguards such as appropriate representations and warranties provided by the seller in the share purchase agreement, regarding the existence of circumstances that could impact the value of the target company (e.g. contingent liabilities or other events that may have material effects), which should also be contemplated in the contractual documents. In certain limited cases, the purchaser may decide to waive such set of representations and warranties, for instance in the event that the seller is a private equity player and the fund through which the relevant investment has been made is about to close, thus limiting the ability to provide any obligations for a period of time after the completion of the transaction.

6.3 Overview of the share purchase agreement

As anticipated in the first chapter, the share purchase agreement is the key document in M&A transactions. It is the agreement that finalizes and crystalizes the terms and conditions under which the ownership of a company is transferred from the seller to the purchaser. The share purchase agreement acts as a comprehensive framework that outlines the rights and obligations of the parties involved, the structure of the transaction, and the mechanics for the transfer of ownership.

This agreement has distinctive complexity and is tailored to the specific characteristics of each transaction, reflecting the results of the due diligence exercise, the strategic objectives of the parties, and the agreed risk allocation. The agreement also typically includes detailed provisions regarding the structure of the transaction, the purchase price, the payment mechanism, the conditions precedent to closing (if any), the representations and warranties of the parties, the covenants, the indemnities, and any dispute resolution mechanisms.

Although, from a local perspective, a share purchase agreement regulated by Italian law can be understood within the broader framework of a typical sales contract (*contratto di compravendita*), as provided and regulated by Article 1470 and subsequent of the Italian civil code, this type of contract has unique features that often deviate from the standard regulations of the Italian legal system. It combines various provisions from other typical contracts outlined in the Italian civil code and incorporates atypical cases (often originating from common law practices).

The reason for this is that the Italian civil code tends to protect the assets that are directly sold (i.e. shares or quotas, as the case may be). However, in M&A transactions, the real need for protection lies in the so-called secondary assets, meaning the assets and liabilities of the company underlying its shareholding. Therefore, the parties involved are compelled to deviate from the automatic application of the Italian civil code that would limit both the seller's and the buyer's protection, by introducing specific tailor-made terms and conditions. The general guarantees provided by the Italian civil code against defects and eviction would only partially ensure the level of protection typically desired by a cautious purchaser, especially if an institutional investor is concerned about undisclosed or potential liabilities that may not fit the definition of "defects" of the sold asset.

As a result, it has become common practice—initially influenced by Anglo-Saxon legal traditions but now also regularly adopted in civil law systems—to develop standard forms of contractual waivers, such as:

1. Representations and warranties provided by the seller relating both to the "primary asset" (i.e. shares or quotas on sale) and, more broadly, the "secondary assets," meaning the company as a whole, whose capital is represented by the shareholding. Linked to these representations and warranties are the indemnification obligations of the seller in case of breach of the representations and warranties. In particular, the parties typically negotiate the specific duration and limitations of such representations and warranties, introducing CAP, thresholds, and/or *de min-*

imis terms to the representations and warranties/indemnities mechanism. This set of negotiated terms serves to prevent the system of representations and warranties and related indemnities from falling under the expiration prescriptions of the Italian civil code, which are not fit for M&A transactions because they are very short, while representation and warranties and related indemnities are meant to be in force for several years.
2. Post-closing agreements regarding termination for breach. Once the contract has been executed in its primary components—transfer of shares/quotas and payment of the price—the share purchase agreement includes certain provisions that survive the main obligations of the contract. If these are breached, for example in the form of a breach of a representation or a failure to complete a post-closing covenant, share purchase agreements usually deviate from the Italian civil code's provisions on termination for breach and provide, on the contrary, that the parties cannot claim any termination for breaches. This is because neither party has an interest in reverting the shares/quotas back to the seller after the sale, especially if some time has already passed and restoring the original situation would be hard, if not impossible, as the company is a living entity that can change significantly from one week to another.

Another point of interest in the construction of this agreement is the timing between the so-called signing, meaning the moment in which the seller and the purchaser sign the share purchase agreement, and the "closing," meaning the moment in which the shares or quotas are transferred to the purchaser. Based on the approach taken by the parties, the timing between these two main events can be classified into one of the following categories:

1. *A preliminary agreement*: The parties intend to commit to signing a subsequent definitive contract (upon the occurrence of the closing), which may involve the endorsement of shares at closing or the signing of a notarial deed required for the transfer of quotas.
2. *A definitive contract*: The parties intend to transfer the ownership of the assets from the moment the contract is signed, subject to the fulfilment of certain conditions. In this case, once the pre-closing conditions are met, the formalities, such as the endorsement of shares or the signing of a notarial deed required for the transfer of the quotas will be an executive act necessary to formalize the transfer. However, the transfer of ownership is considered to have already occurred upon the fulfilment of the conditions that suspended its effectiveness.

In practice, so-called closing is often contingent on the prior occurrence of specific conditions as well as the preliminary fulfilment of obligations by one or both of the parties. As a result, the choice of structure for the acquisition contract is often necessarily that of a preliminary contract.

We now deem it appropriate to highlight some of the main clauses that are usually contained in a share purchase agreement and often the subject of intense negotiations.

6.3.1 Conditions precedent and covenants

Conditions precedent are provisions, facts, or events that must be satisfied or waived before a transaction can be completed. These conditions often include regulatory approvals, obtainment of consents from third parties, acknowledgment of the absence of material adverse changes, and completion of certain pre-closing obligations. They are designed to ensure that all necessary legal and practical steps have been taken to enable a smooth transfer of ownership and to protect the parties from unforeseen liabilities.

Covenants, however, are promises made by the parties to undertake, or refrain from undertaking, certain actions during the period between signing and closing (the so-called interim period). For the seller, these may include operating the business in the ordinary course and according to past practice, maintaining certain financial ratios, or not engaging in extraordinary transactions without the purchaser's consent. For the purchaser, covenants may relate to financing arrangements and efforts aimed at obtaining necessary approvals. The covenants of both parties are fundamental in maintaining the value of the business and providing assurance that the agreed terms will be adhered to until the transaction is finalized.

6.3.2 Payment mechanisms: locked box versus price adjustment

The payment of the purchase price is an essential element of the share purchase agreement and the transaction considered as a whole, and the mechanisms for determining and paying the price can vary significantly. The two most common approaches are the locked box mechanism and the price adjustment mechanism.

The locked box involves fixing the purchase price at a certain date prior to signing the share purchase agreement, based on specific management accounts and relevant financial figures, as agreed upon between the parties. This approach provides certainty of price for both parties and avoids the need for post-closing adjustments. However, it requires the seller to warrant that there have been no value leakages (such as unauthorized payments, dividend distributions, asset disposals, or other forms of distractions in favor of the sellers or their related parties) between the locked box date (i.e. the date based on which the price is agreed between the parties) and the closing date.

Conversely, the price adjustment mechanism allows for the purchase price to be adjusted post-closing based on the actual financial performance of the business of the target company. This typically involves a closing accounts process, where the final price is determined based on the actual financial figures at closing. This method aligns the price with the true value of the business at the time of the transfer but can lead to disputes between the seller and the purchaser over the appropriate adjustments.

6.3.3 Representations and warranties, indemnities, and guarantees

Representations and warranties, as discussed above, are statements of fact made by the seller regarding the shares/quotas to be transferred and the company considered as a whole. They cover various matters, including compliance with laws, the accuracy of financial statements, the condition of assets, the absence of undisclosed liabilities, and several other areas, which can vary depending on the business of the target, the industry in which it operates, its size, and, more generally, the topics which the purchaser is interested in investigating. Conversely, the purchaser is also required to issue certain representations and warranties, which are mostly related to their financial stability and capacity to complete the transaction. These provisions serve as a risk allocation tool, allowing the purchaser and the seller to seek indemnification if the representations and warranties issued by the other party are breached.

Indemnities are contractual obligations set forth to compensate the other party upon the occurrence of certain losses. In the context of a share purchase agreement, indemnities are typically provided by the seller to cover specific risks identified during the due diligence process or for breaches of any of the representations and warranties specified by the seller. For its turn, the purchaser is required to indemnify the seller in the event it is the one to breach its contractual obligations.

Guarantees are assurances provided by a third party, usually a parent company or a majority shareholder, to back the obligations of the seller under the share purchase agreement. They provide additional security to the purchaser, ensuring that there is recourse to a solvent entity if the seller fails to fulfil its indemnification obligations. The purchaser may also obtain that an escrow account is set up on the closing date, to which a portion of the purchase price will be paid and held as security for the seller's indemnification obligations arising from any breach of the representations and warranties. Sometimes the purchaser may also be required to provide guarantees; for instance, if the share purchase agreement provides that the payment of the purchase price is wholly or partly deferred.

In conclusion, the share purchase agreement is a quite complex document that requires careful negotiation and drafting to ensure that the transaction reflects the parties' intentions and adequately protects their interests. The complexity of share purchase agreements and the significant financial stakes involved underscore the importance of meticulous legal work in the M&A and, specifically, in the private equity sector.

6.4 Introduction to portfolio companies and management mechanisms

Portfolio companies are those entities—previously subject to M&A transactions—in which private equity funds invested, with the objective of driving growth and increasing value over a certain period of time, typically with a view to realizing a significant ROI through exit strategies, such as a private sale or a public offering. These companies can range from small startups to large established entities, and they often operate in a variety of industries.

The management of portfolio companies is a critical aspect of private equity investment, as the value creation plan often hinges on the effectiveness of the company's leadership. The management mechanisms of portfolio companies can include strategic planning, operational improvements, financial restructuring, and leadership changes. Indeed, private equity firms often play an active role in the management of their portfolio companies, providing not only capital but also strategic guidance. This can involve appointing experienced industry professionals to the board of directors—although private equity funds often partner their management figures with entrepreneurs and leave it to the latter to continue the growth under the guidance of the new ownership—engaging in regular strategic reviews and setting performance targets.

The role of the management team in a portfolio company is to execute the business plan and drive operational improvements that enhance value. This team is typically led by a managing director (usually supported by a group of senior executives who are responsible for various aspects of the company's operations) and charged with the day-to-day running of the business, implementing the strategies agreed upon with the private equity firm and achieving the financial and operational targets that have been set.

6.4.1 Carried interest as a management incentive in portfolio companies

Carried interest is a form of performance fee that aligns the interests of the top management of the portfolio company with those of the investors of the fund and the fund itself. It represents a share of the profits generated by the divestment from the portfolio company that is paid to the management team that has invested together with the fund, typically after the fund has returned the original capital invested, plus an agreed hurdle rate, to its investors. Such share of the profits is more than proportional to the investment that the management made in the portfolio company, provided that the return for the fund and its investors has been at least equal to the goal originally set when creating the carried interest plan.

The mechanism of the carried interest serves as a powerful incentive for the management of the portfolio companies for several reasons. First, it directly ties the financial reward of the management team to the success of the investment, encouraging them to maximize the value of the company. The prospect of receiving a portion of the profits more than proportional to the investment made (and often growing in direct correlation with the growth of the investment returns) upon a successful exit provides a strong motivation to drive performance and achieve the targets set by the private equity firm.

The structure of the carried interest can be tailored to promote long-term value creation rather than short-term gains. For example, the carried interest may be subject to a vesting schedule or tied to the achievement of certain milestones, ensuring that the management team remains focused on sustainable growth and the strategic objectives of the private equity firm.

However, the use of carried interest as an incentive also comes with complexities. The tax treatment of carried interest can be very advantageous for the management, providing that certain conditions set by the applicable tax provisions are met.

Without dwelling too much on the tax aspects, however, it should be pointed out that the difference in the applicable tax regime can be very significant. In fact, while in the presence of all the requirements prescribed by the tax regulations the applicable tax regime is that of financial interests, in the absence of these requirements the income from a carried interest plan may be taxed as employment income. It is therefore important that carried interest plans are always drafted and negotiated with the help not only of legal advisors but also of tax advisors who can guarantee the best tax arrangement for the company and the management.

In conclusion, carried interest is a cornerstone of the compensation structure in the private equity sector and serves as a significant incentive for the management of portfolio companies. By providing a concrete share of the risks and the benefits of the investment, it aligns the interests of the management team with those of the private equity firm and its investors, fostering a culture of performance and value creation.

7 The Tax Process in M&A and Private Equity

by *Valentina Santini* and *Gianmaria Leoni*

Numerous strategic levers can be used in the planning of M&A transactions; however, from a tax point of view, there cannot be said to be a "magic" formula suitable without any quid pro quo to reduce the "tax effect significantly." The choice that is fiscally less demanding for the transferor, that is, the "indirect" sale of a "company" through a so-called share deal transaction, is, on the one hand, accompanied by a tax burden for the purchaser in the form of lower deductible depreciation, as the capital gains relating to the "company" sold are acquired in the form of shareholdings. *Mutatis mutandis*, the most tax-burdensome choice for the transferor, that is, the direct transfer, is accompanied, on the other hand, by a tax benefit for the buyer in the form of higher deductible depreciation, goodwill for example, and any capital gains paid on individual tax-recognized assets.

The tax differences in the chosen transaction structure are not just theoretical concepts. They are practical tools both the seller and the buyer can use to define the price. However, the choice of these tools is not made in isolation. The economic and financial conditions of the parties involved heavily influence it. This practical aspect of tax considerations in M&A transactions underscores the importance of decisions in defining the price and the need to consider the broader economic and financial context.

In pursuing the correct tax classification of the transactions in question, it's crucial to note that the search for a solution has significant implications on the operational level in civil law and, most importantly, in the tax field. These implications are far-reaching, considering the existence of anti-abuse provisions as well as guidelines of practice and jurisprudence that increasingly steer the audits of the tax administration, altering the principles of good faith and cooperation.

Tax can arise in multiple forms, including corporate taxes, withholding taxes, employment taxes, and indirect taxes (VAT, transfer taxes, and stamp duties), is complex, and can represent a significant cost. Getting it wrong can therefore result in considerable and unnecessary value leakage. However, getting it right can ensure value is maximized.

Tax, therefore, should play a key role throughout the transaction process (Figure 7.1).

Figure 7.1 Deal life cycle and tax inputs

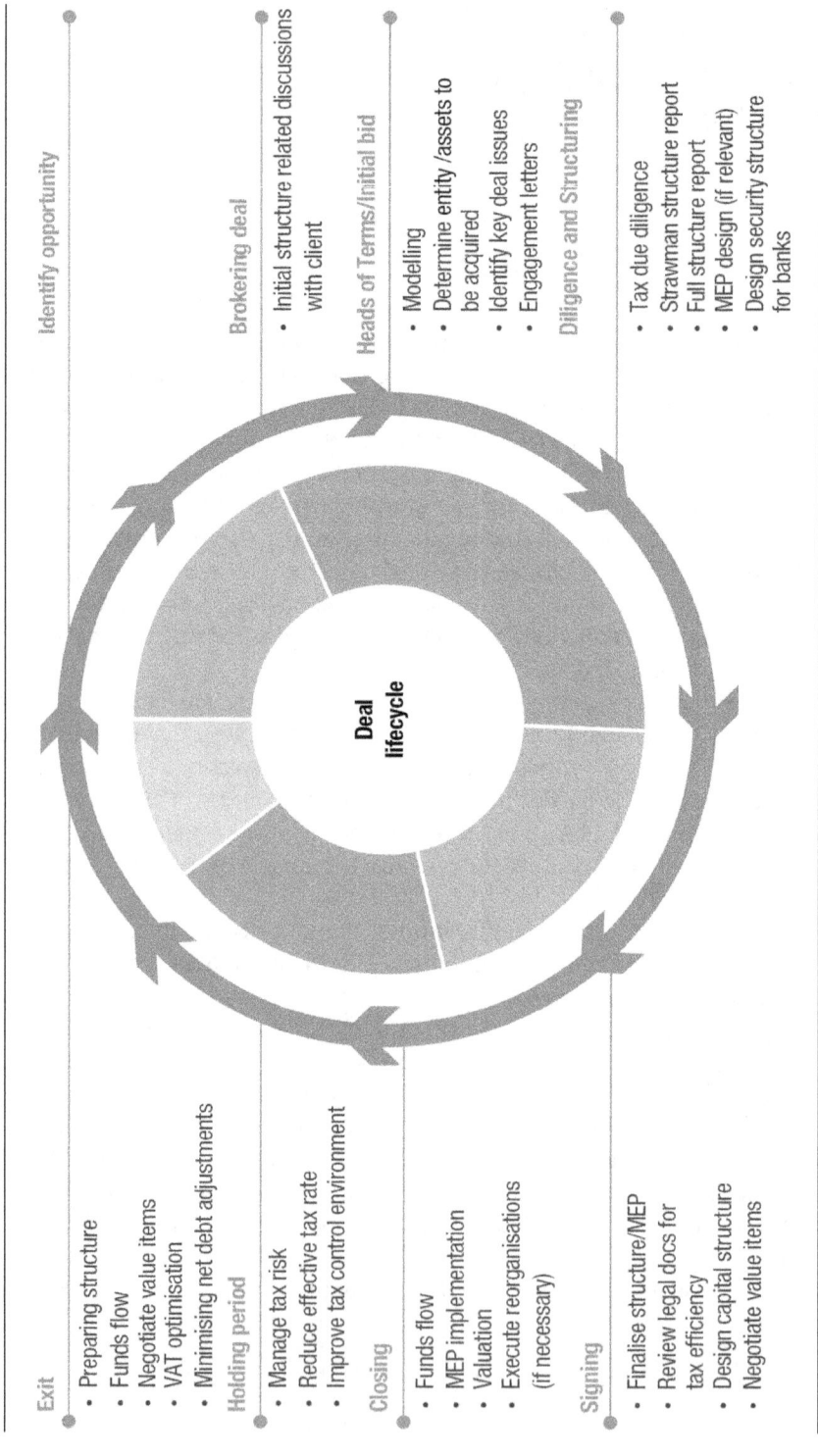

Identify opportunity

Brokering deal
- Initial structure related discussions with client

Heads of Terms/Initial bid
- Modelling
- Determine entity/assets to be acquired
- Identify key deal issues
- Engagement letters

Diligence and Structuring
- Tax due diligence
- Strawman structure report
- Full structure report
- MEP design (if relevant)
- Design security structure for banks

Signing
- Finalise structure/MEP
- Review legal docs for tax efficiency
- Design capital structure
- Negotiate value items

Closing
- Funds flow
- MEP implementation
- Valuation
- Execute reorganisations (if necessary)

Holding period
- Manage tax risk
- Reduce effective tax rate
- Improve tax control environment

Exit
- Preparing structure
- Funds flow
- Negotiate value items
- VAT optimisation
- Minimising net debt adjustments

Figure 7.2   **Why involve tax in a transaction?**

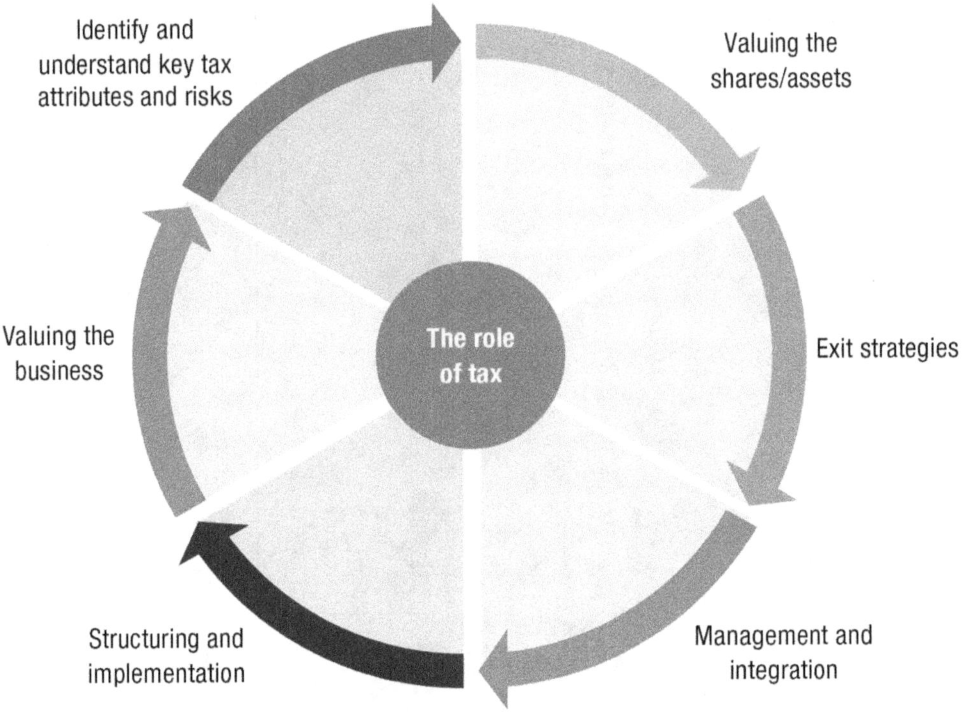

- Identify and understand key tax attributes and risks
- Valuing the shares/assets
- Exit strategies
- Management and integration
- Structuring and implementation
- Valuing the business

The role of tax

7.1   The structure of the transaction

Since around 2014, there has been a real boom in asset acquisitions by (mainly) investment funds. As mentioned, this type of operation has also forced operators in the sector to address the issue of optimizing the tax variable (Figure 7.2).

In this perspective, there are numerous design schemes able to be adopted, the most frequent of which is represented by the creation of a particular purpose vehicle, SPV, in which (generally) the seller contributes all the assets of specific interest to the buyer; just as often, the seller is also interested in the realization of the added value, generated by the interaction of the assets being transferred, and, consequently, the final phase of the "deal" manifests itself in a project scheme that provides for the sale of the SPV to the actual investor (e.g. the private equity fund).

This (last) transaction can be carried out, as mentioned, not only through the direct sale of the "asset" itself, the so-called asset deal, but also through the use of substantially alternative instruments, consisting of the sale of the shareholding, which generally represents the entire capital of the SPV, the so-called share deal or, more precisely, in the shift of the assets to a newly established company with the subsequent sale of the shareholding in the transferee to the entity interested in the

Figure 7.3 Key tax inputs: structuring

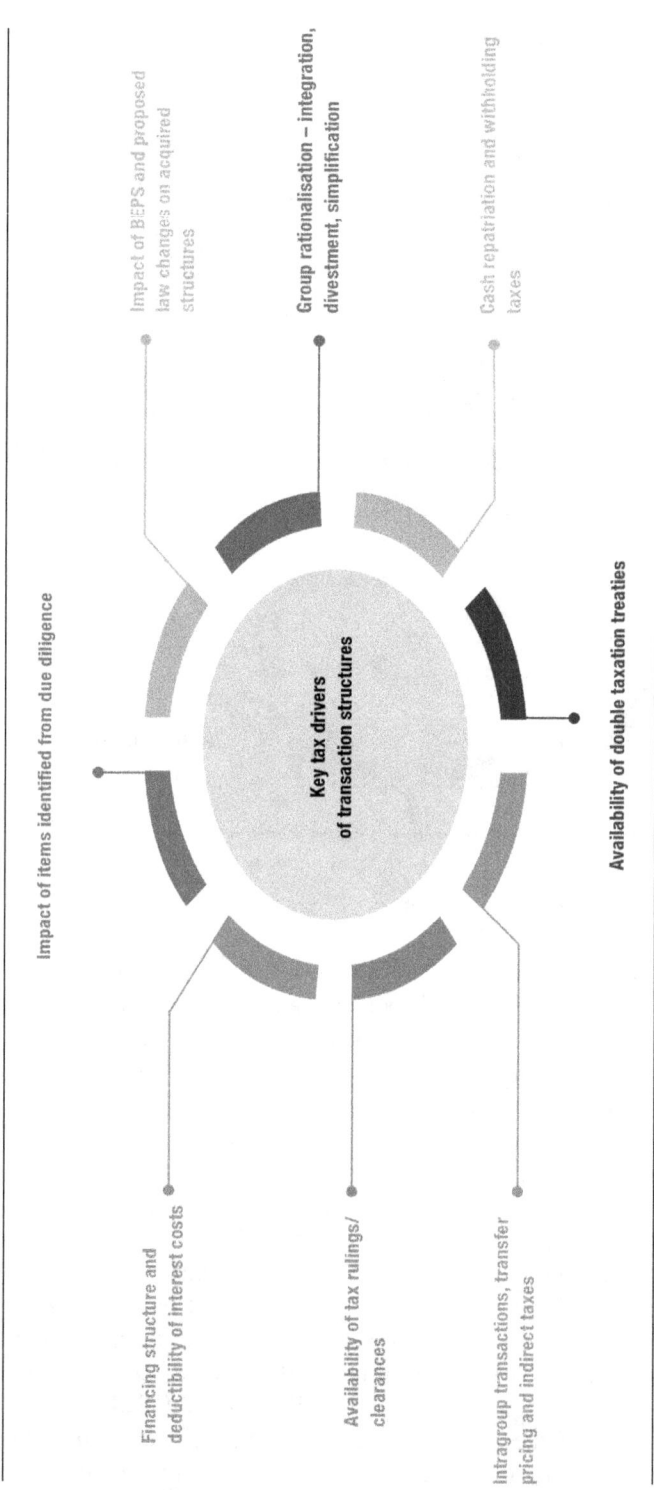

acquisition. The latter party, if it deems it appropriate, may subsequently proceed to carry out a merger by incorporation of the transferee company, through, for example, an LBO transaction.

The choice of sources to finance a given business acquisition (asset deal) or shareholding (share deal) is attributable to the use of debt as "leverage," as will be described later in this chapter. This leverage involves the emergence of incremental benefits (and risks) if the cost of debt is lower (or higher) than the return on risk capital.

The examination of the tax aspects of the agreements governing the sale and purchase of assets (depending on the intended outcome) requires identifying the different methods through which the company as a "complex" entity may be transferred. This is because the ordinarily applicable (tax) regime is not always the same due to the different treatment applied by the legislator to the share deal in contrast to the asset deal, both in terms of direct and indirect taxation; hence, the existence of tax-planning margins available to the parties involved in such transactions (Figure 7.3).

However, the negotiation practice that has prevailed to date fluctuates in identifying the "one" rather than the "other" form, assuming, in the context of these processes, that the tax variable is undoubtedly an essential strategic value; that is, that the analysis of the tax burden of the seller/transferor rather than the enhancement of the potential benefit of the buyer/transferee represents essential strategic variables in the price determination process.

Effective management of commercial and tax issues will drive the acquisition structure, and tax teams will invariably take the lead in designing and developing both the outline "strawman" structure and the final structure. These will be set out in a structuring report, which can potentially be shared with banks and other advisors.

7.2 Variables underlying how the investment is carried out

The formal differences, in tax terms, of the chosen transaction are, first of all, elements of evaluation available to both parties, seller and buyer, for a correct weighting of the so-called pricing of the transaction itself, often related to the economic and financial conditions of the "parties" involved and, therefore, difficult to reconcile with potential ex post reconstructions aimed at denoting any anti-abuse profiles. These also generate significant consequences both from a tax and legal point of view: through the sale of a shareholding, there is an "indirect" circulation of the company's assets, as it is not the ownership of the assets themselves that is transferred directly but the entire shareholding asset (or a percentage of it) of the company that holds such assets.

On the one hand, with the transfer/contribution of assets and a company, the transfer from one legal entity to another of assets, and a set of assets organized for the exercise of the business (such as machinery, contractual relationships, know-how, employees, etc.), is carried out.

The buyer's situation, on the other hand, is often more delicate than that of the seller. The seller is typically required to make short-term assessments, such as determining the fairness of the price relative to the value of the asset being sold and the tax burden, which usually ends once the transaction is completed.

The buyer, *mutatis mutandis*, must make a complex series of forecasts for the medium and long term to realize the convenience of the investment and the opportunity of the price: it is necessary, moreover, to also assess the possibilities of "recovery" of the cost, of the optimal ways of satisfying the financial needs, of the identification of the subject/vehicle through which to carry out the acquisition, and a series of other variables to coordinate the inclusion of the acquired assets better, for example, within the preexisting group (where present).

More and more often, the interests of the parties are opposed: the situation optimal for the seller/transferor to mitigate the tax burden clashes with the interests of the buyer, who may have difficulty obtaining tax recognition over time of the cost of the acquisition.

Moreover, the natural objective that the purchaser sets is that this cost is relevant for tax purposes and can potentially and prospectively be offset against the taxable income generated by the acquired company (or that of other companies in its group).

Technically, this is possible if the cost: (i) is recognized for tax purposes; and (ii) is expendable (through depreciation) in the income statement and, therefore, is fiscally relevant for determining the taxable income for the year.

The most immediate way, according to this view, to maximize the tax lever is to structure the operation in the perspective of the asset deal: by purchasing the assets directly, in fact, the price paid reverberates (as a cost fiscally recognized) directly on the assets acquired and automatically contributes to the formation (by reducing it) of taxable income in the form of depreciation quotas (in this perspective, the only burden that is usually incumbent by contract is that of the registration tax, applicable on a proportional basis).

From the seller's perspective, on the contrary, in the absence of harmful income components capable of offsetting the capital gain (possibly realized), the share deal route is preferable, even more so in the presence of conditions to benefit from the so-called participation exemption regime (i.e. taxation of the "gain" realized to the extent of 1.2%).

On one hand, regarding the tax implications related to the structure of the acquisition, the sale of shareholdings does not allow any liability profiles to be limited/alleviated, since, through the transfer of ownership of the shares (or units), the assets and liabilities of the "target" company remain unchanged, as do as any risks that emerged from the "previous management," which the purchaser must take responsibility for unless they try to significantly reduce them through necessary guarantees relevant for this purpose in the contractual texts. On the other hand, the asset deal allows the buyer to choose, in agreement with the transferor, which elements to include and which to exclude from the compendium subject to "transfer" (e.g. it is possible to exclude debt positions relating to the company, rather than receivables), thus protecting itself from any risks associated with the previous management of the sold/acquired asset.

In the face of the general symmetry, however, the advantages of the circulation of "assets" in the form of shareholdings are linked to the splitting of the latter (it is sufficient to acquire, after all, 50.1% of a company to have control of it), to the formalities with which the tangible assets of the company are burdened (such as, by way of example, registration tax on the transfer, the stipulation of notarial deeds, or transfers of concessions or administrative authorizations), and to the need to regulate the transfer of contracts concerning ongoing legal relationships (supply or employment relationships, for example).

That said, the factors that the parties must take into account in determining the contractual conditions, including, of course, the price of the transaction, are mainly affected by the way that the transactions represented impact tax purposes, without forgetting the existence of anti-abuse provisions and the guidelines of practice and case law, which, with increasing frequency, guide the verification as well as the perspective of tax administration bodies.

7.3 Asset deal versus share deal

From this perspective, the asset deal represents the most direct way to transfer assets.

From a tax point of view, the transaction has significant consequences both for the seller, who realizes a capital gain/loss that is relevant for tax purposes, and for the buyer, who is recognized for tax purposes as having received 100% of the price paid. The same does not, therefore, apply any tax jump, determining the subjection of the transferor to direct taxation on any capital gain realized (the tax burden of which could also be eliminated or significantly reduced in the presence of tax assets, i.e., tax losses carried forward) and offering the buyer the opportunity to record the higher values recognized for tax purposes (at the value indicated in the deed of sale), with the consequent recovery of the consideration paid for the acquisition through the (ordinary) depreciation process.

The purchaser is, therefore, granted the possibility of amortizing all the higher values attributed to tangible and intangible assets, including the value of goodwill, finding itself the owner of both the cost incurred for the acquisition process carried out and the future income that will be generated by the capitalized assets (a factor to be taken into due consideration in the negotiation phase). Moreover, in the context in question, the transaction represents the only possibility for the purchaser to have the value of the goodwill paid recognized. In all other cases (purchase of the shareholding and subsequent merger of the target company or contribution and purchase of the shareholding in the transferee), the purchaser will recognize the tax value of the higher values paid by paying a substitute tax. Furthermore, suppose the transaction is classified as a transfer of a business (or a branch of a company). In that case, the transaction is excluded from the scope of VAT and subject to proportional registration tax (that is, the market value to be taxed corresponds to the total value of the assets that make up the business, including goodwill, net of liabilities resulting from the mandatory accounting records).

Finally, it should be noted that although the asset deal is more demanding from a tax point of view, a provision in this area allows the buyer to limit the transfer of the seller's tax liabilities in quantitative and temporal terms. The reference is to the provision contained in Article 14 of Legislative Decree No. 472 of December 18, 1997, according to which the transferee is jointly and severally liable with the transferor—subject to the benefit of the latter's prior enforcement and within the limits of the value of the company—for the payment of tax and penalties relating to violations committed in the year in which the transfer took place and in the two previous years, as well as for those already imposed and contested in the same period, even if they refer to violations committed in earlier periods. This liability can be limited through specific certification of the outstanding debts relating to the company or business unit.

From this perspective, tax due diligence is a tool for identifying and quantifying transaction risks. Suppose the due diligence activity reveals significant risks and tax liabilities for the target company. In that case, the acquisition structure should be oriented toward an asset deal, given the benefits of the rule that allows the buyer of a business unit to limit the transfer of the selling company's tax liabilities (Figure 7.4).

Figure 7.4   **Key tax inputs: due diligence**

Tax Due Diligence
- Identify historical cash tax exposures not provided for on the balance sheet.
- Consider the tax impact of the transaction (e.g. change of control provisions).
- Identify tax attributes that may impact target's future tax position and cash flow.
- Understand accounting position and drivers of the effective tax rate.
- Impact on pricing.
- Consider risk-mitigation strategies and contractual protection for identified tax exposures.
- Consider effective tax rate/adjustments for modeling purposes.
- Consider implications for proposed acquisition structure.

Findings from tax due diligence will help inform and drive other parts of the transaction process.

7.4 (Merger) leveraged buyout: "typical" structure of the transaction

In this perspective, the LBO is part of the broad phenomenon of "financial restructuring," specifically within corporate M&A planning.

Private equity funds usually specialize in investment segments. Those operating in the LBO deal with transactions that mainly concern unlisted companies with cash generation suitable for implementing value maximization strategies that, through appropriate interventions in the short to medium term (three to five years), will enable the obtaining of a return through sale (exit). That activity consists of acquiring a company or part of its assets, mainly using loan capital, which will be secured through the company's shares or assets and repaid through its cash flow.

Therefore, this architecture aims to make the repayment of the debt contracted by the particular purpose vehicle coincide with the generation by the target company of the cash flows necessary to repay the loan contracted for the acquisition. The transaction can be concluded through direct merger (when the NewCo incorporates the target company) or reverse merger (when the target subsidiary incorporates the parent NewCo).

More specifically, in its typical form, the transaction is carried out through the establishment of a new company (the "NewCo"), or particular purpose vehicle, aimed at acquiring a total shareholding in the capital of another company (so-called target company or target), and then incorporating the latter. The incorporation is (as a rule) necessary at the behest of the lending credit institutions, which hope that the debt from the "acquisition" (so-called acquisition debt) flows into the same legal entity to which the company that will produce the (expected) cash flows necessary for the repayment of the debt itself is part. Therefore, there is a logical-functional relationship between the establishment of NewCo, the indebtedness, the acquisition of control, and the subsequent merger by incorporation.

Generally, the NewCo has insufficient financial resources (or sufficient to cover the "equity" part of the transaction) to acquire the target company and, therefore, to proceed with the acquisition it enters into a loan agreement with financial intermediaries (i.e. banks or other specialized intermediaries), with the expectation of repaying the loan through the cash flow generated by the target entity acquired (at the time of disbursement of the loan).The loan is also provided to grant specific guarantees in favor of the lender. It is often agreed that the loan will be secured by pledging the shares of the target company once the acquisition is completed. However, this type of guarantee is usually temporary, as banks typically prefer the guarantee to be directly tied to the assets of the target company.

Once the acquisition occurs, the purchased shares become part of NewCo's assets. NewCo will have, in assets, the shareholdings in the target company and, in liabilities, the debt granted for acquiring the latter. The transaction typically results in a merger between the acquired company and the acquiring company, a merger that, in the most classic case, can result in the direct incorporation of the target into the NewCo or with the reverse merger of the NewCo into the target (so-called reverse merger).

Following the merger between NewCo and target, the resulting legal entity (from the merger) will have, in assets, the assets of the target, which serve as collateral, and, in liabilities, the loan obtained initially to acquire the latter. Therefore, a merger becomes the only suitable mechanism for transferring financial resources from the target company to the particular purpose vehicle promoting the initiative, whose function is instrumental in the transaction's context. Only in this way can it bear the debt costs incurred by acquiring shareholdings.

The negotiation chain implemented (acquisition with debt and subsequent merger) integrates, therefore, an operational technique used when making investments in the capital of companies evaluated positively as having entrepreneurial and industrial potential and, therefore, profitability. The use of leverage appears to be equally justified, at least to the extent that this does not jeopardize the economic equilibrium of the acquired company (by carrying out such a transaction it is possible to benefit from the financial and monetary advantages deriving from the exploitation of financial leverage).

The evolution of civil law favors the legislator in such transactions. Civil law also increases the contestability of companies, facilitates those who want to acquire control, and allows them to finance themselves more easily by using third parties.

In addition to the clear confirmation of the transaction's economic substance, it is generally impossible to detect any hidden or unclear elements in the individual transactions that form part of the overall deal, especially regarding the merger of the 'container' company with the target company.

As long as the debt remains among the NewCo's liabilities, the company's sources of repayment are mainly the dividends paid by the investee, since the NewCo's operating activities do not generate sufficient cash flow. From a financial point of view, however, this condition does not represent an adequate guarantee of repayment for the institution that granted the loan (and, in general, for any lender that has given credit to the NewCo for the acquisition of the target's entire package of the shares).

From this perspective, debt repayment would necessarily be tied to the distribution of dividends by the target company and indirectly to a future point when profits are generated.

However, the credit institution—an economic entity with a different degree of risk appetite—would have a different point of view. It follows, from the perspective of the lender, that the merger of the NewCo with the target is a key part of the transaction, as this will enable cash flows to be generated (both deriving from activity and the possible disposal of some assets); this will therefore provide a suitable guarantee for repayment. As further proof of this, it is sufficient to recall that the ordinary negotiation practice, between lenders and loan beneficiaries, provides for the inclusion of clauses in the loan agreement aimed at guaranteeing that the NewCo and target will merge. These dynamics are not unknown, however, even to the tax authorities, which, in response to specific anti-avoidance rulings aimed seeking to prevent the enforcement of the restrictive rules on the carry-forward of losses in mergers, have already shown that they fully understand and share the economic motivations of the (merger) LBO transaction.

In short, the negotiation chain should not be characterized by elusiveness. However, none of the individual passages it is composed of meet such requirements. In other words, the operation legitimately planned and carried out according to civil and economic dictates should be translated, from a tax point of view, into an operation generally devoid of any abusive connotation.

The possibility of benefiting from financial and economic advantages deriving from the exploitation of financial leverage by such operations has led the tax authorities to investigate such extraordinary transactions through the lens of anti-abuse legislation.

From the point of view of tax assessments, the configuration of the LBO as an elusive transaction means it is able to neutralize, indirectly, the deductibility of interest expenses, albeit within the limits allowed by Article 96 of the *Testo Unico delle Imposte sui Redditi* (TUIR). The main tax issue (for the purposes relevant here), in essence, is the deductibility of the financial charges that weigh on the debt contracted by NewCo, although other relevant tax issues are related to these transactions, especially when non-resident entities are involved (as lenders or investors).

If LBO transactions are examined only from a tax point of view, it is usual to find, moreover, at least in the short term, a contraction in the taxable income in question, as a consequence of an approach that focuses on the financial efficiency of the acquisition structure and not the underlying cause of the debt, which is a result of acquiring a shareholding. Although there is no doubt that the different tax treatment of indebtedness compared to equity capital (due to the deductibility of interest expenses) influences the financial choices of companies, favoring the use of debt, it has often been questioned whether the use of anti-avoidance provisions to combat such phenomena is excessive and without a legal basis, and whether it is the task of the legislator to introduce, through appropriate corrective measures, neutrality between the different forms of financing, reducing the existing imbalance between the fiscal treatment of debt and that of equity.

Some recent rulings of the European Court of Justice provide some relevant food for thought regarding the application of the prohibition of abuse of rights, currently detailed in (Article 10-bis, of Law No. 212 of July 27, 2000, about the deductibility of interest expenses incurred in the context of such transactions, in this case within the same corporate group (so-called intragroup releverage transactions), without any actual change of control of the acquired company. However, at the national level, given the fluctuating nature of the jurisprudence of the Supreme Court of Cassation and the practice of the Tax Administration in Italy on the subject of avoidance, it is appropriate to handle the expressed principles of law with caution.

It seems both desirable and feasible to radically rethink this approach. While not explicitly codified, this approach increasingly tends to overlook the tax lawfulness of the transactions in question. These transactions should no longer be subject to review under the abuse of rights principle, particularly regarding the tax relevance of financial charges from loans granted by third parties. Even in cases involving intragroup loans, as long as the terms are consistent with market value, the financial charges should be considered legitimate for tax purposes.

Moreover, considering the recent Organisation for Economic Co-operation and Development (OECD) indications on the application of the arm's-length principle to financial transactions and the related additions to the Commentary on Article 9 of the OECD Model Convention on the avoidance of double taxation, the conformity of the interest rate with market conditions should rule out the artificial nature of the transaction.

7.5 Optimizing the seller's tax regime: consequences for the buyer

The taxation (for the seller) of transfer transactions carried out through share deals is more attenuated. Despite being an implementation transaction, the consequences for the seller may vary significantly depending on the subjective and objective characteristics of the shareholding transferred.

In particular, in the presence of a corporation (the transferor), the participation exemption allows the seller's tax burden to be almost eliminated, reducing it to 1.2% of the value of the capital gain realized. However, if the requirements set out in the law to benefit from this preferential regime are not met, the capital gain is taxed in the ordinary way (the capital gain is not relevant for *Imposta Regionale sulle Attività Produttive* - IRAP - purposes).

In terms of tax consequences for the buyer, the sale of the shareholding results in latent taxation, meaning that the additional value (surplus value) paid by the buyer does not receive immediate or adequate tax recognition. This often means the buyer will not benefit from any immediate tax deductions or relief. As a result, during negotiations, the buyer must take into account the lack of tax benefits they will receive, especially when compared to the seller, who may enjoy lower taxation if the participation exemption applies to their sale.

The purchasing company retains the depreciable assets at their historical values, meaning it cannot recover, for tax purposes, the higher price paid due to any surplus value potentially realized by the seller. Instead of being allocated to the acquired company, the investment cost is attributed to the securities representing the company (since the assets themselves are not depreciable). This creates a disconnect between the stable income generated by the acquired company, which continues to form the tax base, and the investment costs, which are tied to the shares or quotas of the acquired company.

Only through a subsequent extraordinary transaction, typically a merger by incorporation capable of bringing out a deficit (e.g. goodwill) and through the payment of a substitute tax, can the purchaser, in essence, realign the tax values to the higher values emerging under civil law and, therefore, to the price paid. However, from the view of indirect taxes, the sale of the shareholding is exempt for VAT purposes and is not subject to proportional registration tax. Finally, regarding the liability profiles incumbent on the purchaser regarding the "inheritance" of the target company's tax liabilities, there is no rule that allows, in substance, their effects to be limited.

7.6 Optimizing the tax management of acquired companies

In addition to the SPV/NewCo vehicle, investment funds (rectus, fund managers) also use other intermediate SPVs through which they indirectly hold the investment. It follows that, regardless of the cause of the transaction, the fund develops a corporate and financial structure articulated on several levels of SPVs. It is thus often necessary to evaluate these in order to apply efficient tax management to maximize leverage and reduce tax burdens, taking advantage of any preferential regimes and seeking optimization of the capital structure.

For example, assuming the investment chain has an Italian holding company (i.e. HoldCo) at its apex, the fund manager, having established the holding company, puts in place the necessary operations for HoldCo to set up a BidCo, which, in turn, acquires an SPV/NewCo. From a tax point of view, the exercise of the option for the national consolidation regime, referred to in Articles 117–129 of the TUIR, allows, in this perspective, the intersubjective offsetting of the financial charges related to the debt capital disbursed to the SPV/NewCo.

The national tax consolidation regime appears to be a valid tool, as it is configured in the same way as a particular optional tax regime that allows the parent entity to determine a single taxable base given by the algebraic sum of the taxable income of the companies of the group that adhere to it.

Specifically, it is a regime that allows the consolidating companies, independently of the statutory obligation to draw up consolidated financial statements, to calculate the *Imposta sul Reddito delle Società* (IRES) in an unitary manner. In other words, the consolidation is carried out by allowing the parent company or entity a single taxable base for the entire group of companies (the initial requirement for this application is the presence, between the companies and commercial entities that adhere to it, of a control relationship referred to in Article 2359, of the Civil Code, No. 1; that is, that the consolidating company must be the holder, directly or indirectly, of the majority of the votes exercisable at the ordinary shareholders' meeting of the consolidated company, so-called de jure control). For income tax purposes, this recognizes the economic reality of groups of companies. The taxable amount is the algebraic sum of each company's taxable income following an optional option.

Among the possible tax advantages for companies that opt for consolidation are:

1. Offsetting tax gains and losses of group companies. Individual tax losses incurred during the period of validity of the consolidation are taken into account to determine the consolidated result, while losses before adherence to the regime in question can only be used by the entities that produced them.
2. The possible offsetting of tax credits and payables between the various companies of the group. Any surplus tax credits, which can be used by the parent company or by the company to which they compete, are transferable intragroup under Article 43 ter of Presidential Decree No. 602 of September 29, 1973.
3. The possible use of surplus tax EBITDA (gross operating income), for the deduction of interest expenses, referred to in Article 96 of the TUIR. That provision provides that excess interest expense, which is not deductible directly by a group company, may be deducted from the group's income if and to the extent that the other companies in the group have a gross operating income relevant for that purpose.

The option to exercise tax consolidation is also possible when a non-resident parent company controls companies that are resident in Italy. In this case, it is envisaged that the non-resident parent company, identifying itself in Italy due to the assignment of the tax code, designates an Italian subsidiary as a "virtual" consolidator in charge of exercising the option for national consolidation. The designation also remains valid for the renewal of the option for group taxation. In this way, the non-resident parent assumes the responsibilities provided for parent companies or entities in Article 127 of the TUIR.

7.7 Taxation of investment return flows

The treatment of loans from foreign shareholders (i.e. "shareholder loans") is also important as these may make up some of the resources necessary to finance the execution of acquisition transactions.

It frequently happens that the total financial resources used in the fund by investors are, through the intermediate structure, made available to the SPV expressly set up for the acquisition of the target company, partly in the form of risk capital (i.e. equity) and partly in the form of financing (i.e. "debt").

The interest expense that derives, specifically, from the portion invested through loans must be subject to the ordinary rules on corporate income tax and, therefore, both the provisions relating to the determination of intragroup fees and the ordinary provisions regarding deductibility.

In intragroup relationships, the interest expenses agreed between the lender and the borrower, in compliance with both domestic and contractual provisions, must not exceed those that would have been agreed between independent parties for similar transactions under comparable conditions (the so-called arm's-length principle).

These are the general provisions contained in the combined requirements of Article 110, paragraph 7, TUIR, and in the Conventions (Commentary on the Model Convention and the OECD Guidelines) typically interpreted using international principles.

With particular regard to shareholder loans, in the context of the overall financial structure of acquisitions, it is also necessary to focus attention on the possibility, in the event of particular and exceptional circumstances, of reclassifying financing transactions into capital injections based on the indications contained in the OECD Guidelines. These circumstances are often attributable, in general, to the mismatch between the legal form of the transaction and its economic substance, in the case of the shareholder loan.

In the context of LBO transactions specifically, this mismatch between form and substance may occur regarding shareholder financing funded by investors' financial resources (e.g. through the investment fund), in relation to these resources fit into the broader structure of financing provided by third-party lenders. This is, essentially, the case in which the shareholder loan has characteristics specific to equity instruments such as, for example, when the remuneration and repayment are:

(i) conditional; (ii) of variable amount and potentially more significant than other forms of financing; rather than (iii) subordinated compared to other loans. The information necessary to capture these indices is generally contained in the contractual documents that comprise the so-called index. The "financial package" refers to the collection of all loan agreements signed by the borrower, its parent company, or its subsidiaries with third-party lenders. It also includes the planning and execution documents that outline the entire transaction from economic, financial, and legal perspectives. An example of this would be the "Structure Memorandum," which details the structure and framework of the transaction. This package serves as a comprehensive overview of the financial arrangements and strategies involved in the deal.

Regarding the above-mentioned indices or similar situations, a mismatch between the form and economic substance of a shareholder loan may be identified. This could lead to the loan being reclassified, for tax purposes, as a capital contribution. As a result, the interest expenses associated with the loan would become non-deductible. Additionally, this reclassification could affect the treatment of outgoing dividends and the payment of interest on the loan, potentially triggering further tax consequences in line with the rules governing capital contributions and distributions.

7.8 The taxation regime at the time of "exit"

In the context of M&A, the exit from the investment by the private equity fund represents the final phase, in which a large part of the structuring activity described in this chapter is finalized.

The main objective is to transfer, as quickly as possible, the financial resources deriving from the divestment to investors, minimizing the tax burden that the "transnationality" of the structures used could generate; that is, reducing, in fact, both the overall return on the transaction and the variable part of the managers' remuneration.

From a tax perspective, how these sums flow to the entities that directly or indirectly control the NewCo/SPV operating company tend to depend on the presence or absence of additional foreign vehicles (i.e. foreign holding companies) between HoldCo (Italian) and BidCo/NewCo/SPV:

- Sale by a foreign holding company of HoldCo (resident in Italy) and, indirectly, of its direct shareholdings. Such an event alternatively generates: (i) a capital gain that is relevant for tax purposes in the state of residence of the foreign holding company in the presence of a double tax treaty; (ii) otherwise, a significant capital gain in Italy (under Article 23, paragraph 1, of the TUIR).
- Sale by HoldCo of the shareholdings in BidCo/NewCo/SPV resident in Italy and subsequent distribution to the foreign holding company (not resident in Italy) of the "capital gain" in the form of dividends which, alternatively:
  – will be exempt from withholding tax under Article 27 of Presidential Decree No. 600 of September 29, 1973;

- will benefit from the "reduced" withholding tax in respect of companies and entities subject to corporate income tax in EU member states and in states party to the Agreement on the European Economic Area, under paragraph 3 of Article 27 of the same presidential decree;
- will be subject to the application of the conventional withholding tax in respect of non-EU subjects residing in states with which there is a double taxation treaty or, finally;
- will discount ordinary withholdings.

Therefore, the following tax effects can be verified:

- Non-taxation in Italy of capital gains from the sale of shares (territorially relevant based on Article 23, paragraph 1, of the TUIR) through the conventional regime that attributes the power of taxation to the jurisdiction of residence of the transferor.
- Non-application or reduced application of withholding taxes to dividends leaving Italy through the exemption under Article 27 or the reduced rate referred to in paragraph 3, as mentioned above.
- No or reduced taxation in the foreign country.

The achievement of these results, when obtained through structures endowed with the necessary economic substance and, therefore, genuine, cannot be reviewed, given the consolidated orientation of community jurisprudence on the subject of freedom of establishment. The condition of genuineness within the structures implemented by investment funds translates into the need to verify that the intermediate entities used by private equity funds (and from which the benefits derive) are characterized by an effective rootedness in the economic fabric of the country of settlement and do not act as mere "conduits" concerning the individual transaction, thus not carrying out a genuine economic activity.

When an intermediate investment structure lacks overall economic substance or when a transaction lacks substantial non-tax reasons, any undue tax benefits gained through such a structure can be ignored by applying the standard tax rules, as would be the case for a direct investment. In other words, under specific or general anti-avoidance provisions found in national, EU, or international law, authorities can combat tax avoidance strategies that rely on artificial interposition, all while respecting fundamental freedoms. This ensures that tax benefits are only granted to transactions with genuine economic substance.

8 The Due Diligence Process in M&A and Private Equity

by *Tamara Laudisio*

In business, due diligence is the process of making sure every aspect of a transaction is working before it moves forward to the finalization of the deal. For example, when a company considers issuing an IPO, potential investors perform due diligence on that company to make sure it's worth the investment. With proper due diligence, all involved parties are educated, informed, and covered in a transaction, an arrangement, or any other kind of agreement. Due diligence should be completed before the close of a deal and provide a buyer with guarantees on what they are getting.

In M&A, due diligence helps buyers and sellers make informed decisions. This process validates the accuracy of the information presented, ensures that the transaction is complied with the criteria laid out in the purchase agreement, verifies that the parties consider all benefits and risks, and gives the buyer clarity about what they are buying.

Due diligence process, first of all, is a cognitive instrument for the target company, which allows the information asymmetry inherent in the purchasing process to be minimized as far as possible and gives the potential buyer as much information as possible for improved planning of the investment process, highlighting any deal-breakers or implicit liabilities as well as strengths and weaknesses, to support their final decision. Performing due diligence helps the buyer determine whether they will make the purchase and how much they should pay.

In addition, due diligence represents an essential phase of the buyer's risk management process, allowing them to identify and manage all risks of a potential transaction. Through due diligence process, a potential buyer might also come to understand target management expertise and if it is necessary to maintain all/part of the preexisting managerial structure, or, alternatively, to identify any deficient areas to be addressed post-transaction. It is important to understand what due diligence is not. Due diligence does not constitute an audit procedure nor other attestation or assurance standards of financials and/or processes of the target company. Furthermore, due diligence does not express an opinion or other form of assurance in accordance with audit and it is realized by the drafting of a report exclusively for the use of the client.

As mentioned, the due diligence carried out by the buyer on the target company can focus on different areas of investigation. Many of these are listed in Figure 8.1.

Figure 8.1 **Main due diligence stream in an M&A process**

Main due diligence stream in a M&A process

Financial	Investigation focus on the analysis of main financial metrics and value drivers of the target company, as well as on leading a consistency analysis between the historical and prospective financial data.
Tax	Investigation focus on tax matters and transaction in order to identify any potential risks and liabilities that the buyer should consider as per valuation purposes, as well as any tax implication on "deal-structuring" solutions for minimizing any tax risks on the buyer's side.
Legal	Investigation focus on legal aspects and transaction in order to identify any potential risks and liabilities that the buyer should consider as per valuation purposes. The Legal DD also supports the buyer when drafting and negotiating the Share Purchase Agreement (also called "SPA") against the seller.
Labur	Analysis focus on the organizational structure of Target company in order to identify any risks concerning the personnel matters, labor existing contracts as well as the correctness of salary treatments.
Commercial	Analysis focus on the top line of Target company P&L aimed at understanding the current and prospective positioning of the company's offerings on reference markets, as well as the potential opportunities and risks might occur.
Industrial	Analysis focus on the main internal processes, the current business model and cost structure through benchmarking analysis with other operators/competitors, in order to identify any efficiency to implement during the investment period.

The list in Figure 8.1 is obviously not exhaustive. A preliminary inspection carried out by the investor, as well as their knowledge of the business, may determine the scope and the analysis to be completed during the due diligence phase. For example, an industrial investor who identifies a potential opportunity in their own sector will have all skills to be able to evaluate the market peculiarity, focusing on legal, fiscal, financial/accounting, or IT streams.

It is important to highlight that each work stream should not be considered on a standalone basis: the outcome of each due diligence could also have impact on other areas of analysis. Thus, it is important to summarize and link the results of each stream, and also to get in touch with the different consultants, to evaluate each aspect from different angles and identify any further risks.

8.1 Financial due diligence

8.1.1 Definitions and purposes

Financial due diligence consists of an analysis of historical and prospective financial data, both at statutory and managerial levels, related to a target company or group. It aims at supporting the investor through the valuation process in an M&A contest, assisting in:

- Knowledge and normalization of key financial indicators as base elements for the definition of the transaction value (i.e. equity bridge computation).
- Knowledge of business cash dynamics, in order to optimize the degree of financial leverage of the operation as well as the composition of the required financial sources.
- Being a guide for the identification of any risks not properly captured by the equity bridge mechanism and, thus, requiring to be addressed through specific "representations and warranties" when drafting the SPA.

When financial due diligence is carried out, different circumstance might arise, such as the type of parties involved in the deal process (i.e. buy side or sell side), the timing of the M&A process, and the type of investor involved in the deal. In particular:

- The due diligence process may be originated both on the buy side and sell side. The latter situation generally arises when a sales process is structured with limited and controlled access to the management team and target company (i.e. through competitive bidding), or when the drawing up of financial data that would be difficult to manage without full access to the target management is needed (i.e. carve-out of financial data and/or turnaround process).
- The buyer, generally, will carry out financial due diligence focused on a review of vendor's due diligence report, completing any potential financial matters not fully addressed by this document. Due diligence, furthermore, may be required in refinancing or debt-restructuring processes by the financing banks.

- Due diligence may be requested at the beginning of process, in order to capture and understand any potential "dealbreakers" might prevent the process completion and, hence, a binding offer submission. Furthermore, it may be extended in a second phase with additional analysis or areas to be investigated more thoroughly. In contrast, when a potential buyer is able to carry out a successful preliminary analysis on the target's financials in order to submit a binding offer to the counterpart ("subject to due diligence"), due diligence can be performed at a later stage, aimed at confirming the assumptions underlying valuation included in binding offer ("confirmatory due diligence").
- The scope of due diligence is generally customized by the type of investors involved in the process. Financial investors (i.e. private equity funds or private debt) will mostly be interested in the knowledge of:
  i. target business;
  ii. indicators determining the price formula definition (i.e. EBITDA, net financial position, and Net Working Capital - NWC);
  iii. cash flow analysis and, hence, whether the target is able to generate cash; and
  iv. understanding existing target management and organizational structure.
- Corporate investors, by contrast, will be more focused on:
  i. revenues and profitability by product, client and/or other business KPI to identify any overlaps with own business;
  ii. the cost structure analysis to identify any potential synergies with own business, rather than;
  iii. the identification of accounting policies adopted.

8.1.2 Valuation drivers: due diligence supporting deal pricing

As mentioned, one of the purposes of financial due diligence is to support the buyer in the asset evaluation process, making use of the normalization of key parameters or indicators (i.e. EBITDA and net financial position) as determining elements for defining the value of the transaction.

As common practice, the pricing considered in a M&A process is generally formalized, as illustrated by Figure 8.2 (the equity bridge formula), and, when tender "formal" processes occur, the seller's advisor sometimes requires that the offer needs to be divided into each of its valuation elements, in order to compare the different proposals received.

In this regard, the key elements essential for the determination of asset value would consist of: (i) the identification of a normal level of profitability of the business; (ii) the identification of a net financial position level consistent with the target company operations at the "closing date" (or "reference date" as agreed between parties); and (iii) an adequate level of working capital supporting the operations of the business. These three parameters should guide the investor during their closing negotiations with their counterpart, leading to the final pricing determination.

8 The Due Diligence Process in M&A and Private Equity   135

Figure 8.2 Equity bridge formula

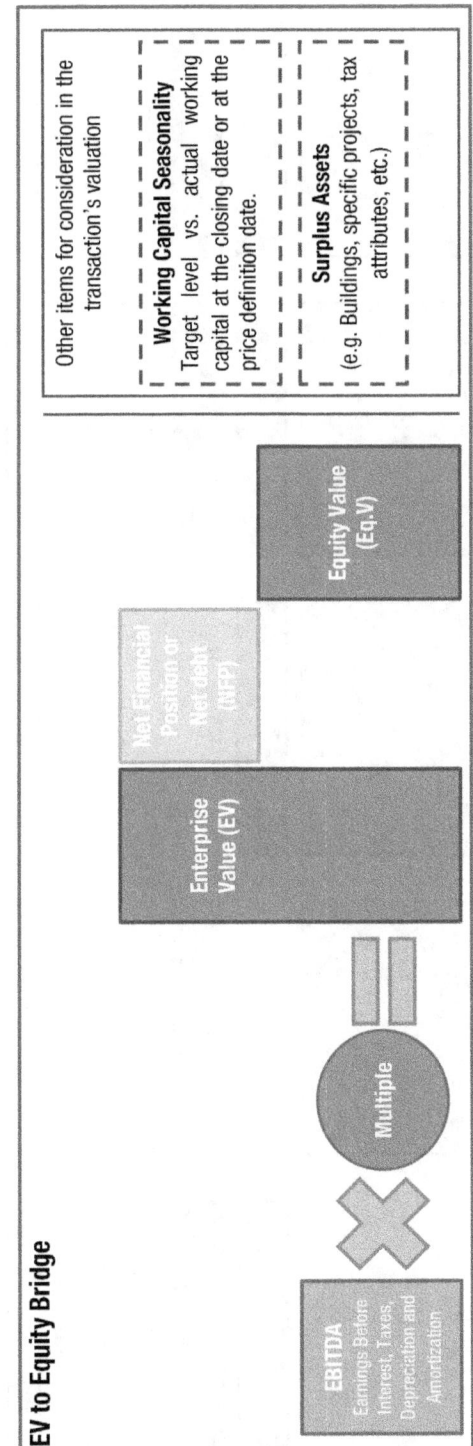

Figure 8.3 **Financial due diligence analysis**

Financial due diligence analysis

- **Balance sheet analysis** and identification of cash or debt-like items to be considered for the net financial position definition
- **P&L analysis** and normalization of the historical profitability, with the objective to identify the valuated elements underlying the EBITDA to be negotiated with the counterpart
- **Cash flow analysis**, focused on the company's ability to carry out adequate investment needed at business supporting, both recurring and non-recurring in nature, as well as working capital dynamics analysis, by looking into its composition and trend
- **Analysis of forecasted data** and their consistency with historical data

EBITDA | PFN | Working capital | Surplus assets

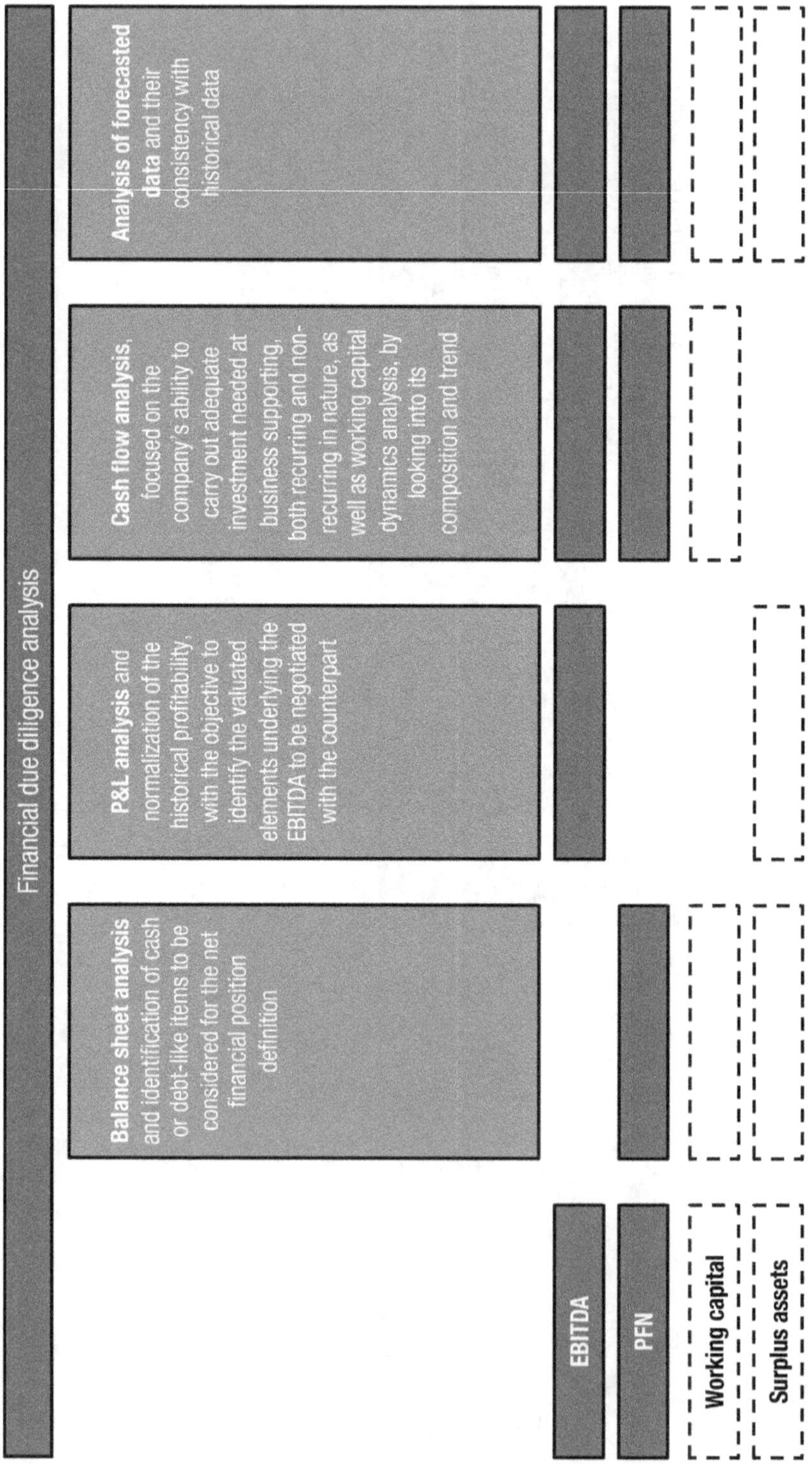

It's crucial that financial due diligence analysis is concerned with the analysis of various equity bridge and other potential elements that should be considered during the final negotiation with the counterpart (as indicated in Figure 8.3). It's important to highlight that financial due diligence must be able eward: to a sort of clear consistency between the various aspects that might influence the determination of different pricing components.

8.1.2.1 P&L analysis and quality of earning

P&L analyses are typically conducted on "managerial accounts" prepared on a yearly and/or quarterly/monthly basis. Such internal reporting prepared by the target management, if compared to the statutory data-level report, is preferred due to a number of reasons, including:

- The possibility of having detailed profit-and-loss information by LoB (line of business), product family, client, and other cluster-defined strategies for the monitoring of the target business by management.
- A different classification prepared by management concerning one-off costs/revenues and/or other extraordinary items to be normalized.
- Addressing the target company's strategic actions and having a better and clearer understanding of the historical and prospective trends of the business.

In detail, profit-and-loss analysis is focused on:

- Analysis of revenue and gross profit on a comparative basis as per business view (i.e. by product category, geography, client, etc.).
- Analysis of sales trends with particular focus on seasonality and price and volume effects.
- Analysis of revenues and profitability on a "like-for-like" basis, considering any change of transaction perimeter that occurred over the analyzed period. This provides an understanding of how much increase was driven by historic business (organic growth) or by acquisition of new businesses (external growth through M&A activities), and identifies the portion of business not recurring because it was sold.
- Analysis of the operating cost base, including commentary on trends and costs by type (e.g. raw materials, internal/external manufacturing, services, office expenses, etc.), by function (e.g. direct, indirect, corporate head office costs), and by nature (fixed vs. variable).
- Analysis of potential one-off, non-recurring, non-cash, exceptional, and/or otherwise unrepresentative revenue and cost items with effect on EBITDA (quality of earnings analysis).
- Analysis of items below EBITDA, including the impact of Foreign Exchange (FX) fluctuations.

As previously mentioned, the objective of such analysis is the understanding and identification of a normal level of EBITDA, excluding all non-recurring, non-inherent, and/or extraordinary items that might affect the level of profitability, that the target company is able to maintain on a long-term basis and in normal conditions.

There is no definitive or authoritative literature or common standard with respect to the calculation and estimate of normalized EBITDA. Therefore, there is no basis for stating whether all appropriate and comparable adjustments have been made during the representation of normalized EBITDA (i.e. QoE analysis) and often this is due to also the existence of adjustments related to target company business specifically.

Adjustments to EBITDA may be largely clustered as follows:

1. Accounting adjustments These refer to items resulting from incorrect accounting classifications, such as cut-off errors, failure to accrue items, or incorrect classification of items as either above or below EBITDA. Accounting adjustments also involve standardizing the treatment of certain entries, including those in line with group rules or guidelines. This can include adjustments for the accounting treatment of financial leasing, factoring, or other specific transactions to ensure consistency and compliance with established accounting standards.
2. Pro-forma adjustments: Items aimed at standardizing historical profitability with the current perimeter of the target company or business involved in the envisaged transaction. Such kinds of adjustments are applied when a subsidiary is carved-out from a group over the period under analysis or when certain business units or significant contracts are excluded for whatever reason.
3. Run-rate adjustments: Items aimed at representing the fully operational impact of changes in the cost or revenue structure that occurred during the period under analysis due to specific cost-saving or restructuring initiatives (i.e. run-rate of rental costs due to market condition alignment or run-rate of personnel costs due to reorganization plan focused on key people not being replaced).
4. Normalizations: Items aimed at neutralizing the profitability from the following matters:
    a. Non-recurring or "one-off" revenue and costs, such as:
        i. Ceasing costs related to initiatives or projects aborted, even if this may represent a recurring item for the company's business.
        ii. Startup costs of new business concern/units not at full capacity.
        iii. Extraordinary trend of average purchase price of raw material without pass-through to final selling prices.
        iv. Impact on profitability arising from extraordinary events such as natural disasters, failure and replacement of strategic suppliers, and, in general, impacts resulting from temporary disruption of the value chain.
        v. Extraordinary accrual of risks such as extraordinary legal claims, extraordinary disputes with suppliers or customers, tax claims for which potential liability is expected going forward, and so on.
        vi. One-off bonuses accruals for employees.

vii. Insurance reimbursements pertaining to prior years or to be reallocated in correlation to relevant operating costs.
viii. Gain or loss on disposal of assets, since these do not represent operating items in nature.
ix. Grants on investment refers to grants or subsidies received for investments that are accounted for above EBITDA, meaning they are recognized as income rather than being used to reduce Depreciation and Amortization (D&A) expenses. This treatment can affect how the company's profitability is presented, as it keeps the grant income separate from the capital cost depreciation.
x. Other grants considered temporary or one-off items. It should be specified that a portion of some extraordinary costs are always incurred, such as overstatement/understatement of invoices to be received or issued, which are endemic to business and, hence, would be considered recurring in nature. Alternatively, from the analysis of accruals and releases of invoice to be received/issued, if understood that management historically tries to underestimate operating costs at year-end, this impact might be reflected as normalization and, hence, a recurring level of underestimation may be estimated accordingly.

b. Operating revenues and costs not included within EBITDA, including:
   i. Forex impact related to trade transactions that represent revenues/costs operating in nature, although these are accounted for within financial items (below EBITDA) according to accounting principles.
   ii. Cash discount applied to customers or by suppliers on a recurring basis to be deducted from operating revenues/expenses, although these are accounted for within financial items (below EBITDA) according to accounting principles.

c. Normalizations of operating costs incurred on a multiyear basis, such as costs for trade fairs or other events held every two or more years, should be linearized on a "pro-rata" basis in each period under analysis despite being correctly accounted for on an accrual basis.

d. Adjustment of no-cash costs (i.e. accrual of bad debt). A common best practice to be performed during the Due Diligence (DD) exercise would be to replace such accrual with the estimate of a recurring level of trade receivable losses on historical revenues over the last five or four fiscal years. The recurring level would represent an estimate and should be corroborated by the specific peculiarities of the target's business (i.e. if the target has specific processes that lead to a better monitoring of customer reliance or to recovery procedures on bad debt, rather than a change in sales mix that might result in changes of risk within the customer portfolio). This approach, in fact, takes us back to the main purpose of the identification of a normalized EBITDA, which is, as far as possible, a proxy of the business's ability to generate cash on a recurring and sustainable basis.

5. The examples indicated are naturally not exhaustive, since the due diligence exercise is not standardized and each business presents its own specific issues that should be understood within its own economic, financial, and accounting dynamics.

8.1.2.2 Balance sheet analysis and adjusted net financial position

In order to calculate the amount payable to the seller, the EV is adjusted for net cash/debt. Under a typical pricing mechanism, the buyer will pay in full for any cash/cash-like items and get a deduction in full for any debt/debt-like items. The purpose of a net debt analysis is, therefore, to provide information on the likely impact of cash, debt, and debt-like items on the consideration to be paid for that business. As a result, the balance sheet analysis of the target company is the second pillar of the financial due diligence, aiming to analyze the composition and quality of the assets and liabilities of the target company and identify any cash or debt-like items to be considered for the definition of the adjusted net financial position.

The balance sheet analysis of the target company generally focuses on the following areas:

- Tangible, intangible, and financial assets analysis by investigating their composition, movement, capitalizations, depreciation policy, and any devaluations or revaluations, including related accounting impacts.
- Net working capital analysis, which includes:
  - Inventory composition, valuation methodology, the rotation, and any inventory write-down policy applied.
  - Trade receivable composition and ageing analysis, as well as the bad debt accruals policy applied by management. The analysis of receivables is also crucial for the understanding of the average collection terms actually applied and their deviation from those defined contractually, in order to understand the actual absorption of working capital, as managed by management. Other points of attention in the trade receivable area include: (i) understanding the management of collections through factoring tools (with or without recourse) or particular payment instruments (e.g. bank receipt) (ii) any advance payment instruments credit (e.g. invoice discounting); or (iii) the use of credit insurance tools.
  - Trade payables composition, average payment terms applied, identification of any positions in dispute, and policies for extending payment deadlines (agreed or not agreed with the counterparty), which are generally implemented to temporarily benefit the available cash and cash equivalents.
  - Other receivables and other liabilities' composition to understand their nature, recoverability, and the presence of any deferrals or overdue items, in order to identify any cash or debt-like item.
- Analysis of risk provisions and provisions for employee benefits (e.g. severance pay), the related accounting and the expected cash profile. This analysis will al-

so extend to any liabilities, not reflected in the balance sheet, for commitments made by the company to third parties or in favor of third parties or financial instruments that may not be recognized in the balance sheet on the basis of the accounting principles used (e.g. derivative instruments, commitments undertaken, and guarantees given by third parties and to third parties in favor of the company). The coordination between the various advisors in this case certainly helps to provide a broader view of any problem that may emerge.
- Net financial position analysis to understand company's composition, the tools used, the quantity and economic terms of the available credit lines, the time horizon of existing loans (short, medium, and long term), and the related contractual terms, including any change of control clauses or the presence of any penalties in the event of early repayment of the debt. These last elements also present aspects of a legal nature, which must be addressed with the consultants who deal with legal due diligence.

The objective of this balance sheet analysis of the target company is to analyze the composition and quality of the assets and liabilities of the target company and identify any cash or debt-like items to be considered in relation to the adjusted net financial position. These adjustments may include the following macro-types:

1. *Accounting adjustments*: As mentioned for EBITDA adjustments, the counterpart of accounting errors or harmonization, if of a financial nature, must be considered as an adjustment to the net financial position (i.e. accounting treatment of financial leasing and factoring). Then there are errors or harmonizations in the accounting that only have an asset classification, that is, lack any confirmation from an economic point of view. An example of this is the incorrect classification of the Ri.Ba portfolio.
2. *Pro-forma adjustments*: The reference Net Financial Position (NFP) for determining the price must also refer to the activities included in the scope of the transaction. The NFP of companies or specific business lines not included in the transaction will therefore be excluded.
3. *Run-rate adjustments*: Apart from its relation to working capital, which we will discuss later in this chapter, run-rate adjustments to the NFP mainly reflect any residual equity balance deriving from such adjustments to the EBITDA as a financial component of NFP (i.e. run-rate of personnel costs due to a reorganization plan where key people are not replaced).
4. *Normalizations*:
   a. Postponement or instalment payments to suppliers, taxes, or contributions to social security institutions or other bodies beyond the deadlines due by law or contractual practice take on the nature of financing instruments, especially for companies in financial distress or with financial covenants to be respected on certain dates.
   b. The accruals of interest expense or income classified as working capital items, being financial in nature, must be included among the adjustments to the NFP.

c. Although correctly accounted, a non-recourse factoring operation can only be carried out at the end of the financial year to generate cash and temporarily benefit the net financial position. This operation is distorting, making the working capital and the end-of-period NFP less indicative of the actual level of capital required by the business on a recurring basis. Therefore, in this case we are not talking about error correction, but about normalization of the NFP and, as we will see later, of the net working capital.
  d. Payables for corporate income taxes, net of the related advances, are generally considered as a financial adjustment item in the NFP.
  e. The fair value of any outstanding derivative instruments is considered an item with a financial nature and included as an element of the adjusted NFP.
  f. Credits for the sale of assets still to be liquidated at the end of the financial year have a financial nature in the event that this activity deviates from the company's characteristic activity and consistently with the adjustment for the purposes of normalizing the EBITDA of related capital losses and capital gains.
  g. Cash or bank deposits that are subject to restrictions should generally be excluded from the NFP.
5. *Other elements*: Those which are typically considered as potential adjustments to the NFP, and which are therefore deducted from the final price in the equity bridge mechanism or addressed with specific guarantees in the Sale and Purchase Agreement (SPA), include:
  a. Provisions for risks. Although they represent management estimate, these must be corroborated through specific due diligence analyses for the reference area (legal, environmental, labor law, etc.), and should guide the quantification of any guarantees to be requested in the contract or the definition of any amounts to be considered for the quantification of the so-called escrow accounts.
  b. Debts for capitalization and investments net of any advances paid, as well as any contractual commitments for capex investments.
  c. Deferred tax assets and liabilities if they refer to balance sheet items considered as debt-like items and if they transform into a future benefit or cash outflow.
  d. Potential debts relating to stock option plans or, in general, to top management incentive plans, even if not reflected in the balance sheet, which represent future cash outflows.
  e. Residual amount of severance pay (TFR) adequately discounted, net of the value of any assets serving such plans.

It is important to clarify that the adjustments and normalizations identified in due diligence work represent a starting point for negotiating the final price, which will only be defined following the negotiations between the buyer and the seller. Some adjustments are not negotiable (e.g. accounting adjustments); however, there are many other items that are of a more negotiable nature (e.g. TFR or amount of stretching on suppliers). There are also a number of adjustments and considerations that are difficult to quantify or unlikely to occur (e.g. legal or tax risks with related future liabilities). With regard to this second case, and on the basis of the findings of legal, fiscal due diligence, or other specific checks carried out by the buyer, it is advisable to include in the SPA adequate and sufficient guarantees to be activated when a specific event incurs (e.g. escrow accounts, pass-through and reimbursement mechanisms, etc.).

8.1.2.3 Cash flow analysis

As we have seen, the profit analysis is aimed at identifying a normalized EBITDA, a conventional indicator of profitability that expresses the target company's ability to produce income on a recurring basis. However, it is very important to understand how much of this income measure is able to be transformed into cash on a recurring basis, that is, to also consider the financial absorption that derives, on the one hand, from the physiological dynamics of the business model adopted and, on the other hand, from the need to support business continuity with investments that maintain or expand production capacity and/or efficiency. Hence the need to add a third pillar to the analysis of financial due diligence: cash flow analysis.

Cash flow analysis in the financial due diligence process adds two fundamental aspects to the P&L and balance sheet analysis:

- The understanding of net working capital dynamics over time. The seasonality of the business is an extremely important factor to investigate during due diligence, as it can have a very significant impact on the level of NFP and on the reference date of the price calculation, as we will see later in this chapter.
- The analysis of the nature of the capitalizations carried out during the historical period. These can be divided into:
  a. Maintenance investments: Ordinary investments required to maintain the production capacity and efficiency of the plants and the production process.
  b. Expansion investments: Investments of an extraordinary nature aimed at increasing the production capacity and, in general, the company's offering, or at changing the business model.
  c. Compliance investments: Investments aimed at adapting structures to the compliance requirements of labor and safety regulations. This must also be corroborated with specific analyses carried out as part of business due diligence or on production plants. Any shortcomings or necessary adjustments must be considered in the negotiation as potential adjustments to the NFP, or, in general, as a price deduction.

8.1.2.4 Working capital seasonality

The seasonality of the working capital is an extremely important point to investigate and incorporate into the price definition. It is in fact appropriate, especially in the presence of seasonal businesses, to include an adjustment mechanism that sterilizes the impacts of seasonality on the NFP level at the closing of the transaction and when defining the price. The value of the acquired company or group, in fact, cannot vary based on the month in which it is calculated, obviously with exogenous and market conditions being equal. This mechanism usually takes the form of determining a target net working capital. The difference between this value and the net working capital at the reference date of the price calculation is generally considered as an adjustment to the equity value.

The definition of a target net working capital allows a normal level of working capital requirements for the business, which must be transferred from the seller to the buyer, to be set. This level can be identified using different methods, for example:

- average of the absolute values of the working capital of the last cycle or of the last year; or
- average of the working capital incidence at each month-end or quarter-end on the revenues of the last twelve rolling months.

However, attention must be paid to some points in this approach:

- The working capital, both for the calculation of the target and for the comparison between target and actual capital at the reference date, must be the adjusted working capital that considers all the adjustments identified in the calculation of the adjusted NET financial position that have an impact on working capital. This exercise must be done on each data point for calculating the average working capital (e.g. each end of the month or each quarter).

In defining the calculation data points, any intra-monthly working capital phasing must also be considered. In fact, it may happen that the end-of-month working capital is itself over or underestimated if the dynamics of payments and collections over the month are not consistent. For example, payments to suppliers may be concentrated at the beginning of the month while collections from customers generally occur at the end of the month. In this case, the level of working capital at the beginning or end of the month may be quite different from the average of the month, and, therefore, the average of the data points taken at each month-end may not accurately represent the working capital (and cash) requirements of the business. Figure 8.4 provides a simplified example.

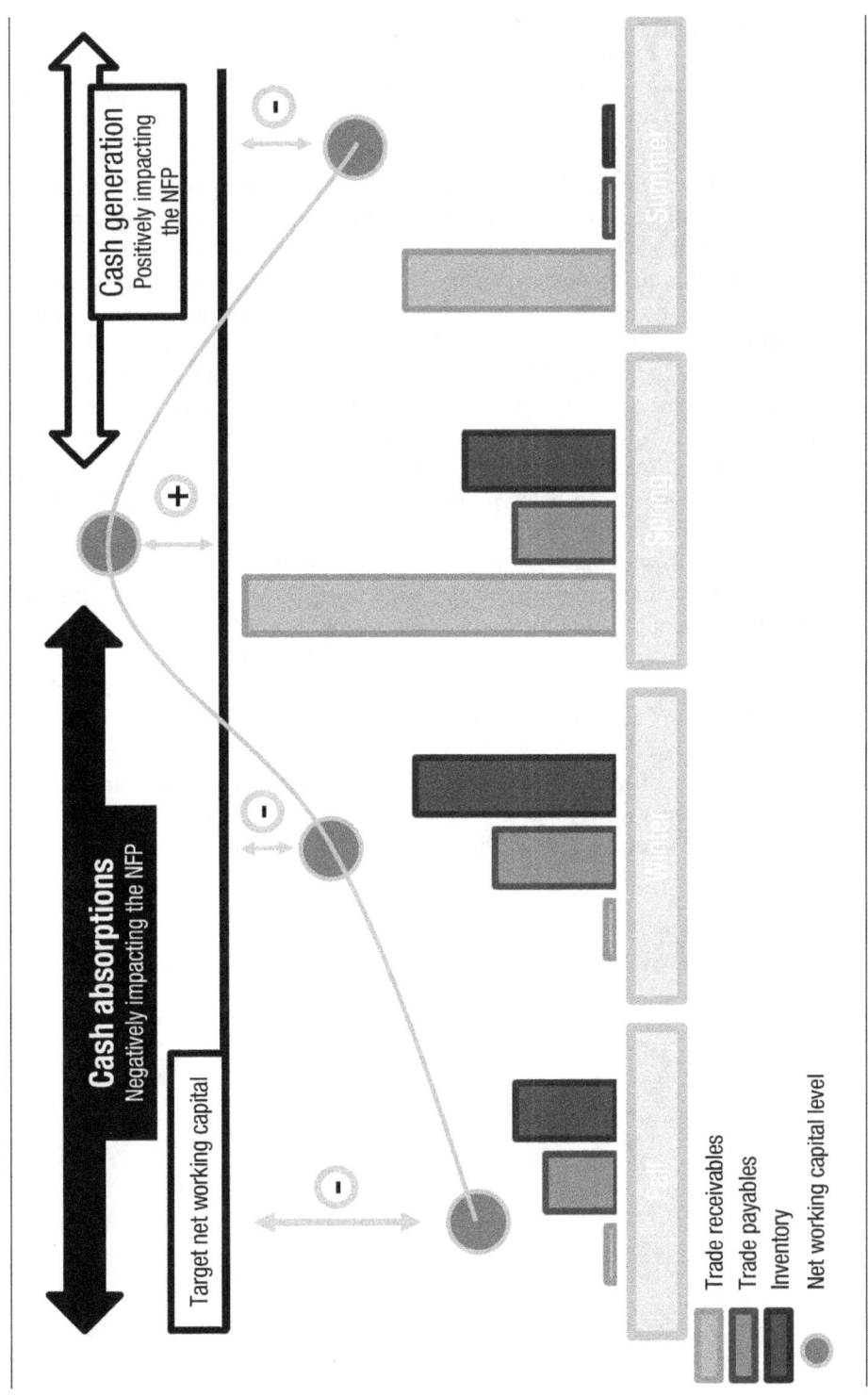

Figure 8.4 Net working capital seasonality

8.2 Conclusions

The advantages and benefits of due diligence for the parties involved and for the transaction itself are:

- *Risk reduction*: Due diligence enables the parties to identify and carefully assess the risks associated with the transaction, allowing them to take preventive measures to mitigate such risks.
- *Better understanding of the target*: Through due diligence, parties gain an in-depth view of the assets and liabilities involved in the transaction, enabling them to accurately evaluate their value and impact on the transaction.
- *Transparency and trust*: The due diligence process promotes transparency among the parties, providing them with a clear view of relevant information. This helps build mutual trust and facilitates negotiations.
- *Dispute prevention*: Identifying and resolving any issues or ambiguities during the due diligence phase helps prevent future conflicts and disputes between the parties after the transaction is concluded.
- *Informed decision-making*: The information obtained through due diligence allows parties to make more informed and strategic decisions during the negotiation and contract drafting process.
- *Optimization of transaction value*: Comprehensive due diligence enables parties to maximize the value of the transaction by ensuring they are aware of all relevant factors and can negotiate more favorable terms.

In conclusion, due diligence provides an opportunity for parties to comprehensively and accurately assess all critical aspects of the transaction, thereby helping to reduce risks, improve trust, and optimize the overall value of the transaction.

9 SME, M&A, and Private Markets in Italy: A Perspective

by *Ernesto Lanzillo*

9.1 General introduction

We are in an international context of current uncertainties that could change investment priorities—due to the timing and outcome of conflicts in Europe and the Middle East; elections in 2024 in seventy-four countries around the world (in particular, with important coalition relocations within Europe's new parliament that lead to uncertainty about Europe's new political and economic lines); risks of financial instability; a level of inflation that is far from central banks' objectives; and continued difficulties in managing the global supply chain, with impacts on the availability and cost of raw material. Nonetheless, the objectives of modernization, growth, and development of our economy are crucial.

9.2 The critical role of SMEs in the Italian economy

In this respect, the involvement of private companies, representing key players who concretely trigger the process of economic transition and act as drivers for investment, remains critical. In Italy, this means that SMEs must embark on a path of growth and evolution in order to continue to play a role as the backbone of the economy, a role which is due to their overwhelming numerical predominance, as well as their contribution to employment and added value.

Regardless of individual actions and their size, it is important that a company is able to evolve rapidly and adapt to new market conditions. Organizations must develop the capabilities necessary to identify, anticipate, and respond to the growth opportunities that arise whenever a disruption event occurs, to avoid taking a defensive attitude and being limited to maintaining the status quo. Having a solid company means being able to value its capital on human, social, operational, financial, and cultural levels. In a scenario such as the current one, where it is crucial to pay attention to development issues and business longevity, it is essential for companies and their leaders to adopt an approach that generates organizational solidity and is able to meet the expectations of stakeholders, even under complex conditions.

According to the data of the last Deloitte Private survey on SMEs in Italy, conducted in fall 2023, it appears that although the perception of confidence of companies in their work is more positive than the view on the economic context, the companies interviewed paid particular attention to the need to monitor phenomena that are exogenous to their organizations. The need to safeguard short-term corporate growth strategy, in addition to inflation and the energy crisis, the risks associated with financial markets, and the geopolitical context, cannot be underestimated. Such criticalities may affect the profitability and the relative margins of the enterprises. According to Bank of Italy, since 2023 the current judgments of Italian companies on the general economic situation and the prospects for their operating conditions have improved, but still remain negative.

9.3 The key role of sustainability

To address the complexity of today's increasingly global and interdependent market scenario, it is worth considering sustainable business models and collaboration logic. While, until a few years ago, the issue of sustainability was perceived as not urgent and not strategic for companies, today it is increasingly relevant in economic terms as well as in environmental terms: Deloitte has estimated that inaction against climate change could cost the global economy $178 trillion over the next fifty years.

In this context, sustainability has become an absolute priority for SMEs, as it is essential in order to maintain competitiveness in the sustainable value chains of their own customers, and it allows companies to preserve their business value, enhancing their capacity to adapt to environmental, social, and economic changes. Being sustainable and in line with the so-called ESG criteria is thus reshaping business priorities, regardless of the size of the company, and is having a disruptive impact on business at all levels; it will also have an increasing impact in the future with regard to access to credit, participation in supply chains, and reputation. Companies are therefore called upon to account for the impact of their activities and to converge toward consumption and investment choices more oriented to environmental and social responsibility. This is even truer for SMEs, the numerically predominant part of the production system in Italy; they must continue to strengthen their commitment to this and assume virtuous behavior in the area of corporate social responsibility.

Long-term value creation and the integration of ESG parameters into business strategies are in fact becoming a new paradigm of economic development that small businesses cannot ignore. The concept of sustainability for companies is not reduced to the environmental footprint of the production cycle, since production is only one of the benchmarks of good business management that today is measured with respect to the already cited ESG attributes.

In order to be socially responsible actors and to implement concrete initiatives to ensure the sustainability of the business, it is therefore crucial to be attentive to social and governance issues as well. And this generates a positive impact on the ecosystem in which the company operates, which is increasingly global and therefore exposed to the influences of actors and stakeholders both internal and external to the company: it is not only investors, financing institutions, and chain leaders who look to the ESG rating. By deciding to shift its capital and interests toward higher

ESG-merit realities It attracts more people, especially younger consumers and talent (both to hire and retain), who belong to a generation that places significant value on sustainability being central to a company's management, organization, and its impact on the surrounding ecosystem.

If a company is sustainable, it can become not only more operationally efficient, but also more attractive in terms of reputation to all those with whom it interacts, creating the prerequisites to be part of virtuous aggregations or supply chains and therefore adherent to the protocols that determine the quality levels thereof. By developing or becoming part of a sustainable supply chain, with reference to the issues of product quality, traceability of raw materials and production standards, labor management methods, governance, and control systems, it contributes to creating value for all the players in the value chain, generating positive economic, social, and environmental returns primarily among the local communities in which these realities operate.

9.3.1 Digital transformation and SME growth

Think also of the contribution that technology can make in accelerating organizations' progress in the field of sustainability. Taking advantage of the fact that many companies currently say they are interested in acting in all areas in which sustainability has declined, investing in digital technologies can become a priority in order to support and improve the reduction of consumption and the energy impact; digital transformation can be particularly effective in achieving green goals that benefit the entire ecosystem.

Agility, clear goals, strong culture, and the ability to maintain a long-term vision that are hallmarks of successful small businesses can help accelerate digital transformation, making these companies' "nature" a competitive advantage.

9.4 Role of private equity in supporting SMEs

A growing number of SMEs are trying to boost growth and increase productivity through digital transformation, which is viewed as a game-changer that can improve the enterprise's growth potential. Digital technologies can enable a leap forward in productivity through improved production process efficiency and higher rates of automation and robotics. The results, however, depend not only on the digitization process itself, but also on the different characteristics of the enterprises and on the productivity dynamics in the sectors in which the company operates. Digitalization increases, above all, the productivity of firms that are already more productive than their competitors, while the more delayed firms are less able to exploit the potential productivity gains from digitization. This means that digitization should not be understood as a "one-for-all" strategy; it must be modulated and adapted so that investment and adoption of digital technologies within enterprises are consistent with companies' current strategies and de facto status.

Another key aspect for businesses is measuring that transformation: leaders who can best bridge the gap between that change, combining strategy, investment, and capacity for change, report an average of 20% more value from their digital initiatives. Businesses must have digital skills and enthusiasm to reap the benefits of this transformation, making digitization part of the company's DNA and corporate culture at all levels.

In today's high-complexity environment, shaped by technological evolution, demographic change, and climate challenges, which all affect the way we live our lives, companies and their leaders need to be more prepared and equipped with the right resources, skills, and tools to successfully address numerous challenges and continue to be competitive and attractive to the market.

A crucial lever in this path is the creation of a corporate culture shared within enterprises, which is also designed to reward virtuous behavior, defined according to the current conception of "virtuosity" recognized by the new generations, and which is able to enhance talent. To attract and retain people with the desired talent, in line with the business expectations and desires of the new generations, to enhance and value their skills, to manage and evaluate performance effectively, and to create teams based on preparation and leadership, these are elements that can position the enterprise in a solid and virtuous way, enabling it to build an organizational culture on which to base its competitive advantage and its longevity.

In recent years, a growing number of employees have been inclined to leave or change their jobs, if not to completely change their professional lives. Talents, in fact, both in the search for a new job, and in the path of growth within a company, are increasingly attracted by the realities that define and adopt appropriate organizational tools and strategies that can enhance the different aspects of the work experience and adopt an agile model, flexible and also attentive to human sustainability, which aims to improve the social and economic well-being of people.

The world of work is undergoing profound changes on the demand side, and companies are facing a highly competitive recruitment environment in a variety of industries. Meeting this challenge—attracting and retaining talent over time—means securing the company's future growth. To do so, organizations need to identify talent with the necessary skills and promote their training and development over time.

Attracting and retaining workers with the desired characteristics includes actions such as the promotion of training and development of current resources (by upskilling and reskilling) and the provision of leadership programs that speed up decision-making and enable the company to adapt quickly to disruptive phenomena. Training is not only a functional tool for the growth and valorization of talent, but it is also a strategic lever for companies to combat the current lack of skills available on the market, by investing in the resources already in staff.

This also applies to family businesses, which, given their nature, must pay particular attention to the training of their leaders in order to ensure continuity of their businesses. Regardless of the contingencies linked to the current macroeconomic and geopolitical situation, family realities address further issues related to their own "nature," which may alter the course of activity and the future of the organization. In fact, a family business must constantly take into account some unique challenges, such as the difficult interaction between business and investment choices, as well as issues related to ownership, generational transition, or family dynamics.

The management of the generational transition and the development of good governance models are central factors for family businesses and promote business continuity, preserve family heritage, improve sustainability impact, and support collaboration with other stakeholders.

Transition planning must therefore become a priority for family businesses: the question of who to put at the company's helm and how to find its future leader, in continuity with family values, traditions, and heritage, is a mandatory and crucial phase for any family-run reality.

The generational change, in fact, can represent an opportunity to reflect on strategy, to review the organization and the processes, and therefore also be open to external figures 'joining the board and in the management.

In the succession phase, it is important to take into account the issue of mentoring, that is, the interplay between the senior leader and their successor for a number of years, and the involvement and preparation of leadership in the case of the new generation, to help the latter understand the business and to promote their intellectual curiosity.

It is crucial that this moment of governance and organization evolution, linked to the change in family leadership, is appropriately prepared and planned. But, to effectively manage business dynamics and adapt to external change, it is equally important to develop a good governance model. Moving in this direction also becomes a great opportunity for smaller family businesses, which can seize the opportunity to grow in terms of entrepreneurial culture and organizational and asset strengths.

This theme of asset and financial consolidation, together with action with regard to human resources, organizational structure, pricing/profit model, business growth through M&A operations, increase in sustainability initiatives, and expansion of the business ecosystem, is one of the strengthening levers to be pursued.

Although Italian companies today have stronger financials, thanks to an improvement in the pre-pandemic decade, in 2023 the liquidity of companies, measured by the value of bank deposits, decreased rapidly (−5–6% per year in August), returning to the pre-pandemic trend, as noted in a study of Confindustria.

Shrinking corporate liquidity and shocks in the economic environment can create a need for some firms to increase their leverage, as in 2022, so it is important that banks' supply of credit remains large, thanks to credit and liquidity measures (e.g. the expansion of the SME Fund's public guarantees and moratoria on bank debts), thereby facilitating business continuity and development.

9.5 Trends and data on private equity in Italy

In this context, private equity has a crucial role for the development of SMEs; in addition to being a significant accelerator of investment, particularly technological and digital investments, private equity portfolio companies are managerialized, adopt advanced governance practices, and are able to implement sustainable behaviors in both environmental and social fields, which make them competitive in the supply chains in which they operate and attractive to the younger generations, both when the latter search for jobs and when they interact as consumers of goods or services. From a financial point of view, private credit provided by private equity is also a development accelerator, a competitive alternative, in terms of money cost, to bank financing. In Italy, this is less common than in other European countries, and therefore interesting because it is poorly explored. Finally, private equity is a useful solution for the development of family businesses when they are struggling in terms of their ability to identify an internal path of generational continuity.

In order to understand how interested private equity is in the Italian industrial landscape of SMEs, it is useful to examine their investment moves in Italy, measured every six months over the last five years by the Deloitte Private Equity Survey series. Private equity has already met expectations for the first half of 2024 in terms of appetite for investment.

The number of private equity transactions shows overall growth from 102 in the first half of 2019 to 239 in the second half of 2023, despite the difficult macroeconomic and geopolitical conditions faced since 2020. The Deloitte PE Confidence Index (Figure 9.1), which measures the confidence of private equity toward Italian industry, has historically seen a positive trend, with such confidence reaching a maximum of 134 points in the second half of 2021, and then stabilizing at 107 (as a preview of the first half of 2024).

Figure 9.1   **Deloitte PE Confidence Index Trends**

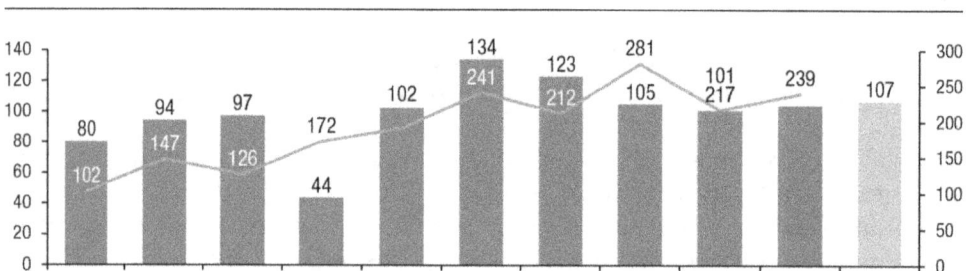

Between the first half of 2019 and the second half of 2023, as can be seen from Figure 9.2, the value of transactions showed significant fluctuations, with a peak of €55.1 billion in the first half of 2022 and a decrease to €13.9 billion in the second half of 2023. The number of acquisitions followed an overall trend of increase, from 90 to 212, while the number of divestments remained relatively stable with slight fluctuations during the six months observed.

9 SME, M&A, and Private Markets in Italy: A Perspective

Figure 9.2   **Transaction Values and Acquisition Trends (2019–2023)**

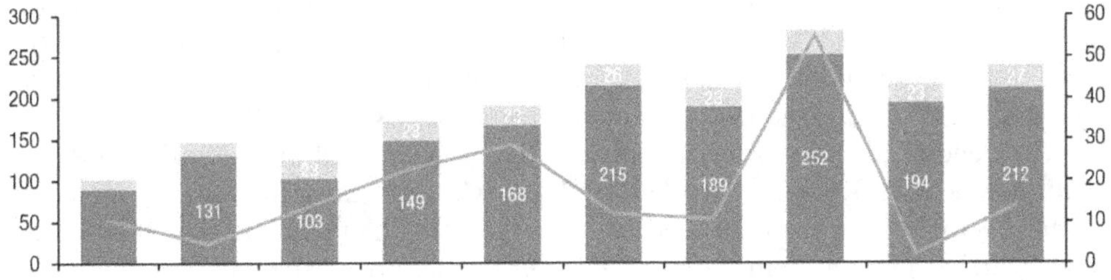

Referring to the average turnover of the companies in the portfolio, 32.8% of survey respondents in the first half of 2024 said that they had an average turnover of between €31 million and €50 million (+9.5% compared to the first half of 2019). Interest for companies with a turnover of between €51 million and €100 million dropped, reaching 27.6% (a reduction of 9.6% compared to the first half of 2019). Finally, 15.5% claimed to have companies with an average turnover of more than €100 million (+3.9% compared to the first half of 2019), while 24.1% fell below €30 million (−3.9% compared to 2019).

In the five-year period, as can be seen from Figure 9.3, there was an upward trend in interest in the consumer goods sector, with overall growth from 12.3% to 14.7%, but volatility in the food and beverage sector, showing a cyclic variation with a peak of 14.3% and a subsequent contraction at 10.1% before a recovery to 13.3%. Healthcare and social services peaked at 8% in the first half of 2023, followed by a slight drop to 7.3% in the first half of 2024.

Figure 9.3   **Sectoral Interest Trends Over a Five-Year Period**

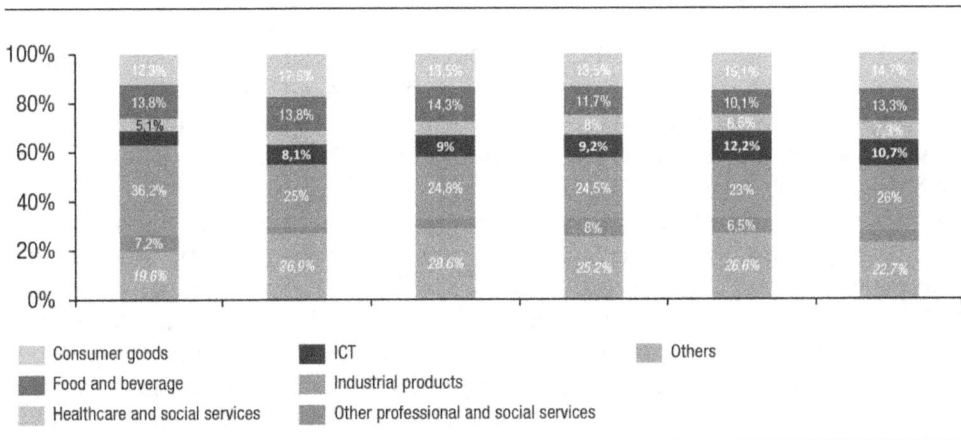

In terms of territorial interest, the northwest region followed a positive trend in the first half of 2019 and the first half of 2024, rising from 39.5% to 44.8%, and being the most important geographical area for operators. The center has seen a total decrease, from 11.6% to 5.2%; south and islands and abroad have shown minor variations, with the south and islands showing a very small presence and interest in foreign countries standing at 6.9% of preferences in the first half of 2024.

The trend for majority transactions has slightly decreased, from 81.4% in the first half of 2019 to 79.3% in the first half of 2024, while minority investments increased from 14% to 19%. Investments and co-investments with others had a marginal presence, which decreases from 4.7% to 1.7% over the period considered.

Investments with multiple EBITDA of less than 2x showed a fluctuating trend, standing at 29.3%. In contrast, those with multiples between 2x and 4x represent the majority, with a significant peak of 78.6% in the second half of 2020. Multiples between 4x and 6x have seen a more variable presence but generally increased, ending at 5.2%, while there were no investments with multiples above 6x in the first half of 2024.

Senior debt increased from 79.1% in the first half of 2019 to 82.8% (+3.7%) in the first half of 2024, with changes over the course of the half-year period. Mezzanine financing had a smaller presence but grew slightly, from 2.3% to 5.2%, while junior debt and high-yield bonds showed a significant increase, from 0% to 5.8%. Vendor's notes/convertible bonds changed, ending at 1.7% (−5.3%).

And finally, in the last three half-year surveys, the appetite for ESG compliance has constantly increased as a selection attribute in an M&A transaction managed by private equity. This is confirmation of what Larry Fink reported in his letter in 2018—that ESG has now become a must for selecting the best investments with a view toward sustainable growth of a company's portfolio and a connected impact on the collectivity involved.

9.6 Conclusions and future perspectives

Both Corporate Sustainability Reporting Directive (CSRD) and Network and Information Security (NIS2) EU Directive, on corporate social responsibility reporting and cyber risk governance respectively, expected to be endorsed in Italy in the next months, with an effective enactment by the end of 2025, imply relevant investment by SMEs. Financing will be crucial to sustain the technological evolution for energy savings and sustainable conversion of the processes, while a more extensive use of technology will increase the level of investments in cyber security, which are not deferrable due to the NIS2 Directive. To stay in the supply chain of their principals, SMEs will be requested to implement important upgrades in governance and production cycles, and the role of private equity will become crucial for injecting money and for pushing portfolio companies into upgrading their governance practice, with a more conscious need for new managers and new strategies based in a new cultural behavior where compliance to the new constraints imposed by the EU Directive have to be considered an accelerator for growth and efficiency.

10 Value Creation and Transformation in Infrastructure

by *Francesco Checcacci*

10.1 Introduction

In this chapter, we will explore the essential role of infrastructure in shaping economies, improving living standards, and promoting sustainable development, and look at how M&A activities can boost value creation for stakeholders.

In the ever evolving landscape of global economies, infrastructure plays a pivotal role in driving growth, fostering sustainable development, and enhancing living conditions. Within this context, the strategic importance of value creation and transformation in infrastructure investments cannot be overstated. As nations and businesses strive to adapt to changing technological advancements, environmental concerns, and shifts in social needs, the ways in which infrastructure assets are valued, acquired, and integrated have undergone significant transformation.

The complex relationship between infrastructure development and M&A activities offers a unique perspective on value generation. M&A transactions in the infrastructure domain are not merely financial deals only; they are strategic moves aimed at enhancing operational efficiencies, achieving sustainability goals, and leveraging technological innovations to meet the demands of the future. By amalgamating assets, expertise, and resources, M&A can serve as a potent catalyst for transforming the infrastructure landscape, thereby creating substantial value for stakeholders, communities, and economies at large.

This chapter aims to explore the foundational concepts of value creation within the infrastructure sector, highlighting the critical elements that contribute to the enhancement of asset worth and operational performance. It will also examine the transformative impact of M&A activities, shedding light on how these transactions can be orchestrated to maximize value, address emerging challenges, and capitalize on opportunities in the infrastructure sphere. By weaving together theoretical insights, strategic frameworks, and real-world examples, this chapter provides a comprehensive understanding of the mechanisms through which value is created and transformed in infrastructure through M&A.

Before analyzing these elements in detail, in an era of continuous evolution and transformation of the infrastructure sector, we believe that it's very useful to distinguish the concepts of core and non-core infrastructure.

Core infrastructure refers to long-term assets that are highly regulated and generally less sensitive to changes in demand and economic distress. These assets provide constant and predictable revenue streams over time. Examples of core infrastructure include network assets such as highways, bridges, water systems, transport links, telecom systems, and electricity grids. Core infrastructure is usually availability-based, meaning that the investor receives payment for the asset if it is available to the public, functioning correctly, and well maintained. This category of infrastructure is fundamental in ensuring the stable operation and accessibility of essential services.

In addition to core infrastructure, "non-core infrastructure" also plays a significant role in the broader infrastructure landscape. This may lack some of the defining characteristics of core infrastructure but is still a capital-intensive sector with significant barriers to entry. Non-core infrastructure assets are typically more exposed to risks such as development risk, inflation, and volume/throughput risk, as well as increased competition. Despite these risks, non-core infrastructure remains vital for its potential to deliver returns and drive innovation in infrastructure development.

10.2 Fundamentals of value creation in infrastructure

Value creation in the infrastructure sector is a multifaceted concept, encompassing a wide array of strategies, processes, and practices aimed at enhancing the worth and performance of infrastructure assets. At its core, value creation is about generating economic, social, and environmental benefits that extend beyond the initial capital investment, offering long-term gains to investors, users, and society at large.

Value creation refers to both economic-financial value and economic-social value in the environment in which the infrastructural asset is developed. When we talk about value from an economic-financial perspective, we refer to the infrastructure's ability to generate cash flows. Therefore, the drivers of this element can be attributed to the following categories:

1. *Operational efficiency*: One of the primary avenues for value creation in infrastructure is through the enhancement of operational efficiency. This involves optimizing asset utilization, reducing costs, and improving service quality. Techniques such as lean management, predictive maintenance, and process automation play a crucial role in achieving operational excellence.
2. *Sustainability and environmental stewardship*: In today's context, sustainable development is a critical component of value creation in infrastructure projects. Incorporating green technologies, renewable energy sources, and sustainable materials not only mitigates environmental impact, but also enhances the long-term viability and attractiveness of infrastructure assets. It also limits potential risks that may arise from possible breaches of local and extra-local regulations, which could lead to the imposition of penalties, and so on.

The main enabling tools used to reach the elements mentioned are:

1. *Technological innovation*: The adoption of cutting-edge technologies such as IoT, AI, and blockchain can significantly enhance the value of infrastructure assets.

These technologies enable smarter infrastructure management, strengthened security, and the provision of innovative services to users. Technological innovation can be considered as a main driver for points A and B, as it enables tools for cost efficiency and for driving sustainable transformation.
2. *Stakeholder engagement and social value*: Engaging with stakeholders and ensuring that infrastructure projects deliver social value are essential for sustainable value creation. This includes considerations of accessibility, affordability, and positive impacts on communities.

All of the above allow for the pursuit of the following strategic approaches to value creation:

1. Asset life-cycle optimization: Managing infrastructure assets across their entire life cycle—from planning and construction to operation and decommissioning. This holistic view ensures that decisions at each stage maximize value and sustainability.
2. Public–private partnerships: PPPs can be a powerful model for value creation in infrastructure, leveraging the strengths and resources of both public and private sectors. These partnerships often lead to innovative financing models, risk sharing, and efficiency gains.
3. Regulatory and policy alignment: Navigating and influencing the regulatory environment is crucial for unlocking value in infrastructure projects. Policies that encourage investment, innovation, and sustainable development can significantly impact the value creation potential.
4. Market positioning and differentiation: Establishing a unique value proposition and differentiating infrastructure assets in the market can attract investment and user engagement, driving up the asset's value.

Through these components and strategic approaches, stakeholders in the infrastructure sector can drive significant value creation, contributing to the economic, social, and environmental prosperity of communities and nations. The following sections will further explore how these elements are transformed and leveraged through M&A activities in the infrastructure domain.

10.3 M&A as a catalyst for value creation in the infra sector

The infrastructure sector is undergoing a significant transformation, driven by global trends, technological advancements, and evolving social expectations. This transformation is reshaping the landscape of infrastructure investment, development, and management, necessitating innovative approaches to value creation and strategic adaptation.

M&A play a pivotal role in accelerating transformation within the infrastructure sector. By facilitating the consolidation of assets, the exchange of technology and expertise, and the pooling of resources, M&A activities can significantly enhance the capacity for innovation and value creation.

1. *Enhancing scale and efficiency*: M&A can create larger, more efficient entities that can leverage economies of scale and drive down costs, thereby increasing the value proposition of infrastructure investments.
2. *Changing demographics and urbanization*: The global shift toward urbanization, coupled with changing demographic patterns and mobility, is altering demand for infrastructure services. Urban areas require modern, resilient infrastructure to support growing populations and evolving urban lifestyles, driving innovation in transportation, water supply, and waste management.
3. *Consolidation for competitive advantage*: In a sector where scale can determine market dominance and operational efficiency, M&A offers a pathway to consolidate assets and capabilities, enhancing competitive positioning and enabling synergies.
4. *Facilitating technological integration*: M&A transactions enable companies to adopt new technologies and innovative practices quickly, speeding up the transformation process and enabling the development of smarter, more sustainable infrastructure. Digital technologies, such as smart sensors, autonomous systems, and data analytics, are revolutionizing the way infrastructure assets are designed, constructed, and operated, leading to increased efficiency, enhanced safety, and improved user experiences. Acquiring startups and technology-oriented firms provides immediate access to the innovative solutions and digital technologies essential for the modernization of infrastructure assets.
5. *Expanding market presence*: Strategic M&A enable companies to enter new markets, access untapped customer bases, and respond more effectively to global trends and demands. Companies can quickly enter new geographical markets or segments within the infrastructure domain, accelerating growth and diversification through strategic mergers or acquisitions.
6. *Addressing regulatory and environmental challenges*: By combining resources and expertise, companies can better navigate the complex regulatory landscape and invest in sustainable infrastructure projects that meet stringent environmental standards. Governments and regulatory bodies worldwide are updating policies and regulations to encourage investment in infrastructure, promote sustainability, and ensure equitable access. These changes can create opportunities for value creation but also require agility and strategic foresight from investors and operators.
7. *Compliance and sustainability enhancement*: M&A allows companies to pool resources to better navigate regulatory landscapes and invest in sustainable and green infrastructure, aligning with global environmental objectives. Growing awareness of climate change and environmental sustainability issues has shifted the focus toward green and sustainable infrastructure solutions. This includes renewable energy projects, green buildings, and infrastructure that supports electric vehicles and reduces carbon footprints.

These considerations find confirmation in any type of M&A operation, whether it involves an aggregation between existing operators or the entry of an institutional investor (e.g. infra fund) into infrastructure assets or private enterprises. For instance, in the case of consolidation among operators in the airport or highway management sectors, the primary goal may be to optimize resources, increase operational efficiencies, and enhance the quality of services offered to customers. This type of operation often aims to create synergies, boosting the competitive capacity of the entities resulting from the aggregation.

However, when an institutional investor decides to invest in infrastructure assets or private operators, the objectives can be different. These investments are generally motivated by the search for stable and predictable long-term returns associated with the inherent nature of infrastructure assets, which tend to be less volatile compared to other asset classes, but also as a way to create value for all stakeholders.

Although the two types of M&A operations—aggregations between operators and institutional investments in infrastructure or private assets—may have different financial return goals and objectives, they are united by the pursuit of the strategies described. In both situations, the key to success lies in the ability to identify and exploit synergies, improve operational efficiency, and maximize value for stakeholders. Effective risk management, attention to sustainability, and adaptation to market dynamics are additional crucial elements for achieving the set objectives.

10.4 Value creation in infrastructure: how to manage the process

While M&A presents significant opportunities for value creation and sectoral transformation, it is not without its challenges. Regulatory hurdles, cultural mismatches, and integration complexities can derail even the most strategically planned mergers. Particularly in the case of cross-border M&A operations, the main challenges to face are those related to the investors' understanding of the regulatory and political context, which can influence the profitability of the project over its lifespan.

Success in this arena requires a keen understanding of the infrastructure landscape, a strategic approach to M&A, and the agility to navigate the complexities of integration and transformation.

Leveraging M&A as a strategic tool for value creation and transformation in infrastructure requires a careful balance of strategic insight, operational excellence, and innovative thinking. As the sector continues to evolve, those who master this balance will not only thrive but will also play a pivotal role in shaping the future of infrastructure development and management.

Mitigating risks and enhancing sustainability are two relevant elements for the successful outcome of the M&A process in the infra sector. Effective risk management, attention to sustainability, and adaptation to market dynamics not only mitigate potential negative impacts, but also unlock opportunities for long-term value creation, resilience, and positive societal contributions.

As infrastructure projects inherently carry long-term horizons and significant societal impacts, integrating these aspects into M&A decision-making processes is crucial. Focusing on sustainability, long-term environmental, social, and economic impacts are increasingly relevant in this M&A process:

1. *Sustainable investment criteria*: Incorporating sustainability criteria into investment decisions ensures that M&A activities contribute to broader ESG goals. This approach attracts socially responsible investors and can enhance the long-term viability of infrastructure assets.
2. *Green financing and incentives*: Leveraging green financing options and government incentives for sustainable projects can enhance the financial attractiveness of M&A deals and support the transition to a low-carbon economy.
3. *Stakeholder engagement*: Engaging with local communities, environmental groups, and other stakeholders can uncover insights into sustainability concerns and opportunities, fostering goodwill and ensuring project support.
4. *Innovation and best practices*: Acquiring companies with innovative sustainable technologies or practices can be a strategic move to enhance the environmental performance of infrastructure portfolios and drive sectoral transformation.

Box 10.1 Key strategies for maximizing value through M&A

Therefore, to develop a successful M&A operation in the infrastructure sector, the steps to follow are the following:

1. Comprehensive due diligence and integration planning: Due diligence that focuses not only on financials but also on operational, technological, cultural, and ESG factors is crucial. This holistic approach helps identify potential risks and liabilities early in the process. Effective integration planning ensures that the combined entity realizes the anticipated value creation synergies. Specifically, for operations involving infrastructural assets, it is essential to perform due diligence to verify implicit risks within the regulatory context. The remuneration of infrastructural assets is regulated to ensure a market return for the investor and to prevent situations of excess profit—consider, for instance, the regulatory system for highway transportation.
2. Focus on innovation and technology transfer: Prioritizing acquisitions that introduce new technologies and innovative practices can significantly enhance the value and efficiency of infrastructure operations, setting the stage for transformative growth.
3. Strategic asset portfolio management: Post-M&A, strategic management of the asset portfolio—identifying core versus non-core assets and making strategic divestitures or further acquisitions—is essential for optimizing value creation.
4. Integration risk assessment and mitigation: Effective risk management involves planning for integration challenges, including cultural alignment, technology systems integration, and operational synergies. Anticipating these risks allows for the implementation of proactive mitigation strategies.
5. Stakeholder engagement and communication: Engaging with key stakeholders—employees, customers, regulators, and the community—from the outset ensures support for the M&A process and facilitates smoother integration and value realization.
6. Flexible financing structures: Given the long-term nature of infrastructure investments, structuring deals with flexible financing that can mitigate the financial risks associated with market volatility, interest rate changes, and project delays.

10.5 Case studies of successful value creation and transformation via M&A

The case of ASTM S.p.A. represents a successful example of value creation in infrastructure. Today, the ASTM Group is a global player in the infrastructure sector, the second-largest motorway concession operator in the world (with a network of approximately 6200 km in Italy and Brazil), and a leader in the realization of large works and in mobility technology.

Originally known as Autostrada Torino-Milano, ASTM was established in 1928 with the aim of constructing a motorway linking the cities of Turin and Milan. In 1969, the company went public on the Turin Stock Exchange and the following year on the Milan Stock Exchange (now Borsa Italiana).

In 1984, the Gavio family (the current majority shareholder of *Azienda Sviluppo e Trasporti e Mobilità* (ASTM)) bought their first stake in ASTM. In 2002, the company underwent a corporate reorganization, spinning off the motorway concessions held by ASTM and *Società Autostrada Ligure Toscana* (SALT) into *Società Iniziative Autostradali e Servizi* (SIAS), which was subsequently listed on the stock exchange.

In 2007, the company completed the reorganization, aiming to concentrate all the motorway concessions in a specific company named SIAS while ASTM became a holding company. Therefore, ASTM directly controlled SIAS, which in turn controlled all the highway concessions.

In 2015, ASTM S.p.A. and SIAS S.p.A., through IGLI S.p.A., completed the closing of the transaction for the acquisition of joint control, together with Primav Construcoes e Comercio S.A., of the NewCo Brazilian company Primav Infraestrutura S.A. This new entity acquired 64% of the shares of EcoRodovias Infraestrutura e Logistica S.A. and 55% of the shares of Concessionária Monotrilho Linha 18—Bronze S.A., which operates in the urban mobility sector.

Based on the agreement, IGLI owns 69.1% of the share capital of the NewCo, which corresponds to approximately 44.2% of the share capital of EcoRodovias.

Following the 2016 agreement for the acquisition of the first stake in EcoRodovias, in 2020, ASTM carried out a capital increase in EcoRodovias in agreement with Primav Construções e Comércio S.A., thereby obtaining a controlling interest in the Brazilian company.

This agreement led ASTM to hold about 51% of the company's capital and further focus on expansion in the Brazilian market, aligned with the group's primary goal of accessing new markets globally. Currently, ASTM manages about 5000 kilometers of road in Brazil through EcoRodovias, which stretch along the country's main logistic corridors. EcoRodovias raised financial resources amounting to 1.7 billion reais through the capital increase, corresponding to a 25% increase in the number of shares issued, which enabled ASTM to consolidate its control over EcoRodovias. This positioned both companies as global leaders in the motorway sector in Brazil.

The expansion in Brazil exemplifies how a group that initially operated on a local scale (Italy only) was able, in a short time and strategically, to expand internationally, bringing about radical structural changes.

In 2016, the group acquired control of Itinera, a company specializing in the construction of transport infrastructure and civil building projects, through which it now operates in the EPC (engineering, procurement, and construction) sector. Itinera ranks among the leading Italian companies in the field for expertise, know-how, revenue, and order portfolio, and it operates globally (Europe, Southern Africa, Middle East, Latin America, and the United States) in various sectors, including road and railroad infrastructure, tunnels and underground works, civil and industrial buildings, ports, airports, hospitals, dams and maritime works, and motorway maintenance. Through Itinera, with an order portfolio of over 4 billion euros, the group is among the main global operators in the construction of major works. The acquisition of Itinera represents not only an expansion in a different but complementary business but also a cost-optimization strategy through a vertical integration strategy.

In 2017, the group expanded its presence in the United States by acquiring the majority shareholding in Halmar International LLC, one of the most significant construction companies operating in the New York area.

The entry of Ardian

In September 2018, an agreement was formalized between Ardian, an independent private equity fund primarily based in France, and the Gavio family. This agreement marked the entry of Ardian as a minority shareholder in ASTM, through the purchase of an indirect stake.

Ardian acquired 40% of Nuova Argo Finanziaria, an entity that held 58.77% of ASTM and 63.41% of SIAS. This transaction involved the signing of an agreement with Aurelia to regulate governance and share transfers, thereby establishing a strategic partnership between the parties. This partnership not only strengthens the Gavio family's position in the infrastructure sector but also enables the exploitation of market opportunities in Europe, Latin America, and the United States. This agreement allows the Gavio family to optimize their access to the capital markets, enhancing operational efficiency and promoting competitive growth both nationally and internationally.

Among the significant events that occurred following the entry of Ardian was the simplification of the corporate structure, through the incorporation of SIAS into ASTM. In 2019, ASTM launched a partial voluntary public purchase offer on SIAS shares, which ultimately led to the incorporation of SIAS into ASTM in 2020.

The merger between ASTM and SIAS has given rise to a global leader in the infrastructure sector, whereby the two companies have combined their respective skills and resources to form a diversified and synergistic portfolio. This union has allowed the group to operate under the title of "One Company." It is important to highlight that the company also operates through its main subsidiaries: Itinera, the construction division (which increases the capacity for business development and risk control and reduces overhead costs), and SINELEC, the technology arm.

From a financial perspective, the merger has also contributed to the rationalization of the capital structure and costs, simplifying access to capital markets and creating a more efficient cost structure.

The primary objectives of the SIAS/ASTM integration operation were as follows:

1. To create a single listed industrial holding company operating as a "One Company" with targeted skills in the sectors of motorway concessions, construction, engineering, and technological innovation, simplifying and rationalizing the corporate structure, and ultimately improving access to capital markets.
2. To promote efficient and competitive growth of the group at both national and international level, reducing holding costs, shortening the control chain, and strengthening industrial synergies to improve long-term operating results.

Following the transformation of ASTM into "One Company," a significant operation was carried out in May 2021. Specifically, the Gavio family and Ardian, through the holding company Nuova Argo Finanziaria 2, launched a public tender offer, making ASTM a private company and thus delisting it from the stock market. Concurrently, a merger between the holding company Nuova Argo Finanziaria 2 and ASTM S.p.A. was executed. Currently, the Gavio family holds 50.5% of ASTM and Ardian holds 49.5%. These operations are aimed at simplifying the group's corporate structure by shortening the control chain, as well as improving management flexibility and reducing organizational levels, thereby speeding up the decision-making process.

Ardian's entry into ASTM's shareholder structure has led to increased international expansion and supported the acquisition of additional highway concessions, resulting in significant investments in the infrastructure sector, especially in Brazil and the USA.

Additionally, as briefly mentioned, with Ardian's entry there has been a focus, after the transformation into One Company, on: (i) technological development through the subsidiary Sinelec; and (ii) stakeholder engagement and social value incorporating sustainability into the strategy and daily business.

Sinelec has developed innovative data collection systems that utilize AI engines and machine learning. These systems allow the connection of physical infrastructure to control centers, travelers, and self-driving cars, creating an ecosystem where real-time data flows ensure proper infrastructure maintenance, safety, and the identification and control of all types of risks.

ASTM's sustainability strategy is based on three pillars: People, Planet, and Prosperity. The group is the first European motorway operator to set targets in terms of Scope 1, Scope 2, and Scope 3.

In summary, the story of ASTM serves as an exemplary instance of corporate transformation, highlighting its transition from a local enterprise to a global player in the infrastructure sector. From its inception, ASTM has demonstrated remarkable adaptability and growth, leveraging strategic opportunities and executing targeted

M&A. These operations have enabled the company to expand its geographical presence and diversify its activities, strengthening its role in the motorway and construction sectors. As described, ASTM, through the M&A transactions carried out, has achieved the following:

1. *Enhancing scale and efficiency*: Through the merger of ASTM and SIAS and subsequent delisting, the group pursued operational efficiency and financial structure.
2. *Changing demographics and urbanization*: In the USA, ASTM promoted and developed a PPP for improving the accessibility of thirteen New York City subway stations so they complied with the Americans with Disabilities Act.
3. *Consolidation and expand market presence*: Following the merger of Ardian—Gavio family, the group expanded its market presence through the acquisition and subsequent consolidation of EcoRodovias.
4. *Facilitating technological innovation*: The group focused on the development of technology through its subsidiary, Sinelec.
5. *Compliance and sustainability enhancement*: The group has been the first European highway operator to set targets approved by the Science-Based Targets initiative.

11 Value Creation and Urban Regeneration in Real Estate

by *Andrea Mucchietto*

11.1 What is urban regeneration?

In recent years, after the diffusion and foreseen implementation of concepts and regulations such as SDGs (Agenda 2030 Sustainable Development Goals), ESG, and SFDR, the real estate industry experienced a trend where any project, from single-building restructuring to entire new neighborhoods' realization, has been labelled as "sustainable development" and/or "urban regeneration" through marketing initiatives aimed at fostering a new perception of real estate developers, ranging from speculative players to (social) value creators.

Even though any modern development initiative may embody an element of positive impact for its users and the surrounding area (e.g. new offices focused on smart working would provide better spaces for workers, require less volumes to be built thanks to desk sharing, and less hours of commuting, thus contributing to the reduction of pollution produced by private vehicles), it is important to understand the deep meaning of "urban regeneration" and how it differs from traditional real estate development (Figure 11.1).

Figure 11.1 **Comparison of Urban Regeneration, Requalification, and Repositioning in Terms of Project Numbers and Value Creation**

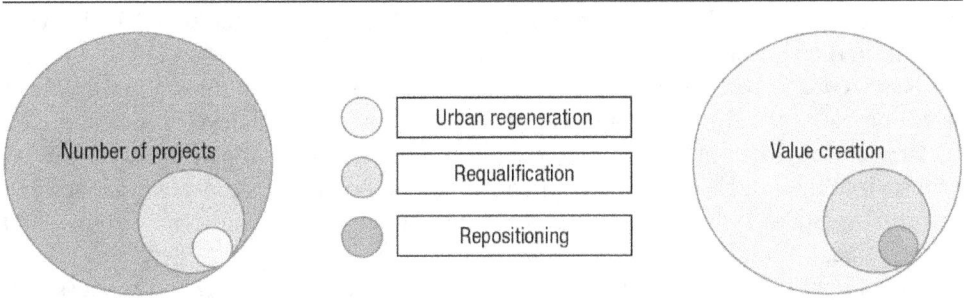

On the one hand, repositioning and requalification strategies often involve a single building and, whilst there are large numbers of these, compared to a proper urban regeneration project, they have very limited value creation (excepting for the investors themselves, if the deal proves successful).

On the other hand, urban regeneration through the substitution of underused assets or brownfields with environment-conscious buildings and the provision of new public spaces (parks, squares, edutainment hubs, etc.) entails the redesign of entire blocks or expansion of the urban context without new soil consumption, creating value for a broad range of stakeholders, not just for real estate developers.

In 2020, the United Nations (UN) World Cities Report estimated that, by 2030, 60% of the global population will live within cities, and that this percentage would increase to 70% by 2050. Urban regeneration projects can foster the enhancement of peripheral districts, creating multicentric cities where existing and prospective inhabitants, as well as city users, can find the services they need and experience better living conditions, especially if those developments include a provision for capped or social housing (from residential to senior living, through student accommodation).

11.2 ESG: from regulatory requirements toward drivers for value creation

Urban regeneration represents a multifaceted endeavor, blending the physical revitalization of urban spaces with the enhancement of social cohesion, economic vitality, and environmental sustainability. Within this dynamic landscape, stakeholders play pivotal roles in shaping the trajectory and outcomes of regeneration initiatives. From property owners and developers to community organizations, government agencies, and investors, each stakeholder brings unique perspectives, interests, and objectives to the table.

Deloitte's report on urban regeneration (November 2023) underlines the importance of ESG assessment as a linchpin for risk mitigation and value creation. Rather than viewing regulatory requirements as burdensome constraints, stakeholders can leverage ESG principles to drive innovation, resilience, and sustainable growth. By embedding ESG considerations into the fabric of urban regeneration projects, stakeholders can proactively address environmental challenges, foster social inclusivity, and strengthen governance frameworks (Figure 11.2).

At its core, urban regeneration is about revitalizing communities and unlocking latent potential within urban landscapes. Property owners and developers are driven by financial returns but increasingly recognize the intrinsic value of integrating ESG criteria into their decision-making processes. By embracing sustainable practices and prioritizing stakeholder engagement, they can enhance the long-term viability and attractiveness of their assets.

Local communities are vital stakeholders in the urban regeneration process, advocating for preservation of cultural heritage, equitable access to amenities, and opportunities for socioeconomic advancement. Governmental entities serve as both regulators and facilitators, establishing policy frameworks, allocating resources, and fostering PPPs to drive sustainable urban development.

Deloitte advocates for a comprehensive approach to urban regeneration, encompassing initial assessment, benchmarking against industry standards, definition of

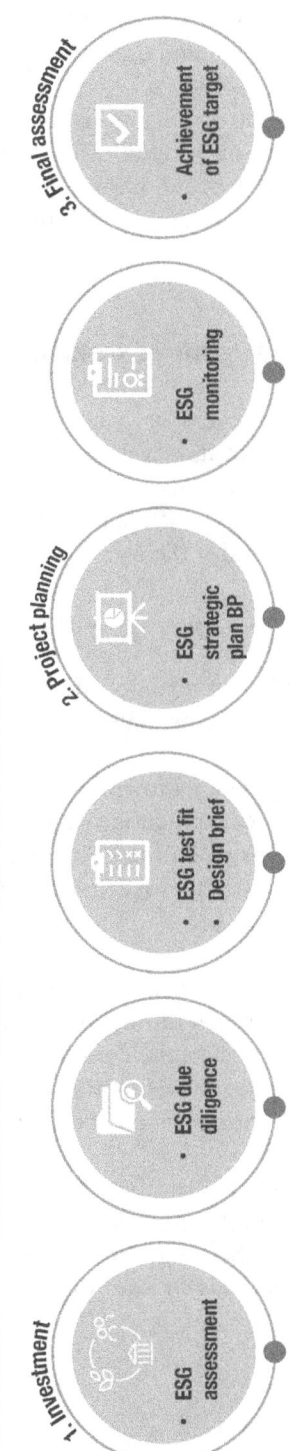

Figure 11.2 ESG Integration Process in Urban Regeneration Projects

KPIs, and ongoing monitoring of ESG performance. This holistic methodology aims to create shared value across economic, social, and environmental dimensions, aligning the interests of diverse stakeholders toward common objectives.

Urban regeneration presents a complex tapestry of challenges and opportunities, demanding collaboration, innovation, and adaptive governance. By reframing regulatory compliance as a catalyst for value creation, stakeholders can harness the transformative power of ESG principles to build resilient, inclusive, and thriving urban communities for generations to come.

11.3 Challenges in urban regeneration: management of stakeholders

When approaching a regeneration project, the investor/developer faces a complex nexus of interests that is not limited to prospective users of its development and the public bodies granting the necessary authorizations for the construction. Urban renewals involve a wide spectrum of stakeholders, which have different expectations and may hinder project success if not managed properly and if their various interests are not fairly balanced.

Some examples of potential conflict between stakeholders may include:

- Heritage preservation versus reuse through conversion of abandoned (or vacant) publicly owned assets versus implementation of interventions aimed to minimize energy consumption (e.g. photovoltaic installation).
- Reducing soil consumption, or even transforming parts of brownfield sites into new green areas, thus concentrating newly built surfaces, potentially altering the urban fabric and increasing construction costs (high-rise buildings), and consequently leading to rent or sale values which would conflict with affordable housing provision.

Whilst stakeholders may be clustered into three groups—developer, government, and public—it's important to adopt a methodological approach throughout the entire urban regeneration process (decision-making, design, construction, use, and management), which, starting from the precise mapping of stakeholders, aims to set up collaborative governance among the groups and build consensus on the sharing of benefits/value thanks to urban renewal.

The implementation of such approach can leverage on the identification of critical barriers (and related management strategies) as depicted in the 2023 study by Z. Liao and M. Liu, "Critical barriers and countermeasures to urban regeneration from the stakeholder perspective: a literature review."[1] They carried out an extensive literature analysis on urban regeneration challenges.

---

[1] Z. Liao and M. Liu, *Critical barriers and countermeasures to urban regeneration from the stakeholder perspective: a literature review*, 2023.

1. *Financial issues*: Urban regeneration projects require huge amounts of capital to carry out the demolition of preexisting structures, environmental remediation, realization of new infrastructures (roads, utilities network, public services, etc.), design of new buildings, and consequent construction. The primary source of capital comes from real estate developers that, due to the high risk level of such projects, aim for significant returns (i.e. double-digit IRR, 2x equity multiple, etc.) but may face challenges when public-oriented uses, such as heritage conservation or rehabilitation projects, are involved, because they might dilute total returns.

   Another item that could discourage developers to invest in urban renewal is represented by its indefinite or protracted lifespan, which could constrain capital turnover, lengthening the payback period.

   In order to solve such issues, the involvement of local government is encouraged. In Italy, for example, the National Recovery and Resilience Plan (NRRP), aiming to support the creation of 60,000 new beds for non-local students' accommodation by mid-2026, provided up to €1.2 billion (i.e. €20,000 per bed) to be distributed to the entities (private as well as public) building them. An administrative fast-track system is also envisaged: for existing buildings (where no cultural restraints are present) it's possible to apply for a change of use to student housing through a certified notice of commencement of works (Segnalazione certificata di inizio attività; SCIA) rather than via more complicated town-planning instruments. Moreover, in case of refurbishment there is a volumetric incentive of 35% of the original volume and no obligation for standard areas and parking lots to be provided.

   With respect to urban renewals benefit distributions, communities generally experience value appreciation following project completions: within the CityLife district (Milan semi-center), average residential sale prices rose from €4700/sqm in 2013 when first residential block was completed, to €9800/sqm in 2022, recording a 110% price increase; the same trend has been experienced for residential for rent, where the average grew from €235/sqm to €360/sqm.

   Whilst developers may obtain huge profits through increased commercial value and local government earn higher tax revenues (through planning fees and property taxes on new built environments), citizens can criticize urban renewals current residents' interests aren't protected and/or there is lack of provision for needed public services and affordable solutions. Therefore, it's crucial to discuss and reach a consensus benefit distribution plan during the decision-making stage of urban renewal projects to avoid hindering, or even interrupting, the project itself.

2. *Demolition and compensation; land redevelopment and planning subsystem*: To enhance land-use intensity, it is often necessary to proceed with the demolition of old and dilapidated buildings that, even if only partially occupied, constitute an obstacle to the realization of real estate developers. In 2007, within the Porta Nuova—Isola regeneration project, a dispute arose between the occupiers of a municipality owned building called Stecca degli Artigiani, which was promised

for sale to the developers Catella-Hines (to realize the so-called Bosco Verticale) in exchange for the provision of new green areas. A citizens' committee, supported by politicians, stood in the way of the developer's bulldozers for days until, after prolonged bargaining, an agreement was reached in order to balance respective interests and find new accommodation for the artisans.

Developers also face challenges in connection with social equality and environment preservation as potential negative externalities for the local neighborhood might arise (e.g. gentrification and pollution). Planning should be overseen by the local authorities to tackle these issues, identifying the appropriate usage of the areas and the synchronization of the development with the existing urban fabric, rationally regulating the plot ratio, building density, mixed use, and so on. The transition toward sustainable urban regeneration can be achieved through the assessment of various planning scenarios that include stakeholders' analysis, coordination, and conflict management. In order to increase engagement on urban renewal projects, it's fundamental that the developer closes the information and knowledge gap as much as possible, highlighting the outcomes of the project for the community and proactively proposing actions that are aimed to satisfy public needs, rather than waiting for claims and consequent bargaining.

The decisional process aimed at sustainability assessment of urban regeneration can be supported by the application of the "Delphi method," which was developed as a forecasting process based on structured communication and multiple rounds of questionnaires sent to a panel of experts. After each round, the results are shown to the experts, who can adjust their answers according to the group response; the ultimate result is considered to be a true consensus of what the group thinks. This method was successfully applied in Latin America in the creation of the eLAC Action Plans, where specific policymaking guidance was determined to foster country development.

In the 2023 study by Z. Pingping, M. A. Zuraini, and A. Yahaya, "Developing indicators for sustainable urban regeneration in historic urban areas: Delphi method and analytic hierarchy process,"[2] the authors developed an indicator-based model that integrates social, economic, environmental, and governance aspects. They discovered that social aspects contribute most to overall sustainability (closely followed by the environmental dimension), whilst building and land use are the most important of the seventeen evaluation categories (followed by economic viability, community involvement, and housing provision), as determined through the survey of international experts.

3. *Public participation and policy support*: Public participation in urban renewal has received increasing attention recently, and residents are becoming more influential, as they may affect public bodies' decision, especially where heritage au-

---

[2] Z. Pingping, M. A. Zuraini, and A. Yahaya, *Developing indicators for sustainable urban regeneration in historic urban areas: Delphi method and analytic hierarchy process*, 2023.

thorities or listed buildings are involved. Various approaches to aid this, including surveys, interviews, workshops, and forums, can be proposed and implemented; however, effective involvement is not straightforward as residents without professional knowledge face difficulties in participating in the decision-making and design stages. They can only indirectly participate in the investigation or consultation of project planning.

Governments and companies usually arrange for (purely symbolic) public participation in order to facilitate the process of urban regeneration rather than absorb the residents' demands and opinions. Superficial involvement, such as simple consultation, informal discussion, and passive participation modes, reduces residents' ability to participate in redevelopment. As a result, residents have no voice in negotiations of interest distribution during the process of regeneration projects, and authentic voices and suggestions from the public might not be heard.

Urban regeneration policies must consider that the sustainability of the development may be negatively affected by ambiguous descriptions, abuse of "public use" issues with defective law articles, and a lack of controls on the demolition of heritage buildings. Policies and planning tend to focus on physical, economic, and social issues, while limited attention is paid to health equality, spatial justice, and vulnerable groups; consequently, in many "top-down" urban redevelopments it can be observed that certain groups, such as the elderly, low-income, and less influential people, are excluded. The urban policies framework should be sufficiently fine-grained to take into consideration continuously changing local demand and flexible enough to avoid creating new barriers while solving a specific one; in this context, a pragmatic partnership between local administration, developers, and public communities is needed to overcome the constraints of rigid regulations.

4. *Social inequality*: Uneven development between renewal and non-renewal areas can be the result of spatial inequality: residents in renovated neighborhoods have more access to public goods and services and live in a more comfortable environment compared to residents in communities without regeneration plans; this gap lowers some residents' sense of social well-being.

   Another concern is represented by gentrification—the process of lower-income residential areas transforming into middle-class neighborhoods through changes in residential use and displacement. This is happening not just in the least appealing areas of the city but also in higher-income communities. Gentrification has positive outcomes as the reshaping of the urban fabric may lead to a better environment, and to enhanced services and infrastructures; however, it also leads to surging housing prices.

To overcome the challenges represented by the critical barriers described, it is necessary to promote and implement effective public participation and multidimensional collaboration between stakeholders, aligning the interests of the public and private sectors. Figure 11.3 recaps the linkage between critical items and the key factors—

Figure 11.3 Linkages Between Critical Barriers, Key Factors, and Research Directions in Urban Regeneration

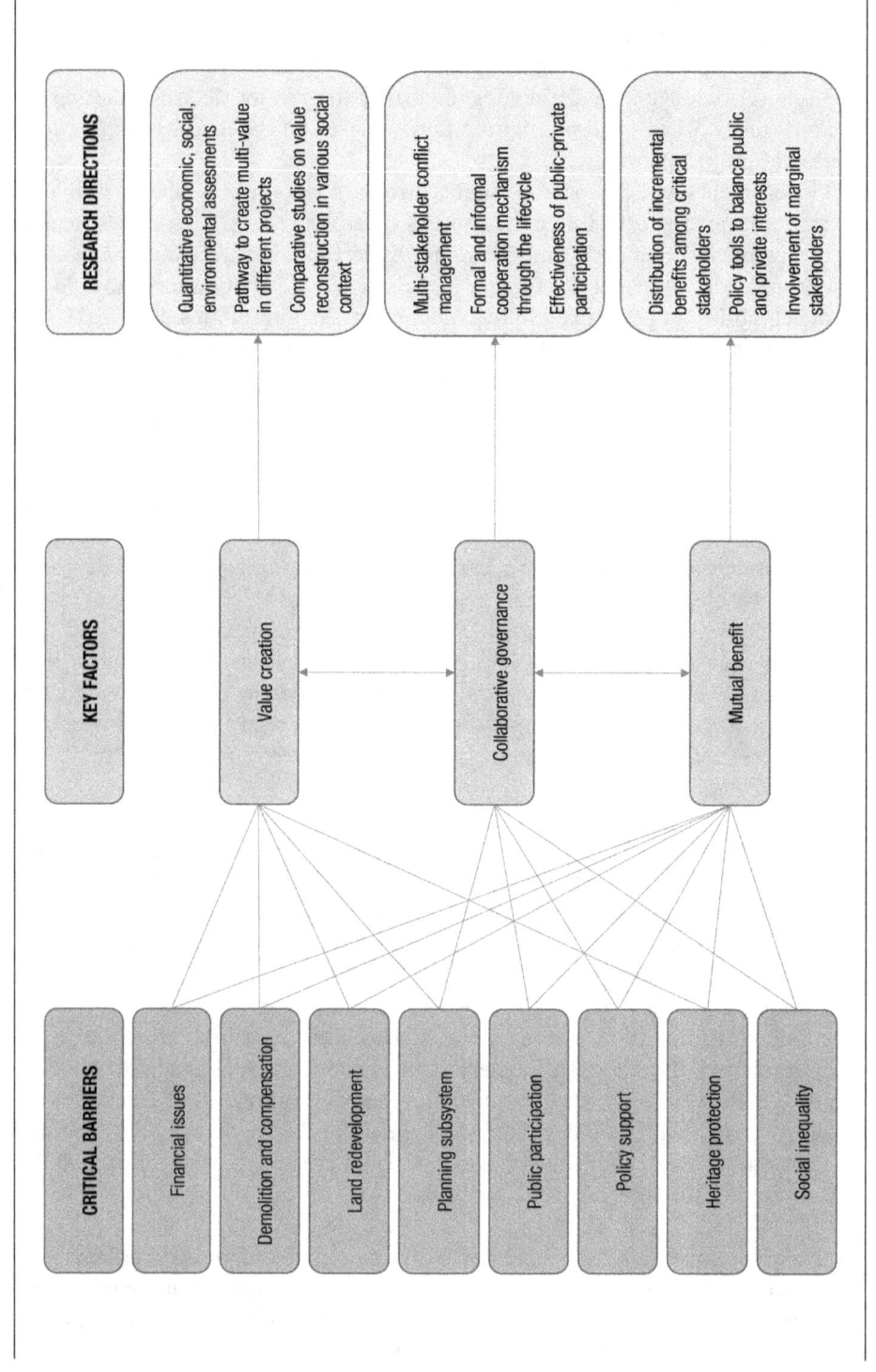

value creation, collaborative governance, and mutual benefit—identifying areas and actions to be further studied/implemented to enhance the valuation and success of urban regeneration projects.

Whilst institutional developers, in order to comply with regulatory requirements and the need to release sustainability balance sheets, might take into consideration the implementation of actions aimed to address all key factors, it's the responsibility of local government to create a supportive environment (through incentive policies and regulatory systems) and promote PPPs establishment in order to attract and leverage social investment. To overcome potential mismatch between supply of new product and demand by existing and future residents, public participation should be incentivized throughout the entire life cycle of renewal projects, by setting up collaborative governance. Mutual benefits can be achieved by establishing coordination mechanisms and negotiation platforms to anticipate potential conflicts between stakeholders and mitigate them.

11.4 Urban regeneration value creation and measurement

As anticipated in Chapter 10, urban regeneration projects are critical for revitalizing cities, enhancing livability, and maximizing economic, social, and environmental value. In recent years, several trends encompassing innovative approaches to design, sustainability, community engagement, technology integration, and adaptive reuse have emerged, aiming at maximizing value creation:

1. *Sustainability and green infrastructure*: Sustainability has become a central focus in urban regeneration projects, with an emphasis on incorporating green infrastructure to mitigate environmental impacts and enhance resilience. Research by by Jennifer R. Wolch, Jason Byrne, and Joshua P. Newell (2014)[3] in "Urban green space, public health, and environmental justice: the challenge of making cities 'just green enough'" emphasizes the importance of green spaces in promoting public health and equity. Integrating features like green roofs, urban parks, and permeable pavements not only improves aesthetics but also provides ecosystem services, reduces heat island effects, and manages stormwater runoff, thus maximizing the ecological value of regeneration projects.
2. *Mixed-use development*: This has gained in popularity as a strategy for maximizing land-use efficiency and creating vibrant urban environments. Articles like "The rise of mixed-use development" by Arthur C. Nelson (2018) discuss how combining residential, commercial, and recreational spaces within a single development fosters social interaction, supports local businesses, and reduces depend-

---

[3] Wolch, J. R., Byrne, J., & Newell, J. P. (2014). *Urban green space, public health, and environmental justice: The challenge of making cities 'just green enough'*. Landscape and Urban Planning, 125, 234-244. https://doi.org/10.1016/j.landurbplan.2014.01.017

ency on cars. Mixed-use developments promote walkability, reduce commute times, and contribute to a sense of community, thereby enhancing the overall value of urban regeneration initiatives.
3. *Adaptive reuse and heritage preservation*: Adaptive reuse involves repurposing existing structures for new functions, preserving architectural heritage, and reducing waste. Research by the Architectural Heritage Center (2016)[4] highlights the economic, cultural, and environmental benefits of adaptive reuse in "The benefits of building reuse." By preserving historic buildings and integrating them into regeneration projects, cities can retain their unique character, attract tourists, and stimulate economic activity while minimizing the environmental footprint associated with new construction.
4. *Community-centered design*: Engaging local communities in the planning and implementation of regeneration projects is essential for ensuring their long-term success and relevance. Articles such *as* "Community engagement in urban regeneration: the case of the Olympic Village in East London" by Matthew Carmona**,** Claudio de Magalhães**,** and Lucy Hammond[5] underscore the importance of participatory processes in fostering social cohesion and addressing community needs. Empowering residents to contribute ideas, concerns, and aspirations helps create inclusive, people-centric spaces that maximize social value and promote a sense of ownership and belonging.
5. *Smart infrastructure and technology integration*: The integration of smart technologies and digital infrastructure enables cities to optimize resource allocation, enhance efficiency, and improve quality of life. Research by by Andrea Caragliu, Chiara Del Bo, and Peter Nijkamp (2011)[6] examines the role of information and communication technologies (ICTs) in addressing urban challenges and fostering sustainable development. From smart grids and intelligent transportation systems to IoT-enabled sensors and data analytics, leveraging technology in regeneration projects enhances connectivity, accessibility, and resource management, ultimately maximizing economic and environmental value.
6. *Health and wellness initiatives*: Promoting health and wellness has emerged as a key consideration in urban regeneration, with a focus on creating environments that support active lifestyles, mental well-being, and equitable access to healthcare services. Articles such as "The impact of urban form on mental health in San Francisco, CA" by Andrew R. Maroko, Kristen Pavilonis, Jared L. Bourgoine, and Christine Grady (2018)[7] explore the relationship among urban design, public

---

[4] Architectural Heritage Center (2016). *The benefits of building reuse.* Architectural Heritage Center.

[5] Carmona, M., de Magalhães, C., & Hammond, L. (2015). *Community engagement in urban regeneration: The case of the Olympic Village in East London*. Journal of Urban Design, 20(3), 326-348. https://doi.org/10.1080/13574809.2015.1044505

[6] Caragliu, A., Del Bo, C., & Nijkamp, P. (2011). Smart cities in Europe. Journal of Urban Technology, 18(2), 65-82. https://doi.org/10.1080/10630732.2011.601117

[7] Maroko, A. R., Pavilonis, K., Bourgoine, J. L., & Grady, C. (2018). *The impact of urban form on mental health in San Francisco, CA*. Urban Science, 2(2), 22. https://doi.org/10.3390/urbansci2020022

health, and social equity. By prioritizing features like pedestrian-friendly infrastructure, recreational amenities, and access to green spaces, regeneration projects can foster healthier communities and maximize human capital, thereby increasing overall value.

7. *Equity and inclusive growth*: Addressing social disparities and promoting inclusive growth is essential for ensuring that urban regeneration benefits all members of society. Research by Karen Chapple and Miriam Zuk (2016)[8] in "Creating equitable, healthy, and sustainable urban regions" examines strategies for promoting equity and social justice in urban planning and development. Measures such as affordable housing mandates, workforce development programs, and anti-displacement policies help mitigate the negative consequences of gentrification and ensure that regeneration projects contribute to inclusive prosperity.

By adopting such strategies, cities can create vibrant, resilient, and inclusive urban environments that enhance quality of life for residents while preserving natural and cultural resources for future generations. Measuring the value created by urban regeneration projects requires a comprehensive approach that considers economic, social, environmental, and cultural factors. Several models and frameworks exist to assess the impact and value generated by regeneration initiatives.

One commonly used model is the triple bottom line (TBL) framework, which evaluates projects based on their economic, social, and environmental outcomes. The TBL framework provides a holistic view of value creation, recognizing that success is not solely determined by financial metrics but also by contributions to community well-being and environmental sustainability. It's often referred to as the 3 P's model, since it takes into consideration the impacts on People, Planet, and Profit and the interactions between the three pillars.

Figures 11.4 and 11.5 show that the three dimensions are present at the same time but will change their momentum and dominance over time: businesses that have been profitably operating in a degenerative environment, with fossil fuel dependence and shareholder primacy, are now facing a so-called poly-crisis or even perma-crisis. To overcome such challenges, business models are evolving to deliver net-zero emissions and circular economies, and are starting to value the externalities that they create as either positive or negative with respect to the planet and the people.

Another model frequently employed is SROI methodology, which quantifies the social, environmental, and economic benefits generated by a project relative to the resources invested. SROI analysis involves identifying stakeholders, mapping outcomes, valuing impacts, and calculating the ratio of social value created per unit of investment. By monetizing both tangible and intangible benefits, SROI offers insights into the broader societal value of regeneration projects beyond purely financial returns:

---

[8] Chapple, K., & Zuk, M. (2016). *Creating equitable, healthy, and sustainable urban regions*. Regional Science Policy & Practice, 8(1), 11-24. https://doi.org/10.1111/rsp3.12085

SROI = (TV + ITV)/(T + M) where:

TV + ITV is the tangible and intangible value to the community

T is the total time invested

M is the total amount of money spent

Figure 11.4   **The Triple Bottom Line (TBL) Framework**

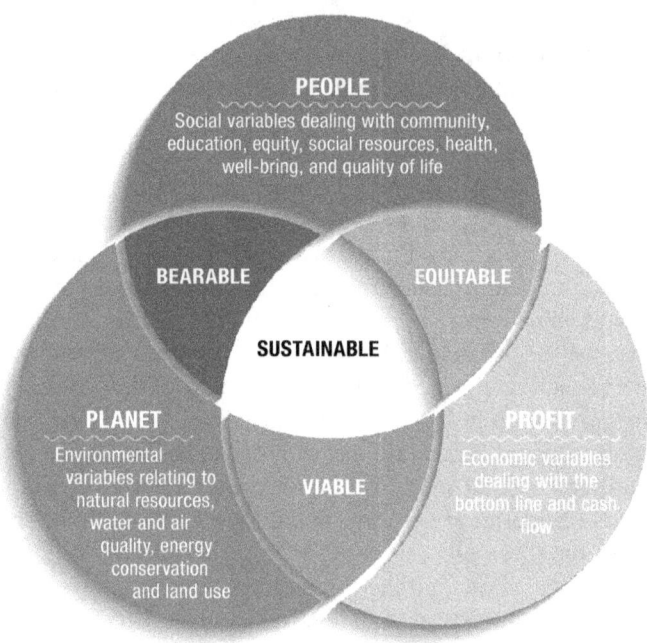

Additionally, the cost–benefit analysis (CBA) approach is commonly used to assess the economic viability of regeneration projects by comparing the costs of implementation to the anticipated benefits over time. CBA considers both monetary and non-monetary costs and benefits, allowing decision-makers to weigh different options and prioritize investments based on their overall net value to society.

Furthermore, frameworks such as the UN SDGs provide a set of universal objectives and indicators that can be used to evaluate the contribution of regeneration projects to global sustainability targets. By aligning project outcomes with specific SDGs, cities can demonstrate their commitment to addressing pressing social, environmental, and economic challenges while maximizing value for all stakeholders.

Selecting the most appropriate model for measuring the value of urban regeneration depends on the specific context, objectives, and stakeholders involved. Integrating multiple models and perspectives can provide a more comprehensive under-

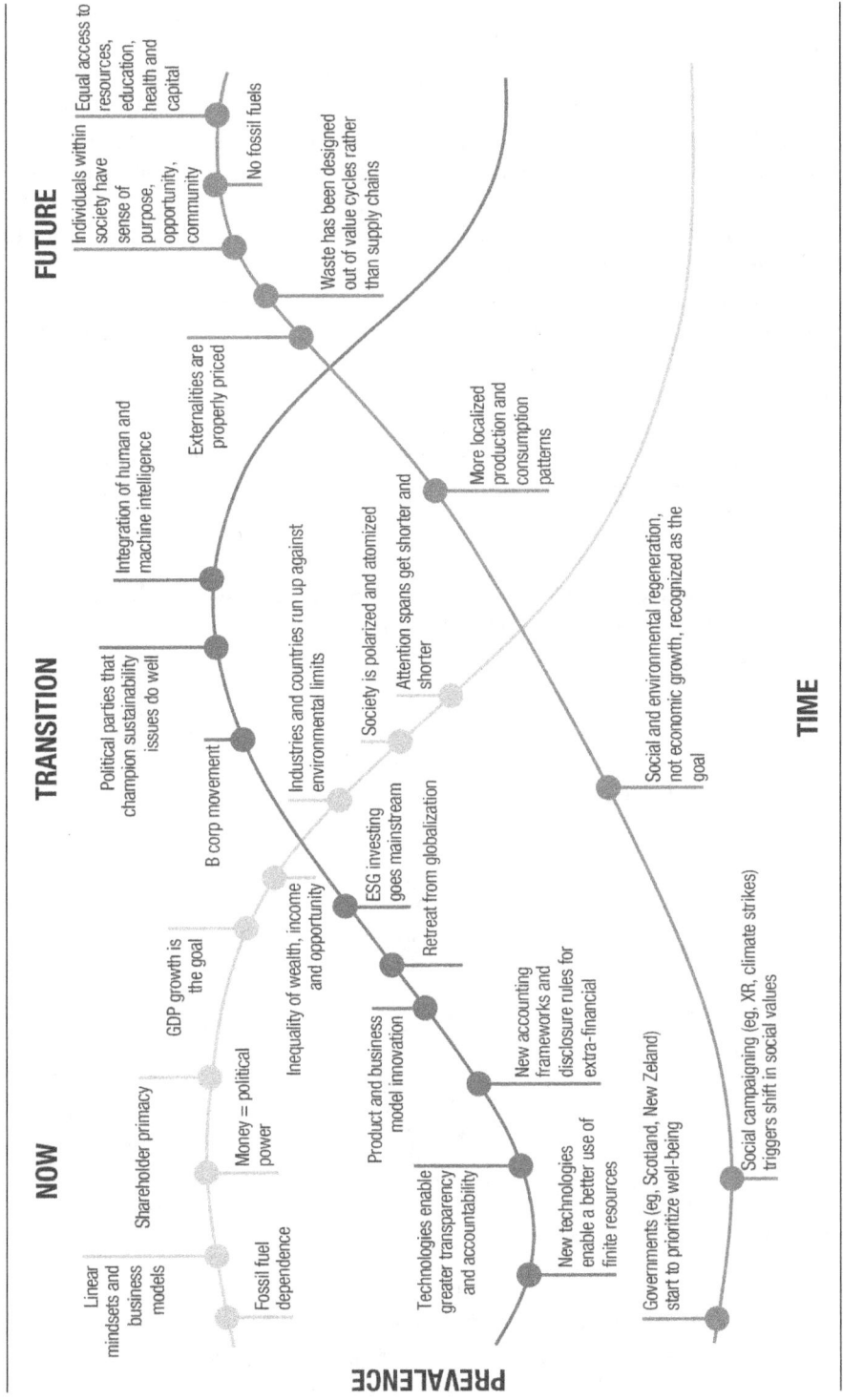

Figure 11.5 The Evolution of Business Models Over Time

diverse impacts and value created by regeneration projects, thereby informing decision-making and guiding future urban development efforts.

As we delve deeper into the realm of urban regeneration, the methodology for estimating positive externalities becomes increasingly crucial. Positive externalities, both social and environmental, are essential for maximizing the value generated by urban regeneration projects. The methodology involves a detailed comparison of two scenarios: the current regulatory context with limited developer commitment (As Is) and a future scenario with a new regulatory framework and long-term developer commitment, aligning interests fully (To Be).

Key dimensions of this methodology include identifying relevant services and classifying them into environmental and social categories. Benefits are estimated in terms of cost reduction, income generation from new jobs, and reduced medical expenses for services with an economic impact, and advantages like time savings and social benefits for services without direct economic impact.

The analysis carried out by SDA (Scuola di Direzione Aziendale) Bocconi School of Management in 2024 of the build-to-rent (BtR) model being developed by Lendlease in the Milan Innovation District (MIND) highlights significant increases in

Figure 11.6 **Positive Externalities of Build-to-Rent (BtR) Model in the Milan Innovation District (MIND)**

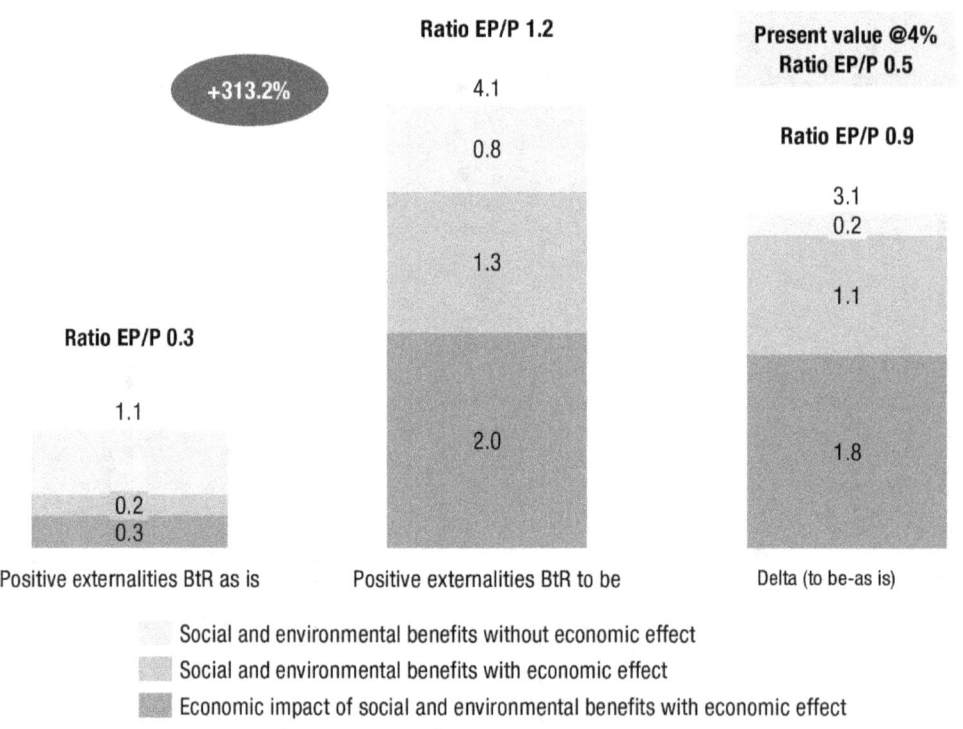

positive externalities in the To Be scenario. The study finds a substantial improvement in social and environmental outcomes by over 300% compared to a standard model (Figure 11.6).

In conclusion, the BtR model showcases how innovative approaches in urban regeneration can yield significant economic, social, and environmental benefits. A consistent regulatory framework is vital to avoid market penalties for energy-inefficient assets and ensure stable long-term investments. This study underscores the importance of aligning regulatory and developer interests to maximize the positive impacts of green housing initiatives.

11.5 An Italian example: the case of MilanoSesto urban regeneration

MilanoSesto is a groundbreaking urban regeneration project located in Sesto San Giovanni, a former industrial area bordering Northern Milan municipality. This ambitious initiative aims to transform the ex-Falck iron production sites, spanning 1.5 million square meters, into a vibrant urban space. It seeks to promote sustainability, economic growth, and social inclusivity by integrating newly built residential and commercial assets (1 million square meters), healthcare facilities (135,000 square meters) with extensive green spaces (45 hectares), through a masterplan developed by Foster+Partners, which leverages the following SDGs (Figure 11.7).

The following paragraphs summarize the results of a study carried out by The European House—Ambrosetti and presented at Cernobbio Forum in September 2021, highlighting the impacts and value created by both the Unione 0 lot (the first private development, spanning over 155,000 square meters) and the broader MilanoSesto project, emphasizing the significant public and private investments involved.

The MilanoSesto project, particularly the Unione 0 lot, is poised to generate substantial economic benefits. The investment in Unione 0 includes approximately €370 million to be spent as capital expenditure, which would activate an additional approximately €600 million in indirect impacts and approximately €85 million in induced impacts. Indirect impacts refer to the economic effects that occur through the supply chain due to the initial investment. For example, the Unione 0 investment will activate various industries and sectors that supply goods and services to the construction and development activities. This includes the value generated by suppliers and sub-suppliers involved in the project. Induced impacts are the economic effects that result from increased spending by employees and workers who benefit from the direct and indirect effects. When workers employed directly by the project or indirectly through suppliers spend their wages on goods and services, it stimulates further economic activity in the local economy.

In summary, indirect impacts refer to the economic activity generated within the supply chain due to the project's investment, while induced impacts pertain to the broader economic activity stimulated by the increased spending of wages by those directly or indirectly employed by the project. This results in a total economic turnover of approximately €1.1 billion; the consequent multiplier effect of 2.8x means

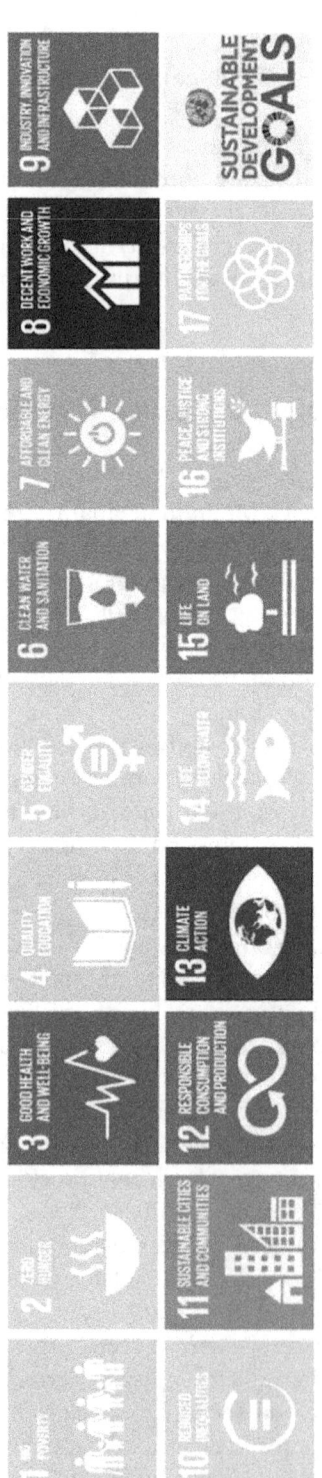

Figure 11.7 United Nations Sustainable Development Goals (SDGs) Integrated in the MilanoSesto Project

that for every €1 invested directly, an additional €1.8 in economic activity would be generated. Such a significant economic stimulus is expected to reverberate through various sectors, driving local businesses and attracting new investments.

Furthermore, Unione 0's development would contribute significantly to local tax revenues. The project is expected to generate over €1.5 million annually in IMU (Imposta Municipale Unica; property tax) revenues and €900,000 in TARI (Tassa sui Rifiuti; waste tax) revenues. Additionally, it is expected to increase the town's IRPEF (Imposta sul Reddito delle Persone Fisiche; personal income tax) revenues by around €170,000 annually due to new residents moving into the area. Overall, these taxes could increase the municipality's financial resources by €2.6 million per year, representing 6.2% of its tax revenues. This influx of funds will enable the local government to enhance public services and infrastructure, further improving the quality of life for residents and new city users.

The construction and development activities associated with Unione 0 will create a substantial number of jobs. Direct investment would generate approximately 500 full-time equivalent (FTE) jobs, with an additional 1100 jobs created indirectly through the supply chain, and 600 jobs resulting from increased local consumption. In total, the project will provide for around 2200 jobs. This impact on employment is a crucial aspect of the project's contribution to the local economy and social structure. The creation of new jobs will not only reduce local unemployment rates but also attract skilled professionals to the area, fostering a more dynamic and diverse workforce.

Public investments play a crucial role in the overall MilanoSesto project. The total investment in the project amounts to €3.5 billion, of which €450 million is to be invested by the public sector. This public investment is essential for the development of the Città della Salute e della Ricerca (CdSR), which will house two major healthcare institutions—the National Institution for Tumors and the Carlo Besta Neurological Institute—with a total of 700 beds. The integration of these prestigious institutions will position MilanoSesto as a center of medical excellence, attracting healthcare professionals and researchers from around the world. This healthcare cluster will not only provide high-quality medical services to residents but also stimulate further economic and academic activities in the region. Public funds are also allocated for the construction of public works benefiting the community, including infrastructure and urban development.

MilanoSesto is committed to sustainability, with Unione 0 lot striving to achieve LEED (Leadership in Energy and Environmental Design) Gold and Platinum certifications. These certifications are based on a range of criteria including site sustainability, water efficiency, energy and atmosphere, materials and resources, and indoor environmental quality. The project also aims for the WELL Building Standard, ensuring that office spaces support health and well-being. These certifications reflect the project's dedication to creating environmentally responsible and resource-efficient buildings, setting a benchmark for future urban developments.

The MilanoSesto project is not just about economic and environmental benefits; it also focuses on enhancing social cohesion and community well-being. The regeneration of the Unione 0 lot will heal a long-standing urban wound, starting to reclaim a space that has been abandoned for over twenty-five years. This renewal will address issues related to urban decay, security, and the attractiveness of the area. By transforming the abandoned Falck sites into a dynamic, mixed-use neighborhood, MilanoSesto aims to boost local dynamism and create a community-oriented environment that operates around the clock. The project will reinvigorate the local area, making it a desirable place to live, work, and visit.

The project will introduce a BTR model, offering an integrated residential experience with professional management and value-added services such as fitness centers, coworking spaces, and communal areas. This approach aims to foster a strong sense of community and long-term residence among tenants. The BTR model is particularly attractive to young professionals and families seeking flexible and high-quality housing options. By providing comprehensive services and amenities, the project aims to create a supportive and connected community, enhancing the overall quality of life for its residents.

MilanoSesto is conceived as a smart city, leveraging advanced technology to enhance urban living. The Unione 0 lot will feature a network of sensors and data systems to monitor and manage various aspects of urban life, including mobility, environmental conditions, and public safety. This digital infrastructure will enable real-time data collection and analysis, facilitating efficient urban management and improving the quality of life for residents. Smart city technologies will also support sustainability efforts by optimizing resource use and reducing waste.

The Unione 0 lot and the Health & Research City will generate an additional €180 million or so in local consumption due to increased activities and population in the area. This increase is comparable to the annual expenses of 33,000 families. The Unione 0 complex will house 800 new families, employ 4750 workers in offices and retail spaces, and attract 160,000 hotel guests per year. The CdSR hospital will deliver 500,000 day surgery services annually, employ 2700 workers, and expect 4000 daily visitors. In terms of additional consumption, this will translate to €22 million in the Sesto San Giovanni area, €54 million in the City of Milan, and €107 million in the Lombardy region (Figure 11.8).

Unione 0 affordable housing will have 285 units, primarily for professionals and families of the CdSR. In the Metropolitan City of Milan, 65% of households pay rent exceeding 40% of their available income. The BTR model includes amenities and services valued at approximately €250 to €500 per month, which constitutes 8% to 16% of the net income of families in Lombardy.

Affordable housing in this project offers 62% more livable space with equivalent rent compared to the Milan average, potentially saving households €9900 annually compared to living in Milan city center. Rent rates are 39% to 52% lower for equal square footage. Affordability is improved, with 29% of households in the area (over 66,000) able to afford a studio, 25% able to afford a one-bedroom, and 13% of couples able to afford a one-bedroom unit. The project also includes a range of amenities. A sixty-spot kindergarten will be reserved for new residents and Health & Research City employees. Additionally, fitness areas, indoor sport facilities, and other common and smart-working areas are planned for the Private Rented Sector (PRS) and affordable housing units (Figure 11.9).

Figure 11.8 Economic and Social Impact of Unione 0 and Health & Research City in MilanoSesto

Unione 0

800 new families

4750 workers in the offices and retail spaces in Unione 0

160000 hotel guests per year

CdSR

500000 day surgery services delivered per year

2700 workers in the CdSR

4000 daily visitors expected

Consumption

€22 M additional consumption in the Sesto San Giovanni Area

€54 M additional consumption in the City of Milan

€107 M additional consumption in the Lombardy region

Figure 11.9 Benefits of Affordable Housing and Amenities in the MilanoSesto Project

Affordable housing

+62% sqm of livable space with equal rent (vs. Milan average)

From −39% to −52% of rent rates with equal square footage

€ 9900 potential annual saving per household (vs. Milan city center)

Affordability

+29% of households in the area (>66000) could afford a studio

+25% of households in the area can afford a one bedroom

+13% of couples in the area can afford a one bedroom

Amenities

A sixty-spot kindergarten will be reserved for new residents and Health & Research City employees

Fitness areas, indoor sport facilities and other areas are envisaged by the project

PRS and affordable housing will have amenities, including common and smart-working areas

The MilanoSesto urban regeneration project, specifically the Unione 0 lot, exemplifies a comprehensive approach to urban development. By integrating economic growth, environmental sustainability, and social inclusivity, MilanoSesto aims to create a thriving urban space that benefits residents, businesses, and the broader community. This project sets a new standard for urban regeneration, demonstrating how innovative and sustainable urban planning can revitalize communities and drive long-term growth.

11.6 Maximizing value through urban regeneration

Urban regeneration stands as a pivotal force in reshaping cities for the better, aiming to generate economic prosperity, enhance social cohesion, and foster environmental sustainability. Across the globe, cities are embracing innovative approaches to transform neglected or underutilized areas into vibrant, inclusive, and resilient urban landscapes.

By integrating sustainability principles, mixed-use development strategies, adaptive reuse practices, community engagement initiatives, technological advancements, and equity-focused interventions, urban regeneration projects aspire to create thriving urban ecosystems that cater to the diverse needs of their inhabitants.

Evaluation frameworks such as the TBL, SROI, and CBA, alongside alignment with the UN SDGs, offer valuable tools for assessing the holistic impact and value generated by these regeneration endeavors. Through rigorous evaluation, cities can gain insights into the tangible and intangible benefits of their regeneration efforts, guiding future decision-making and resource allocation.

The MilanoSesto urban regeneration project in Sesto San Giovanni near Milan exemplifies the transformative potential of urban regeneration. Through its commitment to sustainability, economic revitalization, social inclusion, healthcare integration, and smart city infrastructure, MilanoSesto emerges as a beacon of progressive urban development.

In essence, urban regeneration projects represent a cornerstone in the journey toward creating livable, equitable, and sustainable cities. By embracing a comprehensive and collaborative approach, cities can unlock the full potential of regeneration initiatives, fostering vibrant communities and ensuring a brighter future for all urban dwellers.

11.7 Conclusions and future perspectives

The intricate interplay among value creation, strategic transformation, and M&A in the infrastructure sector is a testament to the dynamism and complexity of today's global economic environment. As explored, M&A serves not just as a tool for financial restructuring or market consolidation, but as a strategic lever for transformative growth, innovation, and sustainability in infrastructure development and management.

Key insights include:

- *Strategic synergies*: The success of M&A in the infrastructure sector hinges on identifying and realizing strategic synergies, whether in operational efficiencies, technological advancements, market expansion, or sustainability initiatives.

- *Risk and regulation*: Navigating the multifaceted risks and regulatory landscapes is paramount. Effective risk management and regulatory compliance are not just safeguards but enablers of value creation and market differentiation.
- *Sustainability as a value driver*: Increasingly, sustainability considerations are moving to the forefront of strategic M&A decision-making. Sustainable, green infrastructure projects not only meet regulatory and societal expectations but also offer long-term profitability and resilience.

Looking ahead, the future of infrastructure M&A is likely to be shaped by several evolving dynamics:

- *Technological integration*: As digital transformation accelerates, the integration of innovative technologies within infrastructure assets will become a key competitive differentiator, driving efficiencies, enhancing services, and opening new revenue streams.
- *Cross-sector partnerships*: The blurring of lines between sectors, such as energy, telecommunications, and transportation, will encourage cross-sector M&A, creating new opportunities for integrated infrastructure solutions and services.
- *Global challenges, local solutions*: Global challenges such as climate change, urbanization, and social equity will demand localized, innovative solutions. M&A strategies will need to be adaptable, focusing on local needs while leveraging global resources and expertise.
- *Resilience and adaptability*: The capacity for resilience and adaptability in the face of economic, environmental, and geopolitical uncertainties will be a critical measure of success. Infrastructure investments will increasingly be evaluated for their ability to withstand and adapt to these challenges.

In conclusion, the role of M&A in the infrastructure sector is set to grow in both scale and significance, driven by the urgent need for sustainable, resilient, and innovative infrastructure solutions. As we move forward, the ability to strategically navigate this complex landscape will determine the success of companies and the sustainability of infrastructure developments. The future of infrastructure M&A holds both challenges and opportunities, but above all, it offers the potential for transformative impact on economies, societies, and the environment.

12 Value Creation and Post-Merger Integration in M&A and Private Equity
by *Tommaso Nastasi*

12.1 Introduction and importance of PMI

With over 60% of M&A deals failing due to poor integration, PMI is crucial to the success of an M&A deal, regardless of the type of acquirer or target. History shows how theoretically successful M&A deals have become failure benchmarks because of poor integration. It is at the exact moment of an M&A signing that PMI starts and that the situation becomes particularly challenging (Figure 12.1).

12.2 Key challenges and strategic considerations

If PMI integration is essential to the success of an M&A deal, it is therefore necessary to understand how to make a PMI a success. PMI is the most crucial phase of the entire merger or acquisition process: this is the moment when all the previous efforts and all the previous precautions can be definitely ruined. In order not to ruin all the efforts, integration must rhyme with value creation. In fact, by observing and analyzing the main reasons behind the failure of several M&A deals, one can quickly notice that PMI constitutes one of the main points explaining these failures. The top five root causes of deal disappointments or difficulties are:

- due diligence failed to highlight critical issues;
- overestimated synergies from combining the companies;
- failure to recognize insufficient strategic fit;
- failure to assess cultural fit; and
- hit problems integrating management teams and retaining talent.

Indeed, most of the main difficulties are related to integration, confirming that PMI is a very hot topic in M&A processes as far as it can destroy all previous efforts.

In view of this, the main purpose of this chapter is to provide specific business guidelines on how to approach and manage the stream of value creation and PMI in M&A both for private equity and corporate.

An effective PMI is critical to realizing the full value of an acquisition. A successful integration involves seamlessly transitioning the acquired entity into the company's systems, processes, and culture by leveraging synergies and executing a defined strategy to create value and enhance the corporate brand.

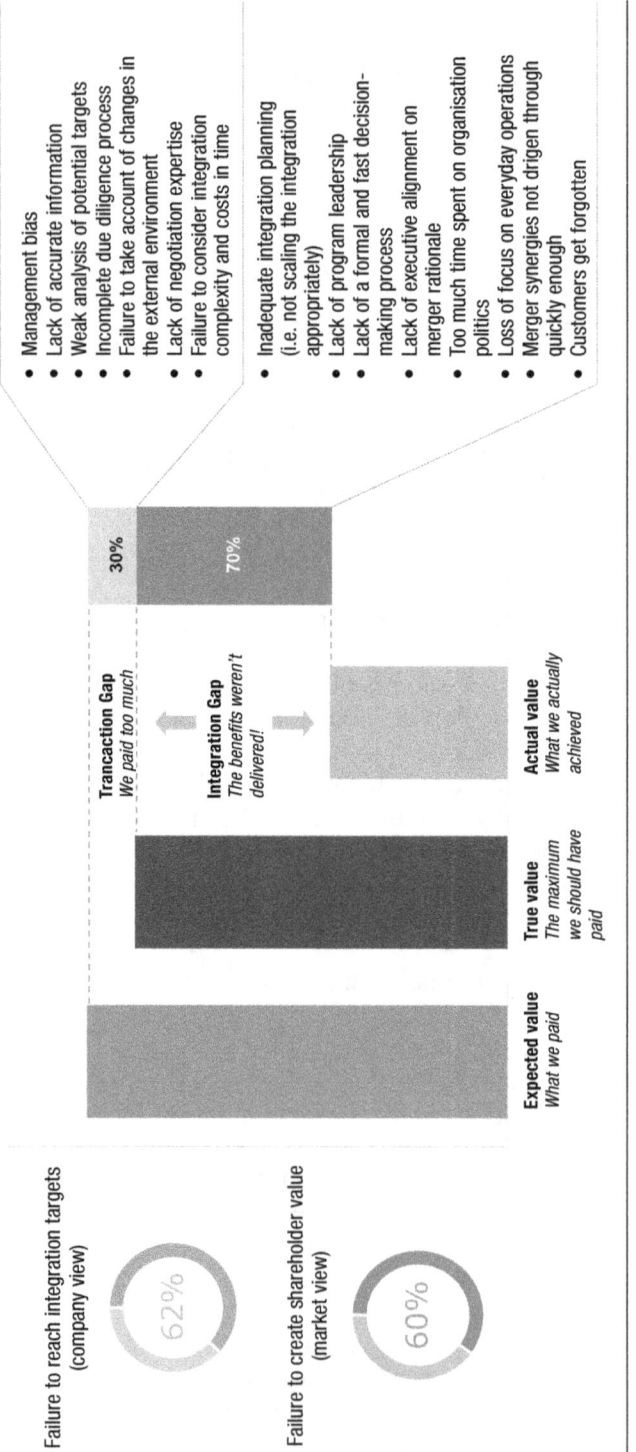

Figure 12.1 M&A transactions: failing to deliver expected results

Essentially, a successful integration will not only benefit the company but will also create value for shareholders. If an integration strategy is not properly planned and executed, the consequences can involve the loss of acquired employees, uncaptured synergies, and missed revenue and EBIT targets.

12.3 Steps for a successful integration

In order to achieve a successful integration, a variety of items must be understood and taken into consideration, such as:

- *Why*? What is the strategic rationale of the deal? What are the deal value drivers? What synergies exist and how will we achieve or exceed them?
- *When*? When will the integration process begin? What are investors' expectations about when value will be delivered by the acquisition? What parts of the integration will take the most time and consideration?
- *Who*? Who are the key company players? Who will be the integration lead? What key personnel will be involved to execute the plan?
- *What*? What are the characteristics of the acquired entity? Will it be fully integrated or stand alone? Have the cultural fit, processes, systems, and resources of the target been closely examined and incorporated in the plan?
- *How*? What steps need to be taken to ensure we comply with corporate policies? How will the processes and systems be integrated? Is there a communication plan in place that will effectively explain the acquisition internally and externally?

Every acquisition is different and there is no standard answer for how to successfully integrate an acquired company into an existing business.

Figure 12.2 shows the main steps of integration process within a typical timeline of M&A deal. All steps in the integration process should be considered early and aligned with the acquisition strategy and transaction timeline.

The full process is divided into main twelve streams, but the steps are not necessarily sequential as many run in parallel. The main principle is that the formulation of the integration strategy needs to start in the early acquisition stages, supporting the business case preparation for Day 1.

Figure 12.3 shows how integration planning is tied into the different milestones/gates within the deal cycle.

In other words, launching an integration and value creation strategy from the beginning is an important critical factor when creating the baseline for a successful deal.

In fact, a common mistake made within a deal is to approach the due diligence and PMI as separate and distinct activities; it is instead crucial to approach both as a joint exercise, to avoid introducing unnecessary risk during the transaction. Figure 12.4 illustrates how mitigate the risk within M&A from the start to the close/end of the transaction.

190 Part III – M&A and Private Equity in Practice

Figure 12.2 Step integration process and timeline

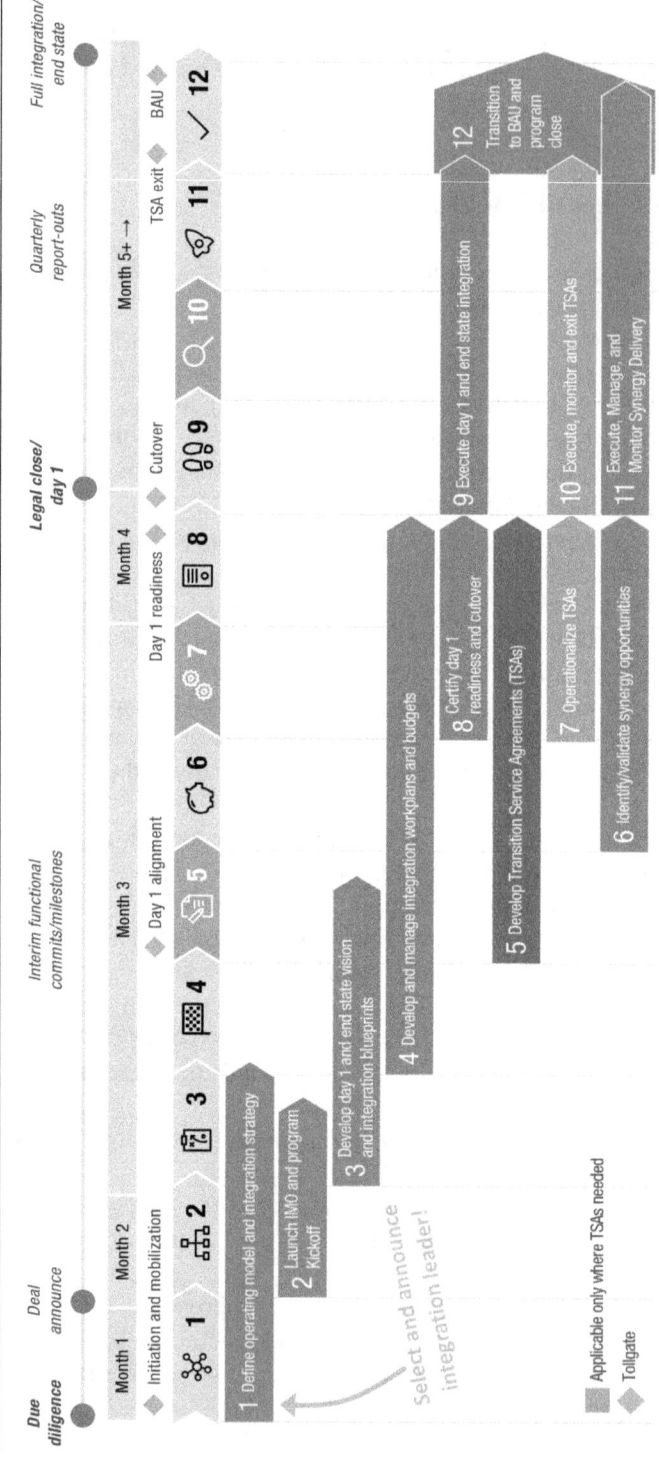

12 Value Creation and Post-Merger Integration in M&A and Private Equity

Figure 12.3 Tying integration into the acquisition process

Strategic Planning Process → Target Identified (Gate 0) → Indication of Interest (Gate 1) → Engage & Study (Gate 2) → Develop Offer → Negotiate (Gate 3) → Agree & Announce (Gate 4) → Close & Execute (Gate 5)

Gate	Description	What is decided	Who	Triggered activities	Post gate owner
0	Theme gate	Set key strategic themes to focus development efforts	CEO/ELT	Proactive theme development	CSD and BA LOB/ BD VPs
1	Interest gate	Begin pursuit – Establish sufficient evidence and interest to engage with entity	BA EVP and CSD	Complete strategic rationale, prelim business care, integration concept, synergy and risk assessments	Deal Executive and CSD
2	Diligence gate	Initial engagement and Due Diligence – Confirm sufficient strategic commitment and interest conviction	BA EVP/CSD (CEO-CFO Notification)	Fully test strategic rationale, refine business care, develop integration synergy, and risk-mitigation plans	Deal Executive, CSD and Diligence Team
3	Negotiation authority (EO review)	Approve proceeding – Establish valuation objective, transaction structure, business/synergy case and integration approach	Delegation Level (CEO-CFO Notice if not Authority)	Make offer, close open difference items, work toward definitive agreements	CSD, Corporate Legal and Integration Lead
4	Final approval (EO approval)	Review and approve changes from negotiation authority, if any	Delegation Level (CEO-CFO notice if not authority)	Finalize and execute definitive agreements, Develop integration metrics	Deal Executive, CSD and Corporate Legal
5	Value capture gate	Verify value creation achieved, modify approach as required	ELT	Periodically review performance to business case and synergy plan	EVP, Integration Lead, CSD

Figure 12.4 M&A risk mitigation

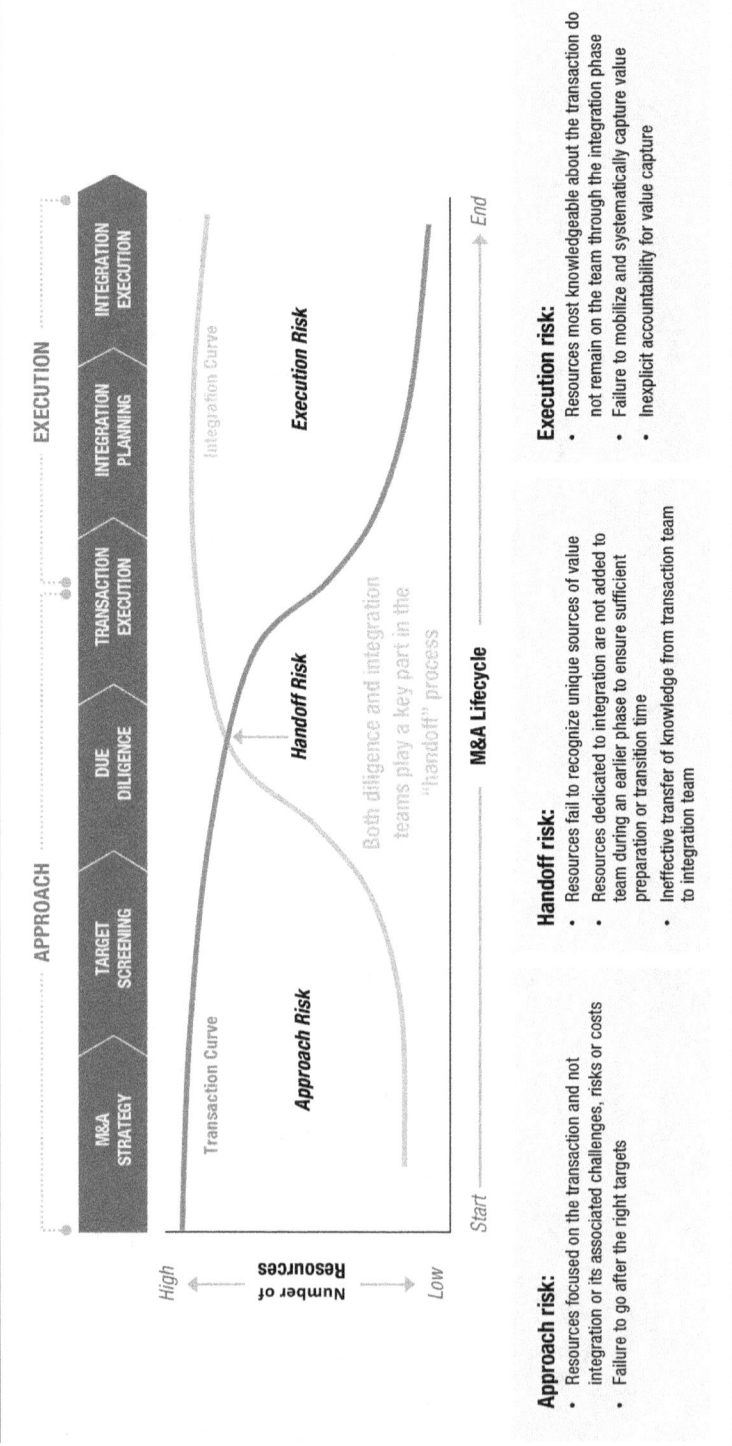

12 Value Creation and Post-Merger Integration in M&A and Private Equity

Figure 12.5 **Integration approach**

	Full integration	Partial integration	Stand-alone integration
Description	Integrating all aspects (e.g. processes, reporting relationships, policies and procedures) of the target into the acquiring firm's model	Developing flexible, transaction-specific integration strategies that meet the specific requirements and needs of the target and the buyer	Leaving the core operational and organizational aspects of the target intact after the transaction is executed
Pros	• Organizational consistency • Greatest influence over cost synergies	• Ensures intrinsic value attractiveness is preserved • Facilitates "partner of choice" reputation	• Facilitates retention of key personnel • Greater likelihood for realizing revenue synergies
Cons	• May destroy the aspects of the target that made them attractive in the first place • May result in exodus of key personnel	• Requires investment in flexibility of integration • Organizational buy-in may be a challenge	• Operational inconsistencies across businesses • Organizational buy-in is usually a challenge

Figure 12.6 **Importance of cultural assessment**

	Intuitive approach	Hybrid approach	Scientific approach
Description	An informal approach to cultural diligence and assessment focused largely on interpersonal issues (e.g. how well liked the target employees are)	An informal but focused approach to cultural diligence and assessment designed to supplement integration planning	A formal, explicit and formulaic approach focused on identifying cultural risks and incorporating them into valuation and integration processes
Pros	• Low cost • Relatively easy to ascertain	• Links due diligence to integration • Provides greater insight into integration risks	• Links due diligence to integration • Allows for explicit management of integration risks
Cons	• Does not identify cross-cultural or cross-organizational issues • Does not assess cultural risk to evaluate probability of integration success	• Lack of thoroughness may result in suboptimal identification of cross-cultural and cross-organization issues	• Gaining organizational buy-in; many companies feel cultural diligence and assessment is unnecessary

There are different options and approaches for integration, with different motivations and performance criteria. Figure 12.5 reports on the different stages and depth levels of integration. It is worth highlighting that each option presents different pros and cons; therefore, it is important to apply a case-by-case adaptation.

In order to transform value creation and synergies into a corresponding NPV there are several factors, some of them are soft elements as cultural, human, and identitarian, that must be taken into account: there is no pre-cooked miracle recipe for an acquirer to guarantee the success of a PMI, but certain key elements that can reduce the risks of a failed integration. Figure 12.6 shows the importance of undertaking a cultural assessment during the deal, because a successful PMI requires a specific underlying change management plan.

In order to properly consider the integration of a company for the acquirer, it is necessary that the acquirer applies a clear and effective roadmap based on the initial motivations underlying the M&A transaction. In particular, it is possible to identify three main roles of motivations with regard to the strategic M&A (see Figure 12.7):

1. Improve the core business.
2. Move into an adjacent market.
3. Create an entirely new business.

In corporate finance, synergy is the concept that the combined value and performance of two companies will be greater than the sum of the separate individual parts: roughly speaking, it is the principle that 1+1>2. Delving deeper into the topic, we now focus on detailing the various steps in the process, with the purpose of highlighting the main rules and activities that will lead to a successful deal.

The initial phases (Steps 1 and 2) include steps geared toward establishing governance structure, engaging with the target, and validating assumptions that underpin the preliminary integration design work.

Step 1: define operating model and integration strategy:

- Establish the strategy for successful integration and create the initial operating model before the target is fully engaged.
- Create an achievable Day 1 approach by outlining must-haves and nice-to-haves.
- Identify which type of integration best aligns with the initial business case for an acquisition (e.g. bolt-on, consolidate).
- Consider realistic assumptions on synergy capture when assessing the feasibility of selecting an initial operating model.
- Utilize due diligence materials to guide the choice of strategy and operating model once the target is initially engaged.
- Understand the level of complexity of the upcoming acquisition to determine the potential level of program management rigor and scope.

Figure 12.7   Role of M&A in realizing corporate strategy

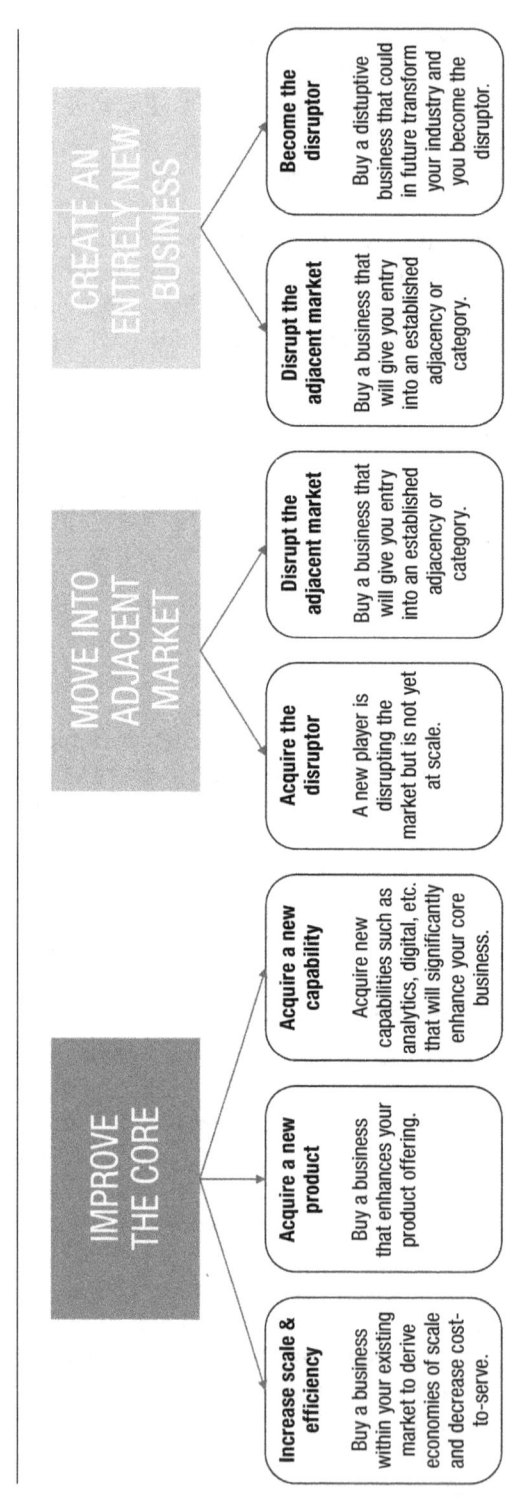

Step 2: launch integration management office and program kickoff:

- Establish the team structure and governance needed for a successful integration and create the initial Day 1 vision and integration design before the target is fully engaged in implementation planning.
- Use workstreams to populate the initial functional and LoB designs, enabling them to identify key interdependencies and corporate shared services. During this stage it's important to prioritize key issues.
- Fully engage with the target and validate assumptions made during the initial design process to finalize functional and LoB integration designs.
- Develop a detailed timeline to integration to help facilitate discussions with the target and build a foundation for the development of a more detailed roadmap.
- Refer to the sale agreement as, in certain cases, services/capabilities provided to the business being acquired may be deliberately excluded.

The planning, from steps 3 to 8, includes transition service agreement (TSA) finalization and operationalization, and Day 1 plan pressure testing and certification, so that any risk to customers, suppliers, and employees is minimized.

Step 3: develop Day 1 and end-state vision and integration blueprints:

- Fully engage the target to finalize the end-state vision of the integration and craft functional and LoB blueprints.
- Develop an integration milestone roadmap that highlights the critical path to the end state.
- Clarify what processes are in/out of scope for the functional and LoB teams, with involvement and input from the target.

Step 4: develop and manage integration work plans and budgets:

- Develop detailed Day 1 and integration work plans from the functional and LoB blueprints.
- Work collaboratively with the target using the finalized functional and LoB designs. Establish key milestones and identify business owners from both sides.

Step 5: develop TSAs:

- Consider entering into a TSA if required. This is a contractual commitment for a target parent company to provide services to the buyer after deal completion
- Focus on the development of comprehensive TSAs that strive to ensure business continuity post-transition while the company develops its own servicing capabilities or finds new third-party providers.

Step 6: identify and validate synergy opportunities:

- Focus on identifying and quantifying synergy opportunities that the buyer will realize from their acquisition of the target.

- Aim to identify incremental cost reduction and revenue generating following integration, to ultimately achieve the target state vision.

Step 7: operationalize TSAs:

- Focus on the development and implementation of TSA exit plans that help manage cross-functional TSA dependencies, identify issues, drive resolution, and facilitate early exit.
- Involve all workstreams in exit planning, isolating and addressing cross-functional dependencies that may preclude timely exit of certain service agreements.

Step 8: certify Day 1 readiness and cutover:

- Focus on confirming readiness and executing cutover while ensuring there is not any negative impact to customers, suppliers, or employees on Day 1.
- Implement four key components of Day 1 readiness planning and assessment to help ensure an issue-free day—readiness certification (including pressure testing), cutover planning, command center establishment, and transition to stabilization.

In the execution phase, post Day 1, the company will monitor and track integration work plans and manage the exit of TSA agreements as soon as possible.

Step 9: execute Day 1 and end-state integration:

- Focus on executing the cutover plan, monitoring and tracking progress against milestones, and actively addressing issues on Day 1.
- Use reporting cadence and governance processes established during the initial integration planning phase (Step 2) to communicate progress and raise issues and risks.
- Reevaluate the overall integration structure, governance processes, and so on, and adjust as necessary based on changing needs of the integration effort.

Step 10: execute, monitor, and exit TSAs:

- Focus on TSA execution and monitoring. This includes effective management of TSAs: tracking delivery, changing services as needed, identifying and resolving any TSA issues, and managing all TSA-related financial commitments.
- Manage the TSAs using information from TSA status reporting and a TSA scorecard.
- Monitor TSA performance and delivery (this applies to both the buyer and the target).

Step 11: execute, manage, and monitor synergy delivery:

- Focus on executing on synergy initiatives identified, monitoring performance, and reporting on progress relative to plans.

- Aggressively drive toward synergy targets and goals.
- Capture synergies as early as possible to allow for a quicker transition to BAU.
- Sync synergy tracking with normal functional status reporting.

Step 12: transition to BAU and program close:

- Focus on transitioning to BAU processes and thus finalizing integration.
- Ramp down the IMO and overall program structure (e.g. meeting cadence, status reporting) based on the needs of post-Day 1 integration activities.
- Move to BAU as quickly as possible to allow the program to be shut down sooner.
- Capture lessons learned from the integration and incorporate them into future revisions of the playbook and for future integrations.

The full deployment of all steps described may not be suitable for all acquisition transactions. Several investors using value creation playbooks as a diagnostic tool to assist IMO program managers at the outset of a new acquisition and provide guidance on integration. Moreover, by assessing the complexity of the acquisition and considering the timing between deal announcement and deal close, each acquisition event can have different rules and implications for value creation and integration planning. Therefore, evaluating the acquisition against several complexity assessment metrics provides the integration lead with a view of the potential challenges for the integration. Figure 12.8 lay outs a general framework to assess the complexity level of the transaction.

Turning to the elements that make up a value creation plan, it's important to highlight that using due diligence results, top-down synergy targets, and other supporting materials can help identify specific value drivers and initiatives that will support achieving the overall business case (see Figure 12.9).

Integrating two separate businesses is a highly complex process. Some challenges must be overcome early, while others can be left for a while or avoided altogether. People at all levels need clear direction on where and how to proceed. Without priorities set from the start, integration will become bogged down in lower- value details. In fact, from the beginning, the acquirer's leaders need to be clear on the strategic logic of the deal. Why are they going to all the trouble and risk of acquiring this company? Is it for cost savings, scale, opportunities for joint efforts, or something else? The answer to this initial question leads to subsequent questions:

- How fast must they move to achieve the expected benefits?
- Will they largely absorb the acquired firm, or take the best aspects from each company?
- Is this a straight integration, or an opportunity to transform the overall business?
- For business processes and IT systems, will they rely mainly on one company's infrastructure, or select the best from both?
- Which parts of the two organizations will they fully integrate and which leave alone, and for how long?

Figure 12.8   Assessing transaction complexity

← Level of complexity →

METRICS	LOW	MEDIUM	HIGH
Acquisition Type	• Specific product line or service offering	• Full business/small BU	• Competitor/large Division
Value of the transaction	• Low value i.e. < $200m	• Moderate value i.e. approximately $200m–$1b	• High value i.e. equivalent of $1+b
Seller Type/ Sophistication	• PE or Strategic/experienced	• PE or Strategic/some experience	• PE or Strategic/inexperienced
Integration Strategy	• Clearly defined	• Recently developed or under discussion	• Not defined
People	• Limited people transfers	• Standard employee transfers	• Challenging employment regulations and high number of FTEs impacted
Contracts	• Limited contracts • Minimal change of contract provisions	• Moderate number of contracts	• Large number of contracts • Large change in contact provisions required
Pro-forma Financials	• Stand alone entity	• Allocations from Target ParentCo. but carve-out financials available	• Significant allocations from Target ParentCo. with carve-out not completed
Go-to-market	• Complementary or adjacent customers, channels, teaming/partnerships, etc.	• Overlapping products/services and channels, conflicting product positioning at end customers	• Conflicting channel partners, commercial + federal end customers, non-US customers
Operational integration/Shared services	• Stand alone • No shared services or reliance on Target ParentCo.	• Clearly defined carve-out • Limited integration of back-office services	• High degree of integrated services from Target ParentCo., especially IT • Full separation by Day 1 not possible
Geography	• Regional or Single location	• Multiple regions/nationwide	• Global/Cross-border[1]

[1] BU: Business Unit
GAAP: Generally Accepted Accounting Principles
SOX: Sarbanes-Oxley Act

METRICS	LOW	MEDIUM	HIGH
Geography	▪ Regional or Single location	▪ Multiple regions/nationwide	▪ Global/Cross-border
Other Operational Considerations	▪ Limited number of parallel commercial activities or initiatives ongoing	▪ Midway through a turnaround plan	▪ Turnaround plan being developed, significant historical issues weighing on performance
TSAs (if already known)	▪ Few or no TSAs required ▪ TSAs signed at time of signing the SPA	▪ Some TSA support required for moderate amount of time especially in Finance and IT TSAs not complete at signing the SPA	▪ Will require high volume of TSAs for up to 12 months (12+ months in certain cases) ▪ TSAs not complete at signing the SPA
IT Environment	▪ Little to no reliance on Target ParentCo. systems or applications	▪ Moderate reliance on Target ParentCo. systems for infrastructure and applications	▪ Systems and applications heavily dependent on Target ParentCo.
Accounting	▪ Limited adjustments	▪ Normalisations	▪ Normalisation + GAAP adjustments + carve-out audit + SOX implications
Regulatory & Compliance	▪ No complex regulatory oversight - one main regulator	▪ Requires engaging more than one regulatory agency (i.e. multiple countries)	▪ Highly complex and stringent regulatory oversight in one or multiple countries
Pensions	▪ No pension scheme arrangement	▪ Defined contribution scheme	▪ Defined benefit scheme
Tax	▪ No issues	▪ Limited issues with standard representations and warranties	▪ Presale reorganisation required ▪ Onerous reporting requirements

Level of complexity →

Figure 12.9 Value drivers of the value creation and integration post-deal plan

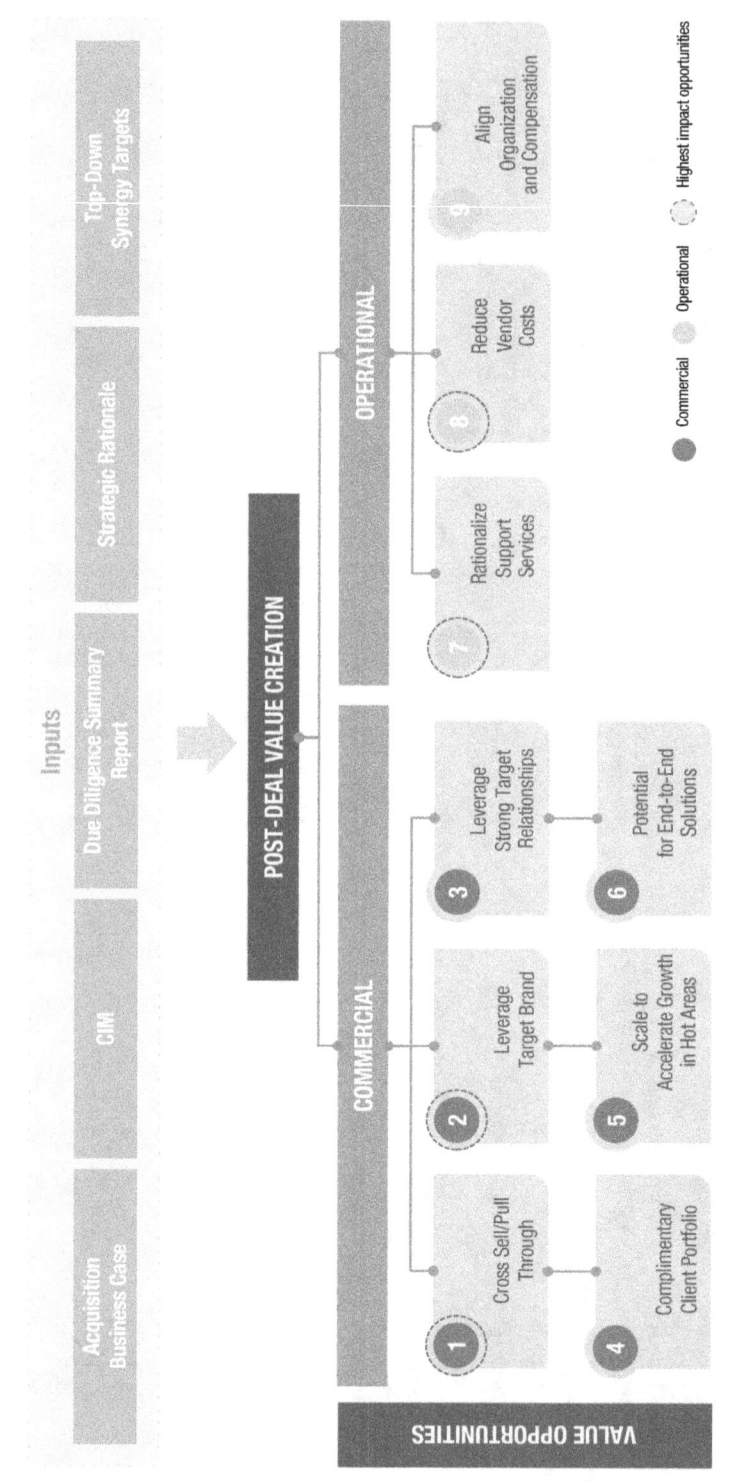

With answers to these questions, leaders can move quickly to three key decisions about: the strategic and economic goals; the value proposition for customers and employees; and expectations about roles, decision rights, and processes.

Having established the overall direction, the acquirer must set up the capture value plan in detail. Most teams will plan the integration and capture value for specific areas, such as business units, regionals, and headquarters' functions. Other teams will work on overall platforms, such as calculations for synergies, talent management, and change management. And still others will handle special issues, such as anti-trust, brands, and customer tracking. Visible leadership is essential because the organization's lower levels will mirror what senior management does, not what it says. Leaders should also manage the essential balancing act of supporting the integration without putting the ongoing business at risk.

In M&A, more often than not, time is money. The acquirer typically puts out a great deal of cash up front (or takes on debt). The faster it captures value from the integration, the higher the return on this investment. Speed also stabilizes the new organization as it reduces uncertainty. But speed in this case isn't about working faster; it's about careful deliberation and making decisions before the close. When established from the beginning, clarity and accountability can reduce delays and expedite the most important work. Advance planning will also ensure business continuity after the close, including reassuring customers worried about service levels. The clean teams are a key element of the advance work, giving acquirers an early blueprint for integration opportunities based on analyses of data that, due to anti-trust reasons, can't be freely shared between both companies. This work enables companies to hit the ground running and capture value on Day 1.

In both the pre- and post-close phase, the integration teams need to pay disciplined attention to synergies. That means an iterative process whereby the steering committee sets stretch targets and tracks results throughout the PMI. Cost synergies are usually easier to quantify and achieve, but, for many acquisitions, revenue synergies matter more in the long run (Figure 12.10).

While moving on the synergies, integration managers must look out for the existing business. Customers may be nervous about the acquisition, fearing disruption or higher prices, especially if they buy from both of the combining firms. Competitors may take advantage of the uncertainty to try to pick them off. In addition to salespeople approaching their accounts, executives need to make the effort to reassure customers directly.

Finally, it is important to prioritize value drivers and opportunities based on their estimated value and ease of implementation, in order to focus and sequence integration efforts on highest priority value delivery areas. This gives guidance in implementing solid post-deal and integration planning (see Figure 12.11 for an example).

The third area of focus during integration is on bringing the two organizations together. This starts with devising the operating model for the combined company. Any new structure can generate conflict, but a clear up-front decision on hierarchies will reduce confusion and establish the all-important accountabilities for achieving synergies.

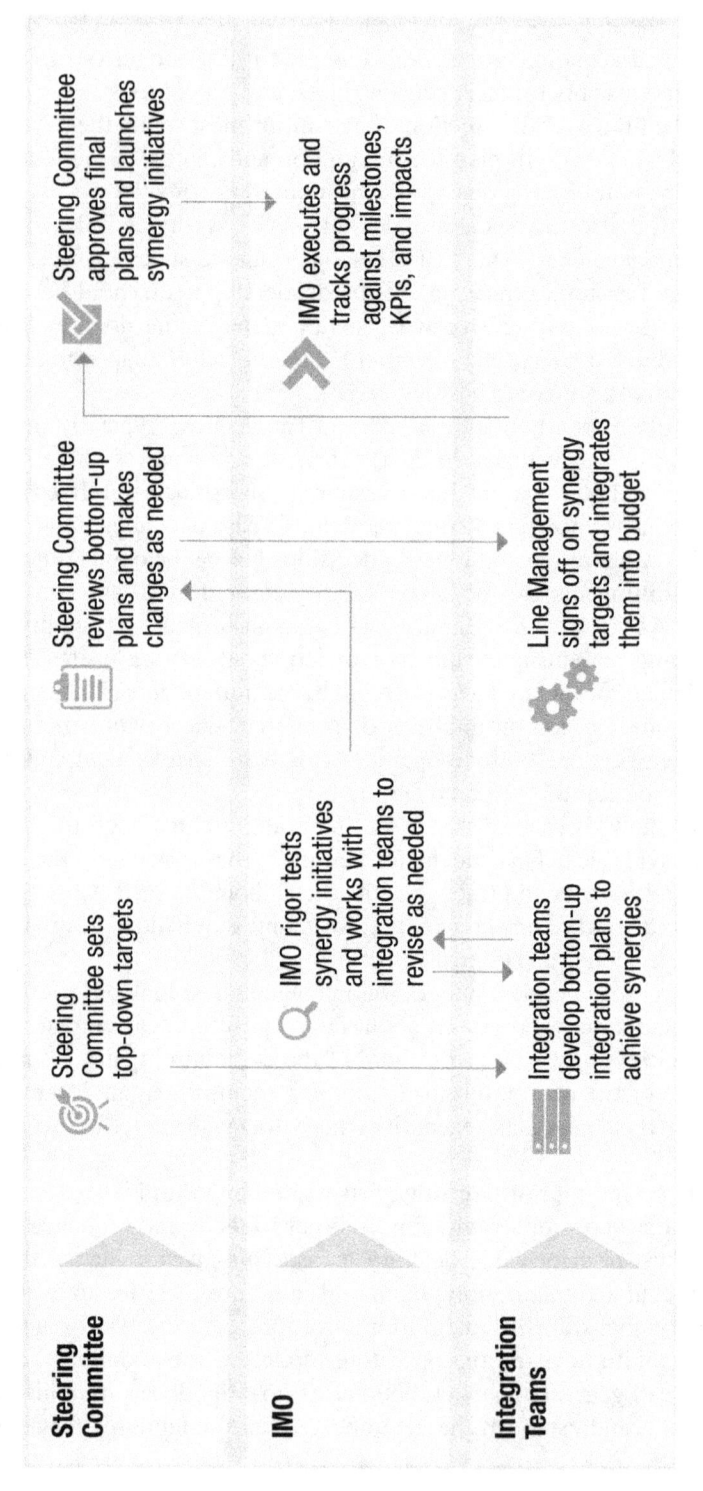

Figure 12.10 Synergy target setting, planning, and capture: an iterative process

Figure 12.11 Value driver and initiatives prioritization matrix

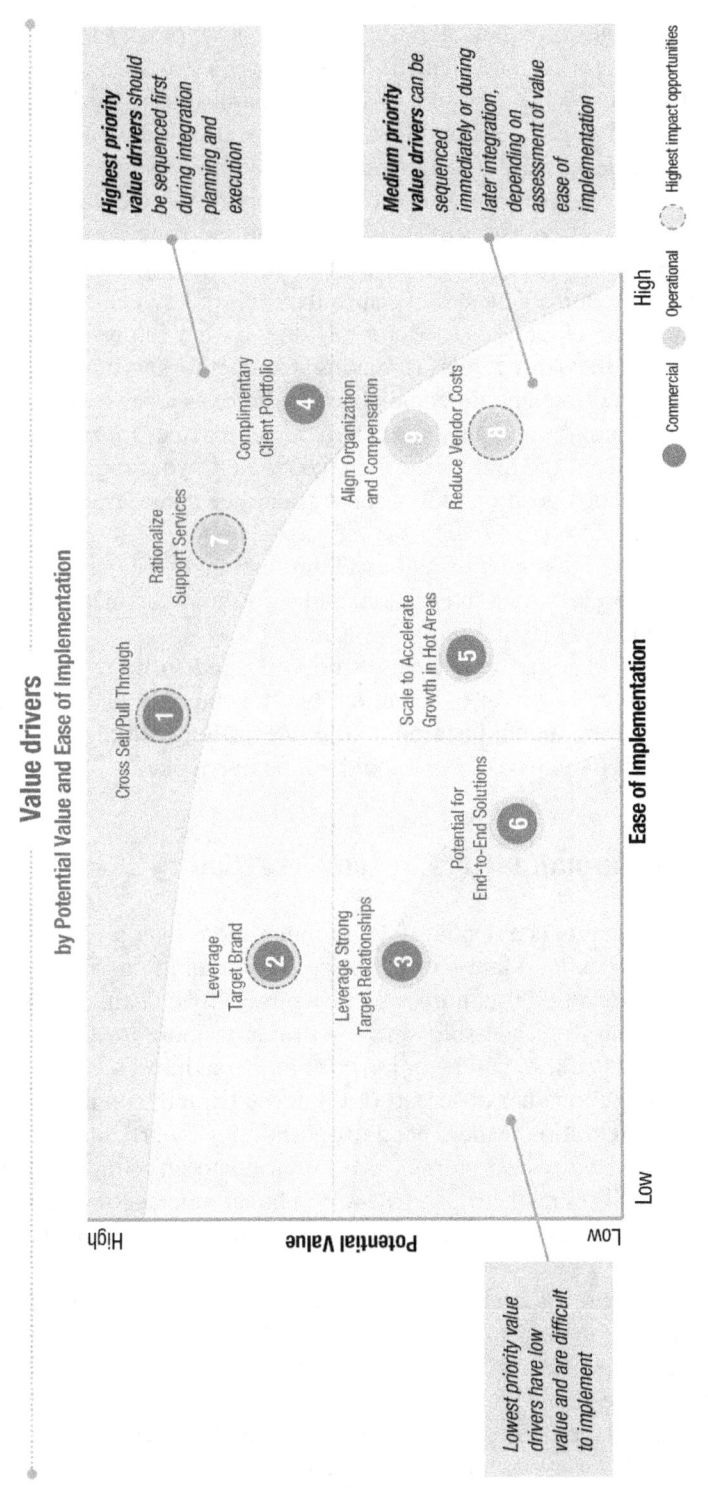

Unless the deal is a merger of equals, the operating model typically follows the acquirer's structure. Acquirers can add elements of the target's structure where relevant to facilitate operations, especially growth areas. Companies often design and staff the first two organizational layers below the CEO before the close. But, in some integrations, clients have designed the full organization before close; while, in others, only the organization level for those who directly report to the CEO has been laid out. It all depends on the circumstances of the deal and the time between deal announcement and close.

As with customers, acquirers must make sure they retain key personnel. Inevitable ambiguities will cause employees to wonder if they have a future in the new organization, especially if their direct boss is leaving. Competitors will make a special effort to lure away the more talented people. The key here, as elsewhere, is to focus on the greatest payoff. Integration managers can divide employees into three groups:

The first is critical talent, the high performers you want in your organization even if you don't know their exact position. All of these should be considered for key roles in the integration program.

The second is the specialist talent, such as IT professionals, whose skills are essential to achieving synergies in the integration, and who should be incentivized with short-term retention bonuses if perceived to be at risk of leaving.

The third comprises all other employees, who still need to be treated with respect. Money is an important driver of retention, but not the only one. Seeing a future role in the organization, being inspired by the integration's strategic vision, and being treated with respect are drivers that should not be overlooked.

12.4 Cultural and human factors in value creation

While hitting synergy targets is essential, PMI is much more than a numbers game. A merger must reknit the human fabric of the organization amid ongoing uncertainty. Integrating two organizational cultures is often more difficult than devising the new structure or selecting the leadership, and it will matter more for long-term success. The new company's culture can be quite close to the acquirer's, a hybrid of the two firms, or something altogether different. But it doesn't emerge on its own. To get the desired outcome, integration leaders need to set the tone by articulating the end-state culture, modeling the key behaviors of that culture, and targeting interventions toward that culture for all employees. A structured change management program is critical to support this process, and it should cover both the target and acquirer's organizations.

In other words, communication is not a nice add-on to the integration, but a crucial driver. Internally, it's central to reducing anxiety, building trust, boosting motivation, and managing expectations. Externally, it makes customers, suppliers, investors, and regulators more likely to support, or at least not block, the process. This relentless work must balance customization to different audiences with consistent themes and messages. A variety of technologies can help reach different stakeholders and reinforce overall messages. Regular pulse checks of the organization can provide vital feedback to integration leadership and be used in the next round of messages.

12.5 Conclusions

Summarizing this chapter, there are twelve key integration challenges should be addressed during a deal in order to ensure a successful integration and value creation for the shareholders:

- Ineffective or weak leadership program.
- Transaction and integration teams don't talk to each other.
- Deal rationale and future operating model not clear and shared.
- Merger synergies not fully identified and value left on the table.
- BAU gets forgotten and performance in both businesses suffers.
- Weak communication and people engagement leads to drop in morale.
- Integration governance not set up in time or inefficiently.
- Exodus of key talent (from both acquirer and target) before and after Day 1.
- Integration planning approach is too complex.
- Poorly executed Day 1 sets the wrong tone for the integration
- Slow IT and systems integration puts brakes on the program
- Decisions are taken too slowly (or not at all!).

Moreover, based on our analysis of the M&A deal data we have compiled as part of our Global Synergy Database of more than 1200 deals, there are five leading principles that help investors achieve greater value and become more effective acquirers; each of these principles in every transaction can greatly boost deal success, opening a path to more reliably create value to deliver the envisioned returns. These five value creation principles are:

1. *Setting aggressive internal targets*: Successful acquirers tend to set internal value creation targets that are more ambitious than the external goals they publicly announce. Successful companies achieved, on average, 1.3 times the synergies they announced to stock market and to investors.
2. *Committing to creating revenue synergies*: Acquirers that apply the same (or a greater) level of rigor and commitment to planning revenue synergies as they do cost synergies often achieve far greater success against their revenue synergy goals. These sources of value are difficult to accurately identify and quantify, and they may be hard to realize. A multitude of factors, such as market conditions, customer reactions, macroeconomic changes, and internal issues, around execution can all potentially hamper capturing revenue synergies. It's no surprise that acquirers' revenue synergy claims are often discounted, at least over the short term. Concurrently, underachieving publicly committed targets can have impacts on valuation or on the board's confidence in M&A. Still, despite the challenges in

managing expectations, revenue synergy goals should be a key component of the deal thesis and should be out in the open to create a level of commitment among management and integration teams. Unambiguous announced targets help foster better governance and accountability to achieve potential revenue goals. Teams become more likely to work together creatively to address customer needs effectively and apply greater rigor to quantifying the opportunities.
3. *Looking beyond workforce reductions*: Reducing headcount is seldom a silver bullet for value creation. Although labor expense is usually a large item on the income statement and thereby a tempting target, headcount reduction shouldn't be the biggest source of deal synergies. Successful acquirers do a better job by expanding sources of non-headcount savings, such that the proportion of headcount synergies isn't the largest driver of value. Further, in deals with an important focus on growth or strategic investments, people are usually valuable assets, often with the ability to redeploy to drive new initiatives. Successful acquirers in most cases identified higher cost synergies from non-headcount sources such as logistics and distribution efficiencies, rationalization of R&D efforts, and development of new operating models.
4. *Investing to obtain value*: Typically, acquirers make bold upfront investments to execute and integrate M&A transactions, with the funds focused on reaching an agreement and realizing anticipated synergies. The kind of new and aggressive projects that can create value in a combined organization demand support. Timely investments for the retention of key talent can help make the integration successful and promote business continuity. Spending on IT system improvements or network optimization can help as well. There may be product development costs that are key to specific revenue synergies. Carving out funding for transformative changes in the manufacturing footprint may be appropriate. Whatever the need for the capital, it needs to be injected in a timely manner, typically early in the process to help create momentum.
5. *Capturing early momentum*: Synergy overachievers reach their announced value creation targets within the first twenty-four months after a deal closes. And the momentum to capture synergies fades away almost completely within thirty-six months. All the successful organizations had dedicated cross-functional synergy teams that were able to quickly identify projects and build momentum. Successful acquirers achieved almost half of their run-rate synergies in the first year.

This leads to the conclusion that, in order to improve the chances of success of a PMI, a corporate acquirer must perform an acquisition with the right reasons and the right value creation and performance monitoring criteria in order to obtain a maximum of synergies. In order to achieve the best possible synergies, these must be implemented quickly, while focusing on the value creation and integration of the target. It became clear that the realization of synergies is an absolute prerequisite for a successful PMI. Nevertheless, these synergies must be combined with successful cultural, human, and identity integration in order to convert these synergies into market value.

13 Sustainable Finance
by *Abulenta Librazhdi*

13.1 Introduction

The principles of sustainable finance are increasingly shaping the landscape of the private equity sector. These principles, rooted in ESG criteria, guide investment decisions to ensure long-term value creation, risk management, and positive societal impact. This chapter explores how sustainable finance principles are integrated into the private equity sector, their implications, and examples of successful implementation.

13.1.1 Integration of ESG principles in private equity

13.1.1.1 Environmental principles

The environmental aspect of sustainable finance focuses on reducing negative impacts on the planet. For private equity, this means:

- *Investing in sustainable industries*: Private equity firms are increasingly channeling funds into industries that contribute to environmental sustainability, such as renewable energy, sustainable agriculture, and green technology.
- *Environmental risk management*: Firms conduct thorough environmental due diligence to identify potential risks related to climate change, resource depletion, pollution, and waste management in potential investments.
- *Enhancing environmental performance*: Portfolio companies are encouraged to adopt practices that minimize their environmental footprint, such as improving energy efficiency, reducing emissions, and adopting circular economy principles.

Climate change is a central focus for many private equity firms. Strategies to address climate-related risks include investing in renewable energy, enhancing energy efficiency, and reducing carbon emissions. Key initiatives include:

- *Renewable energy investments*: Increasing investments in renewable energy projects to support the transition to a low-carbon economy. This includes financing solar, wind, and hydroelectric power projects.

- *Energy efficiency*: Implementing energy-efficient practices and technologies across portfolio companies to reduce energy consumption and greenhouse gas (GHG) emissions.
- *Carbon reduction*: Developing and implementing carbon reduction strategies, such as carbon offset programs **and sustainable supply** chain management.

Case example: renewable energy investments

Private equity firms like KKR and Blackstone have made significant investments in renewable energy projects. These investments not only align with sustainable finance principles but also promise long-term financial returns as the world transitions to cleaner energy sources.

Biodiversity and natural capital are critical components of the global ecosystem, providing essential services such as clean air and water, food security, and climate regulation. The integration of these elements into private equity strategies is increasingly seen as vital for sustainable investment. This approach helps mitigate risks, enhance long-term value creation, and align investments with global sustainability goals.

While not specific cases, here are illustrative examples of how private equity firms can integrate biodiversity and natural capital considerations:

- *Sustainable forestry investments*: A private equity firm might invest in sustainable forestry operations that prioritize reforestation, protect endangered species, and promote biodiversity. These investments can generate financial returns through the sale of timber and carbon credits while enhancing natural capital.
- *Agri-tech innovations*: Investing in agri-tech companies that develop sustainable farming technologies can support biodiversity by reducing pesticide use, enhancing soil health, and promoting crop diversity. These technologies can improve agricultural productivity and sustainability.
- *Renewable energy projects*: Private equity firms can invest in renewable energy projects, such as wind and solar farms, which have minimal impact on biodiversity compared to fossil fuel-based energy production. These projects contribute to climate change mitigation and reduce habitat destruction.

13.1.1.2 Social principles

Social principles in sustainable finance emphasize positive impacts on society. For private equity, this involves:

- *Promoting fair labor practices*: Ensuring that portfolio companies adhere to fair labor practices, including safe working conditions, fair wages, and respect for workers' rights.
- *Fostering diversity and inclusion*: Encouraging diversity and inclusion within portfolio companies' workforces and leadership teams.

- *Community engagement*: Supporting initiatives that benefit local communities, such as community development projects and local hiring practices.

Social impact investing is gaining traction, with private equity firms looking to generate positive social outcomes alongside financial returns. Key focus areas include:

- *Affordable housing*: Investing in affordable housing projects to address housing shortages and improve living conditions for low-income communities.
- *Healthcare*: Supporting healthcare initiatives that enhance access to medical services and improve health outcomes.
- *Education*: Investing in educational technology and infrastructure to enhance learning opportunities and outcomes.

Case example: social impact investments

The Rise Fund, managed by TPG, focuses on investments that deliver measurable social impact. For instance, investments in education technology companies aim to enhance access to quality education in underserved regions, aligning financial returns with significant social benefits.

13.1.1.3 Governance principles

Governance principles ensure that companies are managed responsibly and transparently. In private equity, this means:

- *Enhancing corporate governance*: Private equity firms work to improve governance structures within portfolio companies, ensuring accountability, transparency, and ethical business practices.
- *Aligning interests*: Implementing structures that align the interests of management teams with those of investors, such as performance-based incentives and robust oversight mechanisms.
- *Ethical conduct*: Promoting ethical conduct and compliance with laws and regulations across all business operations.

Case example: governance improvements

Private equity firm Carlyle Group has implemented robust governance frameworks in its portfolio companies, enhancing board oversight, implementing stringent compliance programs, and promoting ethical business practices, thereby reducing risks and improving long-term performance.

13.1.2 Benefits of integrating sustainable finance principles

13.1.2.1 Enhanced risk management

By incorporating ESG criteria, private equity firms can better identify and mitigate risks that traditional financial analysis might overlook. Environmental risks (e.g. regulatory changes related to emissions), social risks (e.g. labor disputes), and governance risks (e.g. fraud) can significantly impact a company's performance.

- *Environmental risks*: Climate change poses significant risks to businesses through physical impacts (e.g. extreme weather events) and transition risks (e.g. policy changes and market shifts). ESG integration involves assessing and managing these risks to protect investments.
- *Social risks*: Poor labor practices, human rights violations, and community relations issues can lead to reputational damage and operational disruptions. Integrating social considerations into investment decisions helps mitigate these risks.
- *Governance risks*: Weak governance structures, lack of accountability, and corruption can undermine business performance and lead to regulatory sanctions. Strong governance practices are essential for sustainable business operations.

Sustainable finance principles help in proactively managing these risks.

13.1.2.2 Value creation

Companies that perform well on ESG metrics often enjoy operational efficiencies, strong brand reputation, and customer loyalty, leading to enhanced financial performance. For instance, energy-efficient operations can lower costs and strong labor practices can reduce turnover and increase productivity.

13.1.2.3 Access to capital

As investors increasingly seek ESG-compliant investments, private equity firms that integrate sustainable finance principles can attract capital more easily. Institutional investors, such as pension funds and endowments, are particularly focused on sustainability, and firms that align with these priorities can benefit from enhanced fundraising opportunities. Institutional investors, such as pension funds, endowments, and sovereign wealth funds, are placing greater importance on ESG criteria when determining their investment objectives. The move is motivated by the acknowledgment that ESG variables can significantly influence financial performance and risk profiles.

An example of this trend is the notable increase in the number of individuals or organizations that have signed the Principles for Responsible Investment (PRI). PRI signatories, comprising numerous prominent asset owners and managers globally, pledge to include ESG concerns into their investing and ownership deliberations. The number of signatories to the PRI has increased from 500 in 2010 to over 3500 in 2022, indicating that they control assets worth more than $120 trillion.

13.1.2.4 Regulatory compliance

Global governments and regulatory agencies are enacting rigorous laws to guarantee business accountability and long-term viability. The purpose of these regulations is to improve the clarity, responsibility, and long-term viability of financial markets. Important rules that have an impact on the private equity industry include:

SFDR

For private equity, SFDR means greater accountability and transparency. Private equity firms must disclose their sustainability risk policies, adverse sustainability impacts, and the ESG characteristics of their financial products. This regulation enhances investor confidence and aligns investments with broader sustainability goals.

SFDR imposes specific requirements:

- *Entity-level disclosures*: Private equity firms must publish their policies on integrating sustainability risks into their investment decision-making process.
- *Product-level disclosures*: Detailed information on how ESG characteristics are promoted within specific financial products, including sustainability risks and their likely impacts on returns.

Compliance requirements

Private equity firms need to adapt their internal processes to meet SFDR requirements. This involves:

- Conducting sustainability risk assessments.
- Reporting adverse sustainability impacts.
- Enhancing transparency with stakeholders through detailed ESG reporting.

CSRD

The CSRD is an EU directive that expands the scope and depth of sustainability reporting requirements. It mandates that large companies, including those in private equity portfolios, disclose detailed information on their ESG practices and impacts.

Implications for reporting and compliance

The CSRD increases the reporting burden on companies but also provides a standardized framework for ESG reporting. This helps investors, including private equity firms, make more informed decisions based on consistent and comparable data.

Key elements of CSRD include:

- *Expanded scope*: More companies are required to report, including large public-interest entities.
- *Detailed reporting requirements*: Companies must disclose information on ESG risks, opportunities, and impacts.
- *Assurance and certification*: External assurance of sustainability information to enhance reliability.
- *Impact on portfolio companies*: Private equity firms must ensure that their portfolio companies comply with CSRD requirements. This involves:
  i. implementing robust ESG reporting frameworks;
  ii. enhancing data collection and analysis capabilities; and
  iii. engaging with stakeholders to communicate sustainability performance.

Other global standards

Other significant frameworks and standards include:

- *UN PRI*: Encourages the incorporation of ESG factors into investment decisions.
- *EU taxonomy*: Provides a classification system for environmentally sustainable economic activities.
- *Task Force on Climate-Related Financial Disclosures* (TCFD): Develops recommendations for voluntary climate-related financial disclosures to help companies provide information to investors, lenders, and insurers about their climate-related risks and opportunities.
- *Task Force on Nature-Related Financial Disclosure* (TNFD): Recommends nature-related financial disclosures. It aims to develop and deliver a risk management and disclosure framework for organizations to report and act on evolving nature-related risks.

13.1.2.5 Long-term sustainability and market opportunities

Investing with a focus on sustainability helps in building resilient companies that can withstand economic, environmental, and social challenges. This long-term perspective aligns with the strategic goals of private equity, which often involves holding investments for several years before exiting.

Sustainable investments open up new market opportunities and can lead to higher returns. Companies that adopt sustainable practices are better positioned to capitalize on emerging trends and innovations. Key areas where sustainability drives market opportunities include:

- *Renewable energy*: Investments in renewable energy sources such as solar, wind, and hydroelectric power are gaining traction as the costs of these technologies decrease and policy support increases. Renewable energy projects offer attractive returns and contribute to reducing carbon emissions.
- *Sustainable agriculture*: Investments in sustainable agriculture practices enhance food security, reduce environmental impact, and promote rural development.

Technologies and practices that improve soil health, water management, and crop yields are critical areas of focus.
- *Green technologies*: Innovations in green technologies, including energy-efficient buildings, electric vehicles, and waste management solutions, are creating new investment opportunities. These technologies help mitigate environmental impacts and improve resource efficiency.

13.1.3 Challenges in implementing sustainable finance principles

13.1.3.1 Lack of standardization

One of the main challenges is the lack of standardized ESG metrics and reporting frameworks. This inconsistency can make it difficult to compare ESG performance across different companies and industries.

13.1.3.2 Data availability and quality

Reliable ESG data is crucial for informed decision-making. However, obtaining accurate and comprehensive data can be challenging, particularly for smaller companies or those in emerging markets.

13.1.3.3 Balancing financial returns and ESG goals

There can be a perception that focusing on ESG factors might compromise financial returns. Private equity firms need to demonstrate that integrating ESG principles can enhance, rather than detract from, financial performance.

13.1.3.4 Resistance to change

Implementing sustainable practices often requires significant changes in business operations and culture. There can be resistance from portfolio companies' management teams, who may be accustomed to traditional ways of operating.

13.1.4 Successful implementation of sustainable finance principles

13.1.4.1 Comprehensive ESG due diligence

Successful private equity firms conduct comprehensive ESG due diligence before making investments. This involves evaluating potential investments on various ESG criteria and identifying any red flags that could pose risks or impact future value creation.

13.1.4.2 Active ownership and engagement

Private equity firms that effectively integrate sustainable finance principles engage actively with their portfolio companies. This includes setting ESG targets, providing resources and expertise to achieve these goals, and regularly monitoring and reporting on progress.

13.1.4.3 Collaboration and partnerships

Collaboration with external experts, industry groups, and other stakeholders can enhance a firm's ability to implement sustainable finance principles. For instance, partnerships with environmental consultants or social impact organizations can provide valuable insights and resources.

13.1.4.4 Transparent reporting

Transparent ESG reporting is crucial for building trust with investors and other stakeholders. Successful private equity firms publish regular reports detailing their ESG activities, performance, and impact, using recognized frameworks like the Global Reporting Initiative (GRI) or the Sustainability Accounting Standards Board (SASB).

Case example: Blackstone's ESG integration

Blackstone, one of the world's largest private equity firms, has made ESG integration a core part of its investment strategy. The firm has established comprehensive ESG policies, conducts rigorous ESG due diligence, and actively engages with portfolio companies to improve its ESG performance. Blackstone's efforts include initiatives to enhance energy efficiency, promote diversity and inclusion, and ensure strong governance practices.

Technology is playing a crucial role in enhancing ESG reporting and management. Tools such as blockchain, AI, and IoT are improving the accuracy and transparency of ESG data. Key technological advancements include:

- *Blockchain*: Using blockchain technology to track and verify sustainable practices across supply chains, ensuring transparency and reliability of ESG data.
- *AI*: Leveraging AI to analyze large datasets, identify ESG risks and opportunities, and enhance decision-making.
- *IoT*: Deploying IoT devices to monitor environmental conditions in real time, providing accurate data on energy usage, emissions, and other critical metrics.

13.2 Overview of the current landscape

The current landscape of private equity is marked by a significant shift toward sustainability. A 2020 survey by LGT Capital Partners revealed that 100% of respondents believe sustainability is relevant to their investment decisions.[1] The growing im-

---

[1] LGT Capital Partners 2020 ESG Report.

13 Sustainable Finance

portance of ESG in private equity is also evident in the increased number of private equity and venture capital firms becoming signatories to the PRI.

13.2.1 Sustainable alternative assets

The total value of assets being managed in private markets reached $13.1 trillion in June 2023. Data shown in Table 13.1 provides a detailed analysis of the AUM in private markets. The magnitude of the value is 7.6% for a sum of $1 trillion.

Table 13.1   **Breakdown of private markets AUM (as of June 2023)**

Asset class	North America	Europe	Asia	Other regions	World
Buyout	18.2%	7.6%	2.9%	0.7%	29.5%
Venture capital	8.2%	1.6%	9.9%	0.9%	20.6%
Growth	4.8%	1%	3.9%	0.7%	10.5%
Other	1.8%	0%	0.3%	0%	2.2%
Private debt	8.0%	3.4%	0.9%	0.7%	12.9%
Real estate	7.5%	2.9%	1.7%	0.6%	12.8%
Infrastructure & natural resources	5.5%	3.7%	1.2%	1.1%	11.5%
Private equity	33.1%	10.3%	17%	2.4%	62.8%
Private assets	41%	13.7%	17.9%	3.1%	75.7%
Real assets	13.1%	6.6%	2.9%	1.7%	24.3%
Total	54.1%	20.3%	20.8%	4.8%	100%

Source: Handbook of Sustainable Finance (thierry-roncalli.com).

- North America holds the majority market share of 54.1% in the industry.
- Europe and Asia have comparable market sizes, with each region accounting for 20% of the market.
- The buyout approach is the most extensive category, with venture capital being the second largest.
- Private equity, including buyout, venture capital growth, and other forms, accounts for 62.8% of the private markets. When private debt is included, the total value of private assets amounts to 75.7%. Out of the total, 24.3% constitutes real assets, with 12.8% allocated to real estate and 11.5% dedicated to infrastructure and natural resources.

Data sources commonly differentiate between private ESG funds and impact investment funds.[2] For instance, Preqin (2023) and PitchBook (2024) categorize these two investment domains in their yearly reports.

- *Private ESG funds*: According to Preqin (2023), the total capital raised increased from $29.4 billion in 2020 to $92 billion in 2022. The total value of assets being managed in private ESG markets has reached $300 billion since 2014. Private equity ESG buyout funds currently hold a majority share of the market, with 50% of total assets. Infrastructure is the second most popular area to attract ESG finance, alongside venture capital, private loans, real estate, and natural resources. Resources allocated to ESG strategies are relatively limited. Europe dominates the market regionally, with over 70% of the market share, with North America and Asia following closely after. In 2023, Article 8 funds were the dominant force in fundraising, but Article 9 funds are gradually gaining traction.
- *Impact investing funds*: Preqin (2023) suggests that this market is 60% smaller than the market for private ESG funds. Regionally, the market is dominated by North America and Europe, which account for 95% of fundraising:

> ESG integration and regulations are more developed in Europe than other regions but impact investment strategies are more concentrated in North America. Rather than looking at when capital was secured, examining fund vintages from 2013 shows that European funds have dominated ESG integration fundraising, securing 76% of the global aggregate. However, among impact funds, North America funds of comparable vintages lead, accounting for 53% of capital raised. (Prequin 2023, p. 12)

One primary factor contributing to development is the prevalence of venture capital funds in the impact investing industry, namely those that focus on renewable energy projects like wind and solar. Consequently, a significant quantity of resources is being allocated to cleantech, a pattern that has been spurred by the 2022 Inflation Reduction Act in the United States (Prequin 2023, p. 12).

Figure 13.1 shows the evolution of total general partner PRI signatories. It indicates that the number of new general partners publicly committing to ESG through the PRI increases significantly in 2020 and 2021. However, they observe a decline in 2022 and 2023. By December 2023, there were 2503 general partner signatories. This represents about 10% of global general partners. The slowdown may be explained by ESG backlash in the USA and the proliferation of greenhushing.

The analysis of Article 8 funds shows a divergence from the global private fund market. Like Preqin (2023), PitchBook (2024) found that more than 60% of assets are invested in private equity (buyouts) and infrastructure (Figure 13.2). Venture capital funds are underrepresented in Article 8 funds due to their small size and the

---

[2] Thierry Roncalli, *Handbook of Sustainable Finance*, http://www.thierry-roncalli.com/. The book is published under a CC BY license (Creative Commons Attribution 4.0 International License), https://creativecommons.org/licenses/by/4.

ESG characteristics of these investments (Table 13.2). Indeed, the primary objective of startup companies is to survive from a financial point of view, which means that sustainability issues are not their main concern (Table 13.3).

Figure 13.1   **General partner PRI signatories**

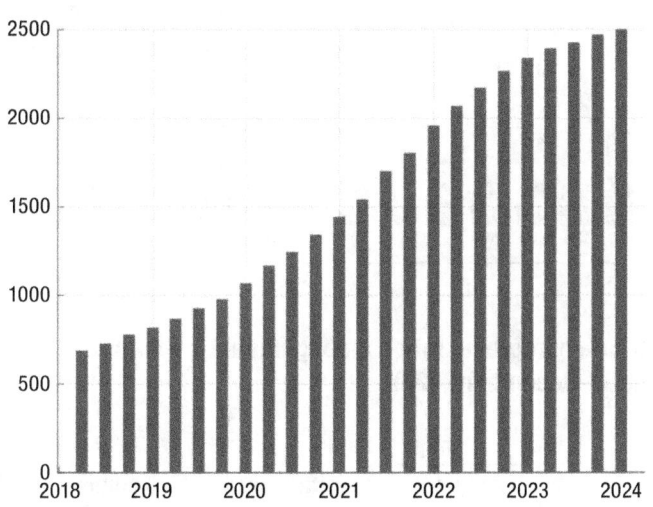

Source: PitchBook (2024, p. 2) and https://pitchbook.com.

Table 13.2   **Strategy representation among Article 8 funds (as of December 2023)**

Category	Article 8 funds		Private markets	
	Number of funds	Capital raised	Number of funds	Capital raised
Private equity (buyout)	25.8%	34.5%	21.92%	37.62%
Venture capital	14.6%	4.4%	46.49%	15.96%
Private debt	20.5%	16.8%	7.08%	14.46%
Real estate	23.2%	14.2%	12.6%	12.34%
Real assets*	12.6%	29.9%	4.16%	9.69%

* Real assets = infrastructure & natural resources.
Source: PitchBook (2024, p. 6) and Thierry Roncalli's calculations.

Figure 13.2   Share of impact capital raised ($m), by impact category

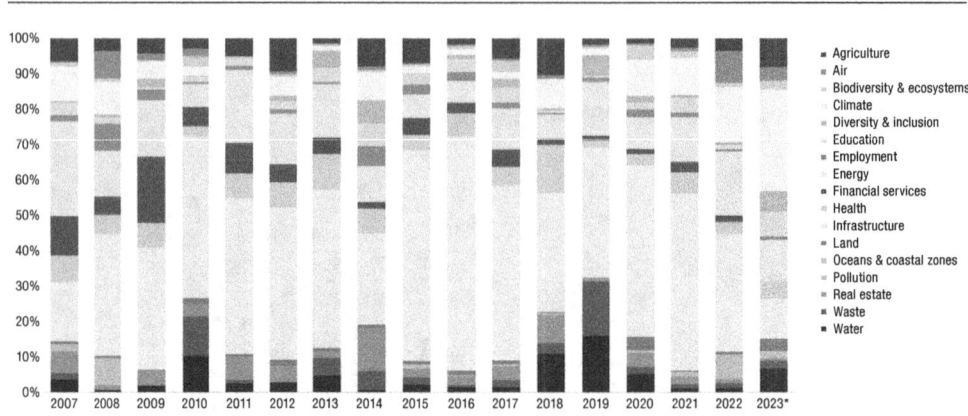

Table 13.3   Strategy representation among impact investing funds (as of December 2023)

Category	Impact funds		Private markets	
	Number of funds	Capital raised	Number of funds	Capital raised
Private equity (buyout)	21.9%	14.49%	21.92%	37.62%
Venture capital	10.18%	7.03%	46.49%	15.96%
Private debt	7.16%	6.26%	7.08%	14.46%
Real estate	5.80%	3.93%	12.6%	12.34%
Real assets*	20.55%	66.96%	4.16%	9.69%

* Real assets = infrastructure & natural resources.
Source: PitchBook (2024), https://pitchbook.com, and Thierry Roncalli's calculations.

13.2.2 ESG private equity and debt funds

Eccles et al. (2023)[3] observe that sustainability considerations are less prominent in private equity businesses as compared to traditional asset management. Historically, private equity firms have placed a high importance on governance as it plays a crucial role in organizing and overseeing companies. However, environmental and so-

---

[3] Eccles, R.G., Klimenko, S., & Stroehle, J.C. (2022). "Private Equity Should Take the Lead in Sustainability." *Harvard Business Review, July*. Reprinted in Young, D. & Reeves, M. (Eds.), *Sustainable Business Model Innovation* (pp. 203-214). De Gruyter.

cial concerns have only gained significance in this business relatively recently. Effective governance is crucial for general partners that seek to exert influence or actively engage in the management of their portfolio firms to ensure optimal performance. Conversely, the private equity industry has been slower to recognize the importance of environmental and social factors. Nevertheless, private equity firms have distinct benefits compared to conventional asset managers when it comes to applying ESG and sustainability policies:

The business model of private equity offers unique advantages for adopting a sustainability agenda in comparison to public equity investors. Private equity firms frequently exert strong control over their portfolio companies, even in cases where they do not possess complete ownership. This control is typically achieved by board representation and the ability to have significant influence over the composition of the board. Unlike public investors, who depend on reported information, they possess extensive access to financial and sustainability data. In addition, private equity firms have the authority to establish executive compensation and can terminate CEOs who do not achieve performance goals (Eccles et al. 2023).

General partners and limited partners generally have a significantly longer investment horizon compared to asset managers and public market investors due to the illiquid nature of their investments. In private equity, active management is necessary to maintain a long-term view. This means selecting assets using a bottom-up approach, with less focus on top-down portfolio creation. Since 2020, the private equity business has experienced a significant change, especially after the pandemic. More and more firms are now incorporating ESG principles into their operations and introducing funds that specifically focus on ESG.

Various inherent reasons indicate that private equity's ESG standards will ultimately converge with those of the asset management business. As a start, limited partners and their beneficiaries, including major asset owners like pension funds and sovereign wealth funds, are placing greater importance on ESG factors. They are becoming more conscious of the widespread effects of climate change and inequality. Furthermore, a significant number of limited partners and general partners hold the belief that incorporating ESG factors is crucial in order to sustain the historically impressive profits generated by the private equity industry. Portfolio companies are becoming more aware of the significance of ESG issues. This is primarily driven by evolving societal expectations, regulatory demands, and the rising emphasis on sustainability by public companies and their stakeholders (Eccles et al. 2023).

These drivers are not unique to private equity but are relevant to all asset owners and managers. Institutional investors, who are common across both private equity and asset management, often invest significantly in alternative assets. Data from institutional allocations indicate a rise in private market investments from 17.3% in 2014 to 27% in 2023, marking a 56% growth over nine years. This shift has coincided with a decline in equity and fixed-income allocations.

The ESG Data Convergence Initiative (EDCI), launched in 2021 by CalPERS and Carlyle, showcases the increasing focus on standardizing ESG data in the private equity sector. At first, a limited number of general partners and limited partners convened to tackle issues related to gathering and reporting ESG data. This ultimately resulted in the creation of a detailed strategy for action. Currently, the project has more than 425 participating general partners and limited partners, with a steering committee headed by Carlyle and CPP Investments. The committee comprises prominent limited partners and general partners from many countries. BCG's 2023 study, utilizing EDCI data, emphasizes significant ESG trends in private markets. Significantly, larger portfolio firms have achieved greater success in their decarbonization endeavors in comparison to smaller ones, and private corporations often fall behind public companies in terms of adopting renewable energy. Private corporations frequently lag behind in board diversity when it comes to social indicators, but they might succeed in other aspects such as employment creation. PRI has created manuals for incorporating ESG factors into private equity and private debt, highlighting the distinct obstacles of involvement and due diligence in private markets as opposed to public ones (PRI 2019b, 2023).

13.3 Key trends in the current landscape

13.3.1 Increased ESG integration

Increasingly, private equity firms are embedding ESG considerations into their investment strategies. This involves performing ESG-focused due diligence, establishing ESG performance objectives, and consistently tracking and reporting on ESG indicators. Core practices in integrating ESG include:

Before acquisition

Deal identification and investment decision-making: Pinpoint potential investments that align with their strategic goals, undertake comprehensive due diligence, and establish valuations alongside the specific terms and conditions. During this phase, general partners scrutinize the potential legal, financial, and business repercussions of climate change on the target company. Here are some sample questions general partners might pose to both existing and potential portfolio companies:[4]

- Understanding climate change impacts: What legal, financial, and commercial consequences might climate change have on your business operations?
- Regulatory knowledge: What existing and anticipated climate change-related regulations and laws could impact your business? How do you stay informed about these regulations? Does your company have a dedicated officer or employee overseeing climate change or environmental reporting and measurement?

---

[4] See Principles for Responsible Investment, "Technical guide: TCFD for private equity general partners" (2020). Available at: https://www.unpri.org/download?ac=10436.

- *Carbon emissions assessment*: What is the extent of your business's direct and indirect carbon emissions? What specific goals and targets have you set to reduce the company's carbon footprint?
- *Competitor actions*: Are you aware of any initiatives your competitors are undertaking to address or evaluate the effects of climate change? How do your strategies compare to those of your competitors?
- *Cost and profit impact analysis*: Have you examined the potential impact of increasing climate-related expenses on your business? Could these rising costs significantly influence your profitability? If so, what mitigation strategies have you put in place?
- *Management of climate-related risks and opportunities*: After identifying climate-related risks, what measures are you implementing to address them? Have you developed a policy and strategy for mitigating climate risks? Do you also consider opportunities arising from or related to climate change? Which departments within your organization are responsible for the measurement, management, and reporting of climate change or environmental factors?
- *Evaluating ESG factors in potential investments*: During the due diligence process, assessing potential investments involves examining various factors such as environmental impact, labor practices, and governance structures to identify both risks and opportunities related to ESG criteria.

Post-acquisition and exit phases

During the post-acquisition stage, it is possible to implement a climate strategy within portfolio companies by developing specific action plans and actively involving enterprises in addressing climate risks. These action plans are customized for each specific portfolio firm, acknowledging that there is no universal strategy to creating them. The plans may encompass the subsequent measures:

- *Creating an ESG policy that specifically targets climate-related issues*: The process entails developing a complete climate strategy that is in line with the specific sustainability objectives and risks associated with the investment. The policy serves as a comprehensive framework that delineates the company's dedication to sustainable practices and their influence on the climate. The approach provides explicit ESG goals that connect specific activities to measurable outcomes in terms of mitigating or adapting to climate change, and it also sets performance requirements. The climate policy is a dynamic document that requires constant assessment and revision to adapt to changing circumstances and integrate the latest sustainability techniques.
- *Allocating resources and assigning responsibility*: Action plans must incorporate the provision of sufficient resources, including both financial and human resources, to ensure the effective implementation of the climate policy. This may entail recruiting specialized ESG personnel or providing training to current employees to assume additional duties. To promote ownership and accountability, it is im-

portant to establish clear and defined responsibilities inside the firm. This frequently involves establishing novel roles or committees (such as an ESG committee) with a special mandate for climate supervision.
- Establishing procedures to execute the policy:
  - Specific procedures are implemented to convert the climate policy into day-to-day activities. This may involve incorporating climate-focused mitigation or adaptation criteria into decision-making processes, procurement, and operational procedures.
  - Additionally, it entails implementing monitoring and reporting systems to measure performance, facilitating ongoing enhancement and transparency.
- Holding the portfolio company's board responsible for their climate performance:
  - The board of directors should have clear and direct responsibility for monitoring and supervising the performance connected to climate issues. This entails establishing climate objectives and guaranteeing that they are incorporated into the most important aspects of strategic planning and supervision.
  - Accountability is typically established by including climate objectives into the board's official responsibilities and by defining explicit targets that the board is accountable for attaining. For example, in the case of a private independent power producer with current assets in thermal power plants that utilize fossil fuels, this could involve decreasing the amount of GHG emissions produced for each unit of energy generated.
- Convening meetings with delegates from each portfolio company to exchange expertise on climate-related subjects:
  - Regularly planned meetings can be arranged when representatives from portfolio companies convene to share ideas, problems, and best practices pertaining to climate action.
  - These sessions can function as a forum for shared learning and cooperation, promoting a communal approach to addressing climate issues that draws on a wide range of experiences and viewpoints. Typically, general partners have a responsible investments framework that is outlined in a policy. This framework can be duplicated or independently created by the portfolio firm as an environmental and social management system (ESMS), in addition to other systems.

While certain organizations may have successfully addressed environment difficulties for a considerable period, others could be less proficient in this area. The general partner will collaborate with individual management teams to harmonize responsible investing objectives with the teams' other duties.

Monitoring and reporting:
- The general partner will be responsible for closely monitoring the portfolio firm to evaluate the extent to which its ESG objectives are being achieved. Additionally, the general partner may be obligated to provide reports to limited partners regarding the management of ESG matters in accordance with any established agreement. Monitoring encompasses regular meetings with portfolio firms, gath-

ering internal data from the company, examining any publicly available sustainability reports, and undertaking on-site visits. Some specific activities are described here in detail:
- Independent monitoring will be conducted through quarterly visits and reports by an independent advisor. This monitoring will continue until financial completion or the achievement of an equal milestone. After this point, the frequency of monitoring may be reduced if it is deemed appropriate, based on the client's performance and contextual variables.
- An environment and social (E&S) manager will conduct site visits at least once a year, or more frequently if necessary, to accompany independent advisers. These visits will continue until financial completion or a similar milestone is reached.
- The continuous support from the broader community, including the identification of any possible challenges to the initiative, will be monitored.

Site inspections can provide a comprehensive understanding of the company's ESG initiatives, validate the accuracy of supplied data, and showcase the dedication of the general partner. General partner site visits can further support climate action by showcasing leadership, offering resources, and supporting the necessary activities to manage and improve climate performance. General partners have the ability to actively participate in the governance of the companies in their investment portfolios by appointing representatives to serve on the management boards of these companies. They can ensure that ESG concerns are consistently discussed in the agendas of corporate meetings. Operationally, this entails actively interacting with the personnel of the portfolio firm and overseeing the management of ESG factors, specifically focusing on the company's climate effect.

Exit

The fundamental assumption behind all ESG initiatives during the period of ownership is that effectively addressing climate-related concerns during the investment process can mitigate risk and increase the worth of a firm, which can be gained following divestment. These endeavors encompass:

- Identifying and effectively managing material ESG challenges to ensure their proper handling. This prevents a customer from discovering unforeseen dangers and bargaining for a reduced price.
- Establishing KPIs from the onset of the holding term, which allows prospective buyers to validate assertions that ESG concerns are effectively addressed.

Demonstrating that the company has taken a professional approach to managing climate issues can signify that the company has been well managed.

13.3.2 TCFD: valuation of private equity

The recommendations of the TCFD have a wide range of uses. The adoption and implementation of the TCFD also encompasses several industries and jurisdictions that are pertinent to private equity. They are specifically developed to simplify the process of generating forward-looking information that is valuable for making decisions and can be included in regular financial reports.

The PRI and INDEFI[5], a consultancy, collaborated on a PRI technical reference guide titled "TCFD for Private Equity General Partners," to offer general partners a strong framework for evaluating climate-related risk and assisting them in navigating the transition. The guide highlights that climate change poses a growing tangible threat to private equity investors:

- Portfolio companies face impacts from the physical effects of climate change.
- Regulatory actions have been rolled out aiming to reduce GHGs.
- Limited partners expect general partners to report on their approach to addressing climate-related risk.

General partners identified several obstacles to evaluating and documenting climate-related risk. Some of the challenges encompass:

- Insufficient understanding of climate-related concepts across investment teams.
- Limited resources and capacity constraints.
- Challenges in accessing climate-related data and determining appropriate metrics.
- The magnitude of tackling climate change across a complete portfolio.

The guide outlines the measures that general partners can implement to tackle the four-pillar structure of the TCFD. The guide is derived from interviews conducted with general partners, limited partners, and service providers. It incorporates illustrations of the prevailing practices employed by the former. Additionally, it emphasizes tangible resources that are accessible to assist general partners in evaluating the significance of climate risk in a portfolio and undertaking scenario analysis for companies in the portfolio.

Step 1: What are the priority objectives and actions for general partners?

The guide addresses each pillar of the TCFD in turn and outlines a series of six priority objectives and actions for general partners, listed as follows:

---

[5] https://indefi.com/

Governance:
Objective 1: Raise climate awareness throughout the organization.
Objective 2: Develop a governance system to manage climate-related risks.

Strategy:
Objective 3: Develop a simplified implementation plan.

Risk management and metrics and targets:
Objective 4: Conduct materiality analysis on current portfolio holdings to identify climate risk exposure and define key climate performance indicators for each portfolio holding.
Objective 5: Fully integrate climate risk into investment processes.
Objective 6: Conduct an annual review of portfolio holdings to assess progress toward climate objectives.

Step 2: How to turn priority objectives and actions into practical steps

The six priority objectives and actions are further cascaded to practical steps and deliverables as presented in Table 13.4:

Table 13.4 **Turning priority objectives/actions into practical steps**

Phase	TCFD pillars	Objectives	Practical steps	Deliverables
Phase 1	Governance	Raise climate awareness throughout the organization	Conduct training for partners, investment directors, and analysts	Training workshops
			Participate in cross-industry workshops on climate integration	Guidebooks
		Develop a climate-dedicated governance structure	Define climate oversight responsibilities at board and executive level	ESG/climate chart highlighting the flow of information and responsibilities
			Define climate assessment and management responsibilities at board and management level	
	Strategy	Develop a simplified implementation plan	Identify macro-level risks and opportunities through sector and scenario analyses	Materiality matrix
				Simplified implementation plans
			Define an implementation plan	

Phase 2	Strategy	Conduct materiality analysis on current portfolio holdings to identify climate risk exposure	Introduce climate components within pre-acquisition due diligence Identify portfolio holdings with the highest exposure and conduct in-depth climate analysis	Portfolio-level materiality matrix Company-level climate reports on main KPIs
	Risk management	Define key climate performance indicators for each portfolio holding	For the companies most exposed to climate-related risks, engage with management to define an action plan to strengthen climate resilience	Portfolio-level climate reports Company-level action plans
Phase 3	Risk management metrics and targets	Fully integrate climate considerations within the investment process Support holdings with tools and recommendations to address climate risks	Integrate climate considerations that affect valuation based on material climate indicators following different scenarios When material risks are identified, define climate targets at portfolio level (e.g. risk exposure, resilience, carbon footprint, 2°C alignment)	Climate valuation models Company climate report models Portfolio-level climate reports on metrics and targets
	Risk management metrics and target	Conduct yearly reviews of portfolio holdings to assess progress toward climate objectives	Pre-acquisition and after climate due diligence, integrate climate covenants for the least resilient companies	Annual climate reports Climate vendor due diligence

13.3.2.1 TCFD pillar 1: governance

The TCFD advises organizations to report on their management and oversight of climate-related risks and opportunities. This entails establishing clear and formalized obligations for both governing bodies and management teams. This can be achieved by explicitly defining climate-related duties, determining the operation and frequency of meetings for climate-focused committees, and monitoring the progress of climate strategy. For general partners to successfully incorporate the TCFD guidelines into their investing procedures, it is crucial to assess their governance and strategy methods at the individual firm level within their portfolio. Training programs for investment committees can be categorized as either theoretical or practical. These seminars aim to demonstrate climate due diligence techniques and provide examples of how climate risks have impacted financial performance. Several general partners have established proprietary training initiatives for their investing teams as part of continuous staff development programs. The objective of these programs is to integrate climate considerations into the teams' analytical processes, augmenting their climate expertise and promoting autonomy in evaluating climate risks during the investment assessment phase.

13.3.2.2 TCFD pillar 2: strategy

The TCFD's second suggestion focuses on the strategic response of organizations to climate-related concerns. Organizations are recommended to clearly express the climate-related risks they identify as major and assess how these risks could significantly impact their business operations, perhaps leading to severe consequences for financial outcomes. The TCFD offers asset managers precise direction within this strategic pillar. It indicates that the parties engaged in financial disclosure:

- Provide detailed information on how climate-related risks and opportunities are integrated into investment strategies or product offerings.
- Explain the potential consequences of transition risks on specific investment strategies or goods.

The differentiation between the strategy and risk management pillars for asset managers is subtle. Strategy focuses on the processes and procedures that asset managers utilize, specifically examining how climate risks impact investment strategies and products. In contrast, risk management is primarily concerned with the implementation of these procedures, including the specific methodologies employed. Despite the possibility of climate hazards occurring after the usual investment retention period, general partners can nevertheless encourage their portfolio companies to formulate strategies that take into account long-term climate changes. Organizations that proactively plan and prepare their operations for the future are more likely to be perceived as valuable by potential investors in the future. When considering strategy, climate risks and opportunities are usually analyzed by looking at how assets are distributed, the length of investments, and the level of exposure to various areas and sectors. General partners lack a consistent method for considering climate-related risks and opportunities in their investment analysis.

13.3.2.3 TCFD pillar 3: risk management

The third pillar of the TCFD focuses on the strategies that companies use to identify, assess, and manage risks associated with climate change. The TCFD provides specific guidelines for asset managers, particularly in relation to the risk management pillar. It advises them to:

- Describe the asset manager's engagement with portfolio companies regarding the disclosure and practices related to climate-related risks, with the aim of improving data availability and the asset manager's ability to evaluate risks.

- Provide a comprehensive account of the methods employed to identify and assess noteworthy climate-related risks for each product or investment strategy.
- Elucidate the mechanisms implemented to manage significant climate-related risks for each product or investment strategy.

13.3.2.4 TCFD pillar 4: metrics and targets

The fourth pillar focuses on the precise transition objectives and the corresponding measures used to measure progress. There exist four categories of objectives that can be established to facilitate the move toward net zero in the private equity sector. These four aims serve as the initial benchmarks for general partners when defining their green goals. Table 13.5 provides more comprehensive definitions of these targets and their corresponding measures.

Table 13.5 **Metrics and targets**

Target type	Description	Metrics
PE portfolio coverage target	A % of invested capital or financed emissions to be managed in alignment with net zero by 2030 and an increased % coverage target by 2040; achieve 100% net zero by 2050 General partners can also set this target for each fund	General partners: invested capital and/or financed emissions Limited partners: committed capital and/or financed emissions
PE engagement threshold target	Complete the specified engagement actions for all (100%) applicable PE investments	General partners: invested capital and/or financed emissions Limited partners: committed capital and/or financed emissions
PE allocation to climate solutions target	Increase investment in climate solutions This target is optional for general partners	% of invested capital
PE portfolio decarbonization reference target	The general partner/limited partner commits to a time-relevant absolute or intensity CO_2 emissions reduction target being set, covering scope 1 and 2 emissions (with scope 3 emissions phased in where possible), aligning with relevant fair share of global and regional decarbonization pathways This target is optional for general partners and limited partners.	Financed emissions

13.4 Conclusions

The principles of sustainable finance are reshaping the private equity sector, driving firms to integrate ESG factors into their investment strategies. This integration not only enhances risk management and value creation but also aligns with evolving regulatory requirements and investor expectations. While challenges remain, successful examples demonstrate that sustainable finance principles can lead to improved financial performance and positive societal impact. As the private equity industry continues to evolve, the adoption of sustainable finance principles will be crucial in building resilient, responsible, and profitable businesses.

14 Elevating Portfolio Companies through IPO Readiness

by *Gabriele Arioli*

When preparing for a change in the equity structure, whether private or public equity, it is essential for a company and its shareholders to be able to assess their readiness to such a disruptive event. In the case of a listing, most of the companies who perform IPO readiness projects before the transaction are able to detect potential issues that might arise and that could lead to the delay or, in the worst scenario, to the abortion of the deal. In addition, being ready in advance allows the company to successfully target the preferred market window (i.e. when the market recognizes the desired value to the company and the company increases the appetite of potential investors).

Deciding to go public is a crucial step in the life of a company. An IPO offers a unique opportunity to: (i) raise capital by diversifying the sources of financing and to accelerate development; (ii) increase visibility and credibility since voluntary compliance with regulatory and transparency requirements enhances a company's public profile and creates recognized added value; (iii) expand the shareholder base with global institutional, professional, and retail investors; (iv) liquidate the investments of existing shareholders; and (v) attract qualified resources as well as enabling the adoption of incentive remuneration schemes such as stock options. However, the IPO brings challenges both during its implementation and throughout the life of the listed company. In fact, during the process the organization of the issuer, in particular the finance department, is often under pressure due to requests by multiple advisors (legal, financial, audit firm, etc.) during the due diligence phase as well as when the relevant listing authority (such as the SEC for US filings or Consob when listing in Italy) perform its review on the offering prospectus. Once listed, the company must be transparent to the market and to investors as well as provide periodical financial reports to the market community.

Timing and planning are critical for creating a strong and thriving public company. Typically, the IPO process is broken down into four distinct phases that are showed in Figure 14.1 and summarized as follows for a better understanding of the key steps required to successfully transform a company from private to public:

- *Assess (pre-IPO considerations and IPO readiness)*: Understanding your organization's readiness to embark on the IPO journey requires answering questions, as well as identifying and filling in any gaps. These may include reviewing the quality of financial reporting (both statutory and managerial); assessing the business

Figure 14.1 Key steps in the IPO journey[1]

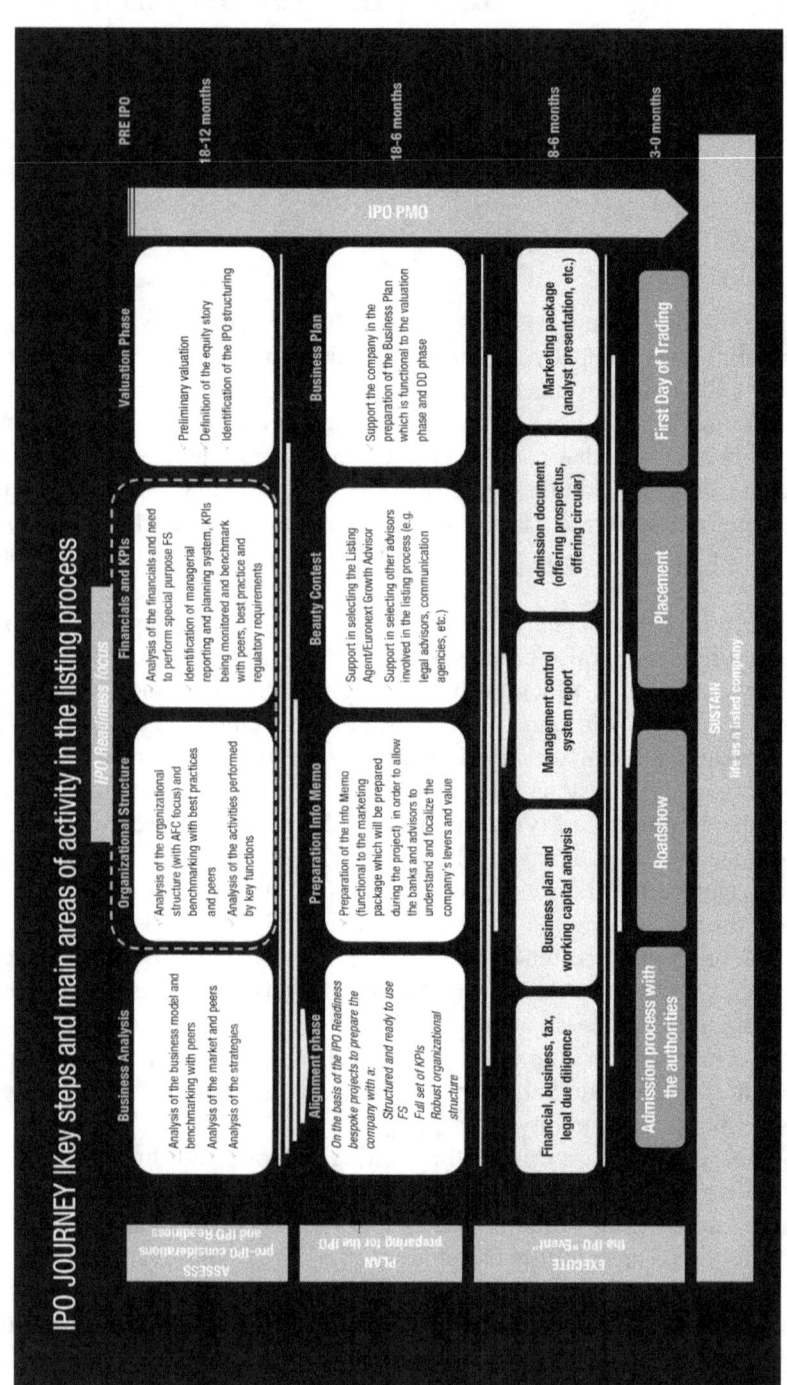

[1] FS (Financial Statements)
AFC (Audit and Finance Committee)

model, the market, and the corporate governance model; considering tax implications; and deciding where to list, along with other legal, regulatory, and ESG matters. In addition, during this phase, the company and the financial advisor start to identify the key success factors, the value levers, as well as making a preliminary valuation. Based on this acquired insight, the choice of either an IPO alone or a dual track can be underpinned.

- *Plan (preparing for the IPO)*: Creating a detailed plan and timetable to track the status of the IPO process is extremely beneficial. A strong project management team will ensure key milestones and objectives are met in time. During this phase it is critical to develop the communication and investor relation strategies, along with ensuring that corporate governance and board of director structures are formalized and robust enough to meet the needs of a public company. Creating a well-structured team of advisors, such as syndicates, legal counsels, and auditors, will be crucial for the IPO's next steps.
- *Execute (the IPO "event")*: Preparing and filing the prospectus are just two aspects of completing an IPO. Ensuring sufficient controls for CEO/CFO certification are in place, maximizing optimal tax structures, and establishing clear reporting processes are all crucial to completing the IPO "event."
- *Sustain (life as a listed company)*: Now that a company is public, it's time to act like it. Developing a plan for ongoing financial reporting commitments, evaluating the status of both internal control gaps, and associated mitigation plans will ensure best practices prevail within the newly public operations. Other considerations during this phase could include: monitoring the effectiveness of the board and management governance structure, creating an ongoing external reporting calendar that includes key timelines, and considering employee training and development needs. Becoming listed often requires a change of culture where new obligations should not stand in the way of the ability of your team.

14.1 IPO Readiness: the project

IPO Readiness is a custom-based assessment whose goal is to analyze, in a relative short-period of time, the key strategic areas that will be involved in the IPO process. It usually takes place twelve to eighteen months before the expected IPO date to ensure enough time for the company to make the necessary steps aligning itself to the relevant listing venue requirements. Usually, such projects last from four to ten weeks, depending on the basis of the complexity and level of maturity of the issuer, the prospected transaction perimeter, the involvement of foreign legal entities (that might also be subject to their country requirements), and the availability of the key personnel from the group. Through a series of interviews and analysis of the documentation already prepared by the company, the first phase of IPO Readiness aims to benchmark the company, as compared to a selected panel of listed comparables and to the requirements of the relevant listing venue. This is fundamental in the IPO process since potential investors will continuously compare the company to its peers in order to understand levers and value. In addition, this is important in order to identify any potential problem that might arise during the due diligence phase before the transition to an IPO.

Markers of IPO Readiness are:

- *Gap analysis*: A report with a IPO risk map summary, which, in graphic form, highlights the main areas of the object of analysis and the improvement required, with evidence of effort to be undertaken and a detailed list including observations, recommendations, deviation from best practices, and requirements of the stock exchange.
- *Master plan*: A report in which the corrective actions in order to align the company to requirements and best practices are identified as well as the relative expected timeline.

14.2 IPO Readiness: areas of analysis

The areas of analysis that the IPO Readiness project covers are:

- The *equity story* is crucial to the success of an IPO, presenting the core investment case for the business and supported by data to generate demand for the shares. This section covers various aspects of the process but primarily focuses on the market in which the company operates, the business model and how its go-to-market strategy compares to peers, the revenue generation streams and profit margins, the expected growth, as well as the key competitive advantages and risks of the company. It also includes an analysis of the company's historical growth (organic vs. inorganic). The equity story assessment is critical in the preliminary valuation phase, as it allows for the identification of relevant listed comparables and the use of appropriate financial metrics.
- *Financial reporting*: This should be both statutory and managerial. The preparation of timely, consistent, and high-quality financial information is essential for the management of the company and allows, among other things, the achievement of the budget data to be verified, thus increasing the confidence of the company's shareholders as well as that of potential investors. During the analysis of the statutory reporting the focus is on financial statements, the accounting principles used, the segment reporting, and the time required to prepare and approve the documents. This analysis is important because the stock exchange sets out specific deadlines for the publication of annual half-yearly financial statements (and quarterly reports if required) both for the Euronext Milan and the Euronext Growth Milan. In addition, during this assessment phase a comparison with the best practices and the information included in the comparables' financial statements is run in order to enhance the company's comparability and ensure investors understand its values. During the analysis of statutory reporting, it is also important to analyze the necessity of preparing special purpose financial statements, especially in the case of acquisitions, spin-offs, or carve-outs. During the analysis of the managerial reporting the focus is on the reports prepared for internal purposes, such as monthly and quarterly reports to understand the recipients

as well as the financial and business KPIs monitored. Also, for the managerial reporting, the stock exchange sets out a minimum set of financial KPIs that must be monitored on a monthly and quarterly basis.
- *Risks and controls*: Every listing company must equip itself with an internal control and risk management system consisting of a set of rules, procedures, and organizational structures aimed at allowing the identification, measurement, management, and monitoring of the main risks. This system is adopted by the issuer and takes into consideration the reference models and best practices existing at a national and international level.
- *Capital structure and treasury*: The preventive identification of the capital structure supported by a structured treasury function is fundamental for the success of the listing process.
- *Fiscal transactions and remuneration*: A company that intends to start a listing process must adopt processes aimed at identifying any ongoing tax risks. Furthermore, in order to align the interests of the shareholders with those of the top management, it would be advisable for company to provide a remuneration policy based on instruments such as stock option plans and so on.
- *Due diligence and working capital*: The implementation of a robust planning system consistent with the managerial view, with a well-defined time horizon and subject to scenario analysis, is crucial for the IPO.
- *Corporate governance*: A listed company must have a good corporate governance system to guarantee, among other things, the decision-making autonomy of its board of directors and the presence of independent directors. A listed company should also have a defined organizational structure, with clear roles and responsibilities. In particular, the Audit and Finance Committee (AFC) structure should be made up of qualified personnel, sufficient to manage the production of the required information.
- *ESG*: Sustainability is becoming increasingly important for both investors and supervisors. From this perspective, the adoption of a clear sustainability strategy, supported by the periodic monitoring of ESG KPIs and the sharing of guidance, could be a decisive factor for the success of the listing.

14.3 Conclusions

The decision to go public is a key milestone in a company's lifetime and allows for the potential to gain substantial returns, both in terms of financial resources and in visibility and credibility on the market. However, if not properly planned, an IPO project can lead to stress and concerns within the company's management, potentially resulting in delays or, in the worst cases, the abandonment of the deal, negatively impacting the company's reputation with markets, customers, and all stakeholders.

In this perspective, preparing and executing an IPO Readiness program that draws a tight, yet feasible and detailed, roadmap is crucial. Running the IPO Readiness program allows for the identification of the necessary steps to equip the management with the tools needed to face the challenges of the market.

References

AIFI (Associazione Italiana del Private Equity, Venture Capital e Private Debt), "Il mercato italiano del private equity, venture capital e private debt" (2016). Available at: Report AIFI—2016

AIFI, "Il mercato italiano del private equity, venture capital e private debt" (2017). Available at: Report AIFI—2017

AIFI, "Il mercato italiano del private equity, venture capital e private debt" (2018). Available at: Report AIFI—2018

AIFI, "Il mercato italiano del private equity e del venture capital" (2023). Available at: Report AIFI—2023

Eccles, R.G., Klimenko, S., & Stroehle, J.C. (2022). "Private Equity Should Take the Lead in Sustainability." *Harvard Business Review*, July. Reprinted in Young, D. & Reeves, M. (Eds.), *Sustainable Business Model Innovation* (pp. 203-214). De Gruyter

Financial Times, "Alternative investments lose steam as fundraising slows down" (August 29, 2023). Available at: Alternative investments lose steam as fundraising slows down (ft.com)

Gredil, O., Griffiths, B. E., and Stucke, R., "Benchmarking private equity: the direct alpha method" (2014). Available at: Benchmarking Private Equity: The Direct Alpha Method by Oleg Gredil, Barry E Griffiths, Rüdiger Stucke: SSRN

Hamilton Lane, "2023 market overview" (2023). Available at: Performance - 2023 Market Overview (hamiltonlane.com)

Hamilton Lane, "2024 market overview" (2024). Available at: Performance - 2024 Market Overview (hamiltonlane.com)

Invest Europe, "Mid-market private equity: Europe's engine for growth" (October 2023)

KKR, "Investor day" (April 2024). Available at: https://ir.kkr.com/app/uploads/2024/04/KKR-2024-Investor-Day.pdf

LSEG | Refinitiv Workspace (2024)

Morningstar, "What is smart beta?" (June 2021). Available at: What is smart beta? | Investing Definitions | Morningstar

PitchBook, "2023 annual European PE breakdown" (January 2024). Available at: 2023 Annual European PE Breakdown | PitchBook

PitchBook, "2024 European private capital outlook" (December 2023). Available at: 2024 European Private Capital Outlook | PitchBook

PitchBook, "Q1 2023 European PE breakdown" (April 2023). Available at: Q1 2023 European PE Breakdown | PitchBook

S&P Global, "Private equity dry powder swells to record high amid sluggish dealmaking" (July 20, 2023). Available at: Private equity dry powder swells to record high amid sluggish dealmaking | S&P Global Market Intelligence (spglobal.com)

Scardovi, Claudio, *Investire bene in Italia* (EGEA 2023)

Scardovi, Claudio, *Speranza e capitale. Un modello per trasformare e innovare il paese* (EGEA 2021)

List of Contributors and Their Roles

Foreword

Antonio Arfè, Strategy, Risk and Transactions Leader, Deloitte

Part I

Claudio Scardovi, Senior Partner Deloitte, Head of Private Equity and Real Assets; Academic Executive Fellow, SDA Bocconi School of Management and Adjunct Professor, University of Turin

Part II

Mario Ciunfrini, Director, Private Equity and M&A, Deloitte; Adjunct Professor, University of Turin

Part III

Carlotta Robbiano, Partner, M&A and Investment Management Leader, Deloitte Tax & Legal

Daniele Cevolo, Senior Manager, M&A, Deloitte Tax & Legal

Valentina Santini, Senior Partner, M&A and Equity Leader, Deloitte Tax & Legal

Gianmaria Leoni, Senior Partner, Tax and M&A, Deloitte Tax & Legal

Tamara Laudisio, Partner, M&A Transaction Services, Deloitte

Ernesto Lanzillo, Senior Partner, Deloitte Private Leader, Central Mediterranean Region

Francesco Checcacci, Senior Partner, Head of Valuation & Modelling, Deloitte

Andrea Mucchietto, Partner, Real Estate, Deloitte

Tommaso Nastasi, Senior Partner, Deal Transformation & Value Creation Leader, Deloitte

Abulenta Librazhdi, Partner, Sustainability Risk & Resilience Leader, Deloitte Climate & Sustainability

Gabriele Arioli, Partner, Capital Markets & Transaction Assurance, Deloitte Audit & Assurance

www.ingramcontent.com/pod-product-compliance
Lightning Source LLC
Chambersburg PA
CBHW081523210426
43595CB00040B/618